Race, Gender and Educational Desire

'This book is a great genealogy of black women's unrecognised contributions within both education and the wider social context. I think it constitutes an important piece of work that is totally missing from the existing literature'.
– Diane Reay, Professor of Education, Cambridge University

Race, Gender and Educational Desire reveals the emotional and social consequences of gendered difference and racial division as experienced by black and ethnicised women, teachers and students in schools and universities. It explores the intersectionality of race and gender in education, taking the topic in new, challenging directions and asking:

- How does race and gender structure the experiences of black and ethnicised women in our places of learning and teaching?
- Why, in the context of endemic race and gender inequality, is there a persistent expression of educational desire among black and ethnicised women?
- Why is black and ethnicised female empowerment important in understanding the dynamics of wider social change?

Social commentators, academics, policy-makers and political activists have debated the causes of endemic gender and race inequalities in education for several decades. This important and timely book demonstrates the alternative power of a black feminist framework in illuminating the interconnections between race and gender and processes of educational inequality. Heidi Safia Mirza, a leading scholar in the field, takes us on a personal and political journey through the debates on black British feminism, genetics and the new racism, citizenship and black female cultures of resistance. Mirza addresses some of the most controversial issues that shape the black and ethnic female experience in school and higher education, such as multiculturalism, Islamophobia, diversity, race equality and equal opportunities.

Race, Gender and Educational Desire makes a plea for hope and optimism, arguing that black women's educational desire for themselves and their children embodies a feminised prospectus for a successful multicultural future. This book will be of particular interest to students, academics and researchers in the field of education, sociology of education, multicultural education and social policy.

Heidi Safia Mirza is Professor of Equalities Studies in Education at the Institute of Education, University of London, and Director of the Centre for Rights, Equalities and Social Justice (CRESJ). She is also author of *Young, Female and Black* (Routledge).

Race, Gender and Educational Desire

Why black women succeed and fail

by Heidi Safia Mirza

Routledge
Taylor & Francis Group

LONDON AND NEW YORK

First published 2009
by Routledge
2 Park Square, Milton Park, Abingdon, Oxon, OX14 4RN

Simultaneously published in the USA and Canada
by Routledge
29 West 35th Street, New York, NY 10001

Routledge is an imprint of the Taylor & Francis Group, an informa business

Typeset in Sabon by
Keystroke, 28 High Street, Tettenhall, Wolverhampton
Printed and bound in Great Britain by
CPI Antony Rowe, Chippenham, Wiltshire

British Library Cataloguing in Publication Data
A catalogue record for this book is available from the British Library

Library of Congress Cataloging in Publication Data
Mirza, Heidi Safia, 1958–
    Race, gender and educational desire : Why black women succeed
and fail/Heidi Safia Mirza.
        p. cm.
    1. Discrimination in education—Great Britain.   2. Sex
discrimination in education—Great Britain.   3. Educational
equalization—Great Britain.   4. Feminism—Great Britain.
    I. Title.
    LC212.3.G7M57 2009
    370'.82–dc22   2008018506

ISBN10: 0–415–44875–1 (hbk)
ISBN10: 0–415–44876–X (pbk)
ISBN10: 0–203–88865–0 (ebk)

ISBN13: 978–0–415–44875–8 (hbk)
ISBN13: 978–0–415–44876–5 (pbk)
ISBN13: 978–0–203–88865–0 (ebk)

Contents

Illustrations

Figures

Acknowledgements

This book is a culmination of several years of scholarship and political activism. I therefore have far too many friends, colleagues and family to thank along the way. Like the Oscars, I can only select a few for mention! This book is only possible because of my intellectual journey with Diane Reay, Reena Bhavnani and Dave Gillborn, whose shared scholarship I acknowledge in these pages. I would not have begun this intellectual journey without the constant mentoring and encouragement of Miriam David and Sally Tomlinson. They have both been academic role models who believed in me.

I was lifted up and propelled along by the inspiring feminist collegiality and academic energy of the CRESJ team at the Institute of Education University of London – Veena Meetoo, Jessica Ringrose, Barbara Cole, Mano Candappa, Anjali Kothari, Shirley Franklin, and Penny Jane Burke, and from afar, in Australia, Cynthia Joseph. I have enjoyed my long and stimulating intellectual exchanges with Lucinda Platt, a sister-friend whose standards of scholarship have been my yardstick for this project. My publisher, Alison Foyle, needs special thanks for her vision for the book, and Amy Crowle for keeping me on track. I will be ever grateful to Gillian Klein who convinced me of the need for such a book over lunch on a warm summer's day. Thank you too to Suzanne Pollock who told me to 'just do it', Aliya Mirza who knew I could, and Stewart Phillips who stood by my side until it was done.

Introduction
The intersectionality of race and gender in education

The inaugural seminar for the Centre for Rights, Equalities and Social Justice (CRESJ) at the Institute of Education, University of London, was a turning point, not only for me, the newly appointed Director of the Centre, but for the several women of colour[1] now associated with the Centre. As a group, we could collectively celebrate our research and writing in a small corner of a powerful, consumingly white institution of higher learning. We settled on a theme to embrace our commonality, 'Black feminism and postcolonial paradigms: researching educational inequalities'.[2] We had sessions on gendered racialisation of refugees in the UK, ethnic identity among Chinese, Indian and Malay schoolgirls in Malaysia, tensions between globalisation and traditionalism for middle-class career women in India, and feminised working-class Caribbean grassroots educational movements in Britain. Emails and notices went out across the UK inviting a broad range of participants. Responses flowed in: they were celebratory and uplifting. Women of colour from the length and breath of Britain wanted to join us and share their scholarship in a safe place – and then there was the one email which signified the turning point. It was from a young black woman. She wrote enthusiastically: 'Thank you for organising this; I thought black feminism was dead!' I was taken aback and it made me think. I have been long consumed by the desire to celebrate black feminist scholarship and naively assumed that out there black feminism as a body of scholarship was alive and well. We have established a small but important community of women scholars of colour in Britain. I belong to a generation of postcolonial women who have struggled together in the world of academe since the 1970s, and many of us are now professors. There is also a new generation of hopeful young women of colour challenging the traditions of the academy – but even then we are so few in number. Data on staff in higher education show there are just 15 black and 80 Asian women professors in the UK out of a total of 14,305 professors.[3] Perhaps I was deluded by our newfound status and assumed that a few black feminists having a place in the academy means we are no longer considered an endangered species.

The email's sense of loss and desire for the articulation of a body of black feminism in Britain triggered the genesis of this book, which explores my evolving black feminist thought in educational research over the past decade. I needed to be reassured that there is a place called 'black feminism', and share with you the patterns of power and ideology that reproduce inequalities based on race and gender differences in education, which, to me, reveal themselves everywhere I look. Drawing on a range of essays, including public lectures, academic papers, book chapters, policy documents and political pamphlets, this book is a personal and political journey illuminating the struggle of 'the black woman' in education. The different sources and styles of writing demonstrate my passionate belief that as academic researchers we need to talk to different audiences. The range of essays have different purposes; some address the scholar in the university, others, the teacher in the classroom, or the policy-maker in government offices, and the activist on the front line. My intent is that all need to be simultaneously mobilised in the anti-racist, anti-sexist struggle for an equitable and socially just world. To tackle race and gender inequality in education, it is imperative to understand the nature of power relations and the ways in which racialised, classed and gendered boundaries are produced and lived through black/postcolonial female subjectivity in our places of learning and teaching.

The book asks the still necessary and fundamental questions that underpin the black feminist struggle to find a voice in the educational landscapes of school, college, university and into the world of work. First, 'how do racial and gender distinctions come to structure the experiences of black and ethnicised women in places of learning?' This addresses the issue of black and ethnicised female identity and subjectivity and the way her 'difference' is systematically organised through social relations in our political and economic structures, and polices and practices. Second, I ask 'why, in the context of endemic race and gender inequality, is there a persistent expression of educational desire and optimism among black and ethnicised women?' To answer this I take an insider's (black feminist) view of the ways in which gender and race difference is lived out in the contingent historical specificity of twenty-first-century Britain. The book aims to clarify our understanding of the multiple and complex ways in which structures of power reproduce social divisions in the everyday lives of black and ethnicised women. It examines the processes of social inequality and systematic institutionalised discriminatory practices in the context of raced and gendered human agency which frames the black female struggle for life chances and educational opportunities.

Black feminism and 'embodied intersectionality': a framework

Black feminism as a body of thought seeks to reconfigure the complexities of black female marginality in an intersectional analysis where race, class, gender, and other social divisions are theorised as lived realities. Intersectionality, a term coined by Kimberley Crenshaw (1989, 1991),[4] rearticulated concerns about black female marginality in mainstream theorising voiced in the scholarship of African American black feminists such as Angela Davis, Patricia Hill Collins and Audre Lorde (Prins 2006). Intersectionality provides a complex ontology of 'really useful knowledge' which systemically reveals the everyday lives of black and ethnicised women who are simultaneously positioned in multiple structures of dominance and power as gendered, raced, classed, colonized, sexualised 'others'. Intersectionality signalled a move away from the inadequate additive models of double or triple jeopardy and the seemingly meaningless listing of never-ending hierarchies of multiple social positions and identities (Butler 1990). Black and ethnicised women, of different ages, with various caring responsibilities, coming from particular cultures, religions, nation states, with or without citizenship/human rights, live in the dominant modalities of race, class and gender (Brah 1996; Skeggs 1997). A black feminist epistemology is contextual and contingent and examines the differentiated and variable organising logics of race, class and gender, and other social divisions such as sexuality, age, disability, culture, religion and belief that structure women's lives in different historical times (Yuval-Davis 2006) and geographic places (McKittrick 2006).

A theme of 'embodied intersectionality' runs through the chapters in the book. Such a notion seeks to make sense of the black female/'othered' woman's symbolic and narrative struggle over the defining materiality of her educational experience (Ahmed 2000). The focus on the women's 'embodied' lived experiences however is not to privilege the notion of experience when constructing a theoretical and methodological framework. Experience is a problematic epistemological concept yet it is fundamental to black feminist theorising. Appeals to experience risk obscuring regimes of power by naturalising some experiences as normative, and others as not, leaving the processes that structure dominance intact. Thus experience should not be an explanation or justification in itself, but be seen as an *interpretation* of the social world that needs explaining (Scott 1992). Experience, as revealed by black and ethnicised female narrative voices in school ethnographies, research interviews, oral histories, autobiography, historical diaries and photographs, demonstrates the ways in which regulatory discursive power and privilege are 'performed' or exercised in the everyday material world of the socially constructed 'black woman'. In this book, I draw on such personalised 'embodied' methodologies to demonstrate the processes of 'being and becoming' a gendered and raced subject of academic and educational discourse (Gunaratnam 2003). However, black and ethnicised women continually resist and rename the regulatory effects of discourses of educational inequity and subjugation. Such resistance is played out in the subjecthood of black and ethnicised women, whose agency challenges and transcends such dominance – such educational desire, which they show, is a key theme of the book.

About the book

The book takes our knowledge of the intersectionality of race and gender in education in new and challenging directions. In particular, it introduces debates on black *British* feminism, genetics, citizenship and black female cultures of resistance. It addresses controversial issues such as multi-culturalism, Islamophobia, diversity, race equality and equal opportunities in school and higher education from a racialised, gendered perspective. Gendered and raced inequalities, outcomes, and aspirations in education have remained on top of the educational agenda for several decades and continue to intrigue and challenge political and social commentators, academic researchers and activists. With the gender Millennium Development Goals[5] and new equality legislation in full swing,[6] it is important to continue to develop our thinking about the universal interconnections between race and gender inequality and its integral relationship to educational opportunities. The book takes up this challenge within the four themes of *inequalities*, *explanations*, *transcendence* and *reflections*, to which I now turn.

Understanding race, class and gender Inequalities

The first theme *Inequalities* sets the scene for understanding race, gender and class differences in educational outcomes by examining the dynamics that reproduce inequalities of race and gender. Chapter 1 gives an overview of research, focusing on young African Caribbean women's meritocratic outlook and egalitarian negotiation of educational pathways to success. It examines their desire for qualifications against the odds. 'Young female and black' opened up a public debate on African Caribbean female success and raised the vexed question as to why black girls are doing better than black boys. This is a popular but divisive question which suggests that gendered cultural differences are the root cause of black academic success and failure. Clearly, the experiences of young black girls are shaped by the effects of racism and sexism as much as those of boys, only in different gendered ways. The dynamic of differential achievement lies in understanding structures of gendered and racialised opportunities in schooling, and the raced and gendered segmented labour market. For young black women, doing well based on passing exams has not translated into success in the workplace or better access to other learning opportunities.

The dynamic of systematic race and gender inequality is developed in Chapter 2, 'Mapping race, class and gender'. This chapter reviews statistical and policy research on the differential attainment of pupils and argues that while standards are rising overall, the race gap in educational achievement remains evident even when accounting for social class and gender differences. This study had a substantial policy impact as it clearly demonstrated how the intersectionality of race, class and gender operates to disadvantage young people in the British education system. This pattern of raced gender gaps in education remains endemic (DfES 2007; Skelton *et al.* 2007; Gillborn 2008).

Theorising race and gender differences

The second theme of the book is *Explanations*. Part 2 focuses on theories and ideologies that have been mobilised to account for the persistent race and gender inequality experienced by black and ethnicised women. The focus here is the relationship between power and ideology on the one hand, and racial and gender differences experienced by black women on the other.

Chapter 3, 'Race, gender and IQ', argues strongly that ideas about differential intelligence between racial and gendered groups still remain popular despite the racist ideology and suspect pseudoscience that underpin them. It concludes that old ideas of biological racial difference have a new respectable mantel in the guise of DNA and genetic arguments. This type of popularist discourse has led to dangerous and consuming beliefs about differential hereditary ability. Our trend in educational policy and practice towards testing, setting and streaming in schools has seen racialised young black people as the ultimate losers.

Chapter 4, 'A genealogy of black British feminism', charts the history of black British feminism rooted in the postcolonial activism and struggles of black women migrants from the Caribbean, Africa, Asia, and the Indian sub-continent.[7] As a critical social force, black British feminism is an intellectual and activist movement that is contingent in nature and confronts the intersectionality of race, class and gender exclusion in academic discourse. The chapter emphasises the marginalisation of black women from feminist debates and the masculinity of the race debates, and examines the critical scholarship of black women oriented around issues of identity and difference, placing the embodied 'self' at the centre of theorising about racialised power and patriarchy.

The next two chapters continue the theme of theoretical marginalisation, but in the context of the changing ideologies of equality, multiculturalism and Islamophobia. Chapter 5, 'Intersectionality and the marginal black woman', examines the consequences of the invisibility of black and ethnicised women in policy, education and employment. Black women appear to fall between the separate constructions of race, class and gender in official education and equality legislation, yet they are highly visible in negative ways when they are included, such as the recent media spotlight on Muslim women wearing of the veil. Only by understanding how the intersectionality of patriarchy and power operates to maintain disadvantage and mask privilege can we begin to get to the root causes of persistent multiple discrimination. The chapter concludes that black women, through determined activism and social commitment, can show us what a feminised prospectus for a multicultural future could look like.

Chapter 6, 'Multiculturalism and the gender trap', picks up the vexed issue of multiculturalism and explores the gendered risk which young ethnicised women face within their own communities and families. Young women growing up in minority ethnic communities who are subject to specific forms of cultural domestic violence, such as honour killings and forced marriage, are caught up in the contradictions of the cultural relativism of British multiculturalism on the one hand, and the private/public divide which characterises our approach to domestic violence on the other. This chapter looks at some of the tensions and confusions involved in dealing with the hard and sensitive issues of gendered human rights violations in the context of rising Islamophobia, which has become an issue for young Muslim women in our multicultural schools.

Transcending race and gender expectations

Part 3, attempts to theorise the persistent expression of educational desire and aspirations among women of colour in Britain. The key issue here is black female agency and subjectivity. How is the black and ethnicised woman constructed in racialised and gendered discourses, and how in turn are these discourses resisted and refuted through black female educational desire and urgency? The chapters focus on the strategies black women employ to transcend racialised expectations, enabling them to access educational opportunities for themselves and their children.

Chapter 7, 'Black women and real citizenship', demonstrates the collective work among black women educators to transform their communities. Women in African Caribbean communities set up Saturday schools, which, on the surface, may appear individualist and about self-improvement, but are really about radical social change. Although it is not recognised in our masculinist discourses of social change, black women's agency and collective action represents a new form of gendered social movement and gendered citizenship.

Chapter 8, '(In)visible Black women in higher education', maps the marginalisation of black women's experience at the institutional level, both as staff and students in higher education. The chapter explores the embodiment of difference and the limitations of the diversity discourse in higher education. It reflects on the power of whiteness to shape everyday experiences in such places of privilege. The powerful yet hidden histories of black women in higher education, such as the Indian women suffragettes and Cornelia Sorabji in the late nineteenth century are symbolic of the erasure of an ethnicised black feminist/womanist presence in mainstream (white) educational establishments.

Reflections on race and gender

Part 4 is about *Reflections*. The two chapters here are autobiographical and tell of my journey into black feminist thought. It is a personal and political insider's account of the complex and multiple ways in which gender and race difference is negotiated in everyday life. Autobiography is a reflexive method that empowers the teller's interpretation of the past, written in the present (Cosslett *et al.* 2000). As I write, my contingent story shifts and changes, demonstrating the destabilising effects of the experiential as a basis of theorising. Nevertheless, autobiography illuminates the collective effects of discursive processes that construct our social and political worlds through individual stories. By placing the 'self' in the process of hegemonic meaning-making, we can reveal the technologies that conceal the intersectionality of dominant structures of difference. It is a privilege to be able to write from such spaces of conscious reflection.

Chapter 9, 'Race, gender and educational desire', is a personal reflection of migration, multiculturalism and gendered racism and how this influenced the development of my thinking. This chapter interrogates the pervasive myths that link race with underachievement, low aspirations, and exclusions in education. In an autobiographical mapping of educational disadvantage and discrimination, I reflect on the positive meaning of education for black communities and its location as a radical site of resistance.

Chapter 10, 'Writing about race and gender', is a reflexive interview with Jacqui MacDonald, a fellow black female colleague and head of staff development at the Institute. The interview is aimed at supporting new and emerging scholars in the task of writing. The chapter describes the pain and pleasures of writing as a postcolonial woman of colour living and working in Britain, while thinking through crucial moments in creativity. A reflexive and experiential positioning of the 'self' in theory is fundamental to a black feminist position.

Conclusion

This book explores the intersectionality of race and gender in education, taking it in new and challenging directions. It introduces debates on black *British* feminism, genetics and the new racism, citizenship and black female cultures of resistance. It addresses some of the most controversial issues that shape black female experiences in school and higher education, such as multiculturalism, Islamophobia, diversity, race equality and equal opportunities. The chapters address two core questions:

- How does race and gender structure the experiences of black and ethnicised women in our places of learning and teaching?
- Why, in the context of endemic race and gender inequality, is there a persistent expression of educational desire among black and ethnicised women?

The book argues that black women's educational desire for themselves and their children embodies a feminised prospectus for a successful multicultural future. It is a personal and political and academic attempt to demonstrate the alternative power of a black feminist framework in illuminating the interconnections between race and gender and processes of educational inequality.

Part 1

Understanding race, class and gender inequalities

Chapter 1

Young female and black[1]

It is now established that significant numbers of young black women do relatively well at school.[2] However, understanding relative black female success is an aspect of social enquiry that has vexed educational researchers and policy-makers for many years. An examination of the contemporary educational discourse over the past three decades reveals an interesting paradox of exclusion and inclusion with regard to young black women in educational research. The former, the *exclusion* of young black women in race and education studies, appears to be fuelled by political undercurrents which, since the 1960s have sought to maintain the myth of black under-achievement (Mirza 1992). On the other hand, when young black women were *included* in educational research in the 1980s and early 1990s,[3] their relative success was explained within the problematic context of 'the strong black female' (Mirza 1993). With its reification of motherhood and marginalisation of the black male, this popular theoretical construction appears to be the outcome of an attempt to explain achievement within a discourse whose underlying premise maintains the 'idea' of under-achievement.

If the contemporary discourse on race and education renders black female success invisible and the myth of the 'strong black mother' appears to be the outcome of inappropriate, ethnocentric theories of female oppression that dominate educational research, then how do we attempt to theorise the black female positive orientation to education? In a critical evaluation of these existing explanations I argue that young black women engage in a dynamic rationalisation of the education system. My findings show that young black women, who identify with the notion of credentialism, meritocracy and female autonomy, strategically employ every means at their disposal in the educational system and classroom to achieve a modicum of mobility in a world of limited opportunities, an aspect of enquiry that is often either ignored or misunderstood by policy-makers and educational researchers for whom black women still remain invisible.

The study[4]

For the purpose of rethinking black female academic achievement I examine the experiences of second-generation African Caribbean women living in Britain. These young women are the British-born daughters of migrants who came to Britain in the 1950s. Encouraged by the British government's recruitment drive for cheap skilled and semi-skilled labour these West Indians came from their newly emerging postcolonial countries to work mainly in the hotel and catering, transport and hospital services. The recipients of crude anti-immigrant hostility, and later, the more subtle workings of institutional racism, these black migrants and their descendants have experienced many obstacles to their social economic and political advancement.[5]

The overall aim of the project was to investigate the complex influences that affect the career aspirations and expectations of young black women. The 62 young black women in this study, who were aged between 15 and 19 years, attended two average-sized secondary schools in two of the most disadvantaged inner city boroughs of South London. Comparative data were collected on the aspirations and expectations of young white working-class women and men as well as young black men. These data, which acted as a 'control', are not reported here in detail, as the findings discussed relate to only one aspect of this research project; that is, the educational orientation of young women of African Caribbean descent.

In each school a random sample was drawn from pupils in the fifth and the sixth year of their secondary schooling. All pupils and schools were given fictional names. From St Hilda's, a co-educational Catholic school, 128 (65 per cent) black and white male and female pupils were taken whereas 70 (35 per cent) were taken from St Theresa's, a single-sex Church of England school. The study combined a longitudinal survey approach with a school-based ethnographic study. The young black women and their black and white male and female peers, who numbered 198 in all, and who could be objectively identified as coming from working-class homes, answered questionnaires, and were interviewed and observed in their homes and classrooms over a period of 18 months. Of these, 62 (31 per cent) were African Caribbean young women; 13 (7 per cent) were African Caribbean young men; 77 (39 per cent) were young women from other (mainly white) backgrounds; 46 (23 per cent) were young men from other (mainly white) backgrounds.[6] Several parents and teachers of these pupils also participated in the study.

The data reported here highlighted three influences on black female educational motivation. First, the cultural orientation of working-class migrants towards meritocracy and credentialism. Second, the strategic rationalisation of post-16 education and careers. And third, the expectation of economic independence and the prevalence of relative autonomy between the sexes. Each of these three factors is explored below.

Migration and meritocracy: the origins of a new social movement?

Gilroy (1987) argues that the struggle for educational opportunities among Britain's black communities merits recognition as a new social movement. Such 'fragile collectivities', he explains, are characterised by their mobilisation around the collective consumption of services, develop a distinct cultural identity and operate by means of a self-managed political autonomy. Indeed, among the West Indians' collective but autonomous political struggle for better educational conditions, a distinct community identity did evolve (Pearson 1981). Gilroy suggests that while these collectivities or movements are not necessarily agents for social change they are nevertheless symptoms of 'resistance to domination'. It could be argued, as indeed I wish to suggest here, that the extent, direction and intensity of the black female positive orientation to education is significant enough to qualify their collective action as an educational movement. An investigation into the rationale and internal dynamics of such a movement offers a new direction in the investigation of black female achievement.

My research findings show that the first-generation African Caribbean migrant identification with the ideology of meritocracy is important in shaping the characteristics of a second-generation black females' educational movement. Positive attitudes to education and the lack of restrictions on female labour market participation within African Caribbean families were major factors in accounting for the high educational aspirations of the young women in the study. A detailed consideration of African–Caribbean, working-class, migrant cultural characteristics, which I undertake here, revealed that in fact, young black women were strongly influenced by their parents. The explanation for young black women's positive orientation seemed to lie within an understanding of the transmission of the African Caribbean migrant working-class ethos, the values of which had filtered down to the girls from their parents, and had subsequently been modified.

It is often the case that people migrate for 'a better life'. This is as true of the West Indians who came to the UK as of any other group of people. West Indians came to Britain in the 1950s in what may be argued as both a male- and female-headed migration, in search of better opportunities for themselves and for their children. While objectively occupational opportunities for migrants are restricted by specific constraints with regard to their dis-advantaged labour market position there is another dimension to migrant life: that of their own subjective occupational orientation. This internal cultural dynamic of migrants, what I call the 'migrant effect', refers to the degree to which migrants themselves pursue the goal of upward occupational mobility, particularly for the next generation, by striving for educational achievement and qualifications. The influence of this 'migrant effect' on educational outcomes may vary according to the culture of the migrant group, the country of settlement, and economic and social conditions (especially significant is the extent of racial exclusion and discrimination), but it nevertheless remains a characteristic feature among many migrant groups (Alba 1985).

Glazer and Moynihan (1963), in their study of American migrant society *Beyond the Melting Pot*, discuss the drive for educational credentials among the many migrant groups in the USA. They describe the Jews' 'passion' for education; the Italian concept of (family) social status through the professional occupations of their children; the Puerto Rican capacity for hard work and the value they place on schooling. Of the Caribbean migrants who came to the USA in 1920 to 1925, Glazer and Moynihan write, 'The ethos of the West Indians . . . emphasised saving, hard work, investment and education . . . buying homes and in general advancing themselves' (p. 35).

They remark that West Indians, such as Marcus Garvey, 'furious' at the prejudice they encountered in America (which they felt was far greater than that among the whites in their home islands), turned to radical politics. Leggett (in Bettelheim and Janowitz 1977) supports this thesis of political involvement, claiming that blacks, having the lowest ethnic status, have therefore the highest level of class consciousness.

Indeed, a degree of political consciousness among early black migrants to the UK has been demonstrated by the 'Black Education Movement' set up by this generation of migrants (Chevannes 1979; Pearson 1981; Tomlinson 1985). The struggle for basic educational rights has been a political focal point for the 'black community' since the 1960s. However, as Tomlinson observes, it is not so much a radical movement as one that seeks to ensure equality of opportunity for migrant children within the education system. Confirming that migrant parents have strong educational aspirations for their children, Tomlinson (1982) writes, 'The parents very much aware of the discrimination their children could face in seeking employment after school placed great faith in the acquisition of educational qualifications to help overcome this' (p. 34).

Parental recognition that the British education system discriminates against the black child has resulted in the establishment of black supplementary schools, spearheaded by the action, in particular, of black women. These separate black schools embody the belief that education will ultimately help black children to succeed in an 'English' system by providing them with the credentials necessary for employment, or further education and training in the majority society. It was found in the study that black parents wanted improved educational standards for their children, and despite the general feeling of disillusionment and mistrust towards the schools their daughters attended, still retained their faith in the meritocratic ideal. Among the parents interviewed it was clear that securing educational opportunities for their children was of central importance, as one father explained:

We work to give our children opportunity. We earn to pay rent, buy a little food. Man, there was no time for bettering ourself. Our children, they now have the benefits to better theyself, education and so on. We didn't have these opportunities our childrens now have these opportunities and we's work hard for them [*sic*].

(Mr Burgess, London Transport maintenance)

Clark (1983) puts forward a thesis on why poor black families succeed in education. He argues that too often studies emphasise family composition (i.e. single-parent families) and not family disposition (i.e. beliefs and values). This is an important point; black girls in the study did seem to derive much of their determination for 'getting on' from their parental orientation and both the passive and active support this engendered. It was apparent that African Caribbean parents did encourage their daughters and were proud of their successes in many different ways. Many of the young women in the study described how their parents had an important role to play in influencing not only their cultural identity, but also in shaping their specific educational outlooks, both of which combined to make them what they were today:

Both my parents brought me up in the West Indian way. They brought me and are still bringing me up in the way their parents brought them up. I would like to pass this West Indian tradition down to my children so that this tradition lives on and never dies.

(Karen, mother: nurse; father: London Transport maintenance)

Nancy Foner (1979, p. 217) makes the following observation about the orientation of African Caribbean migrants' children towards education in the years to come. She writes,

The struggle to get a good education may, however, become a central focus in their lives; the second generation set their goals higher than their parents have and measure their achievements and prospects by English rather than Jamaican standards.

Indeed, as Foner predicted, the second-generation African Caribbean girls in the study did show a strong commitment to education and in particular identified with the meritocratic ideal as a means of 'getting on'. This was clearly illustrated in the girls' optimistic statements:

Black people work hard and want to really make something of themselves. I want to get on in my life.

(Maureen: aspiration social work; mother: office worker; father: carpenter)

I believe you can really change things for yourself, it is up to you but you really can.

(Laurie: aspiration sports woman;
mother: secretary; father: BT engineer)

A fundamental belief these young black women share is that, no matter who you are, if you work hard and do well at school you will be rewarded in the world of work. The goal of 'equality of opportunity' it encompasses suggests that the occupational outcomes of pupils should be a reflection of their educational achievements regardless of class, race or gender. It is ironic that such an outwardly individualistic ideology which centres around the notion of credentialism and meritocracy, expressed in the desire for personal academic qualifications, should engender a collective social movement. It is equally ironic that this 'meritocratic ideal, while a fundamental pillar of liberal democratic society, and hence enshrined in the British educational system, should also be a central ideology of the black female educational movement: a movement whose motivation appears to be the strategic rationalisation of the very system that oppresses them. Whatever the ideological orientation of such a movement, it nevertheless enables young black women to 'resist domination' and achieve social change in a world of limited opportunities.

'Strategic rationalisation': the challenge to subcultural theory

In the 1980s the notion of 'subcultures of resistance' became the perceived wisdom for not only explaining the persistence of working-class inequality, but also sexual and racial inequality. This notion of subcultures of resistance was developed from the influential work of the cultural reproductionists who, in the late 1970s, dominated the analysis of social inequality in Britain.[7] This theory, which suggests that through their own activity and ideological development young working-class men and women reproduce themselves as a working class, appeared to offer the ideal framework for developing an understanding of positive black female orientation to education.

The preoccupation with subculture, which dominates the small but distinct body of scholarship on young black women in Britain, has had far-reaching consequences for our understanding of black female academic motivation. Today, romantic, celebratory notions of black female 'subcultures of resistance' prevail in both our commonsense and academic discussions. The notion of subculture appears to have been employed because it first offers an imaginative and interpretive account of the girls' 'lived-out experiences' of racism in the classroom. Second, it offers an understanding of creativity, activity and resistance, while leaving intact the pervasive myth of black underachievement. Emphasising the subcultural features of youth remains descriptive, diverting our attention away from the structural issues which determine the quality of the experience of those being studied; issues such as unemployment, compulsory miseducation, the prospect of low pay and dead-end jobs.

Challenging the existing and popular explanation of positive motivation that is subcultural identity, I argue instead that young black women engage in a dynamic rationalisation of the education system. My findings show that young black women strategically employ every means at their disposal in the educational system and classroom in order to negotiate the institutional practices and overcome the limited resources that shape their educational opportunities. An examination of the schooling of young black women revealed a challenge to the central characteristic of black female subcultures; that is, the strategy of resistance within accommodation or the anti-school/pro-educational position. Often the young women would sit at the back of the classroom and carry on with 'prep' or homework, being neither disruptive nor participating. Fuller (1982) suggests that the negative classroom stance which she also observed among the girls in her study was a manifestation of the 'subcultural' resistance to the negative connotations that arose from being black (in school) and female (at home). She suggests that the forms of action by the black girls in her study were strategies for trying to effect some control over their present and future lives by publicly proving their own worth through their academic success. Ten years on, employing a more celebratory account, Mac an Ghaill (1993) suggests that the mixture of rebellion and acceptance displayed by the 'black sisters' in his study was an extension of the historical survival strategies found among the oppressed. In Gillborn's (1990) interpretation of the female subculture in his study, he asserts that the strategy of resistance and accommodation revolved around protecting younger pupils from experiences of sexual harassment and racism suffered at the hands of the teachers, together with a solidarity borne out of the common experience of future domestic roles.

However, there was little evidence to support any of these views of the often obvious classroom dissent among young black women. The girls simply appeared to be getting on with their own work as a means of rationalising what they considered to be unproductive and wasteful lesson time. It was clear that the young women had developed a strategy by which they gauged those lessons and teachers that were worth listening to. Their response to certain teachers was the outcome of the girls' particular and unique orientation to education, which was clearly the outcome of their identification with meritocratic ideals, a product of their African Caribbean migrant social class background. Clearly the young women held similar expectations about education and success as their parents. This accounted for their often stated preference for strong discipline in the classroom, which they identified as 'control', and organised, structured lessons which they regarded as 'good teaching'.

It was a fact that in many cases the girls' academic energies were often diverted to strategies aimed at avoiding unpleasant scenarios within the school environment, rather than in the activity of learning. It was not uncommon to find teachers expressing openly their misgivings about the intellectual capabilities of the black girls in their care. During informal conversation and formal interviews I had with them, 75 per cent of the teachers in the study made at least one negative comment about the black girls they taught. I was told by one fifth-year teacher and careers teacher that:

> Most of these girls will never succeed . . . they are just unable to remember, the girls just can't make it at this level (GCSE and CSE), never mind what is demanded in higher education. There is what I call "brain death" among them . . . unable to think for themselves.

All too often the recognition of these negative assessments led the girls to look for alternative strategies with which to 'get by'. These strategies, such as not taking up a specific subject or not asking for help, were employed by the girls as the only means of challenging their teachers' expectations of them, and as such were ultimately detrimental to the education of the pupils concerned.[8] If the overall effect of the young black women's schooling was to restrict opportunity rather than facilitate it, then the strategy of 'staying on' in pursuit of educational qualifications may be seen not as a subcultural stance but as a rational response to their impoverished secondary school experience. In her study Fuller (1982) observed the girls' commitment and resoluteness in their efforts to achieve their goals. While she was right to do so, she was less correct in describing this positive orientation as a 'subculture of resistance', the outcome of a reaction to negative parental and societal pressures towards them as being black and female. In my study, 'staying on' was the way many working-class black women expressed their aspirations for 'getting on' in life, when clearly their educational experience had restricted them.

Literature examining the educational characteristics of young black women suggests that they, more than any other group, and in particular in contrast to their white female counterparts, endeavour to pursue their education beyond the statutory minimum requirements.[9] My study upheld these findings, demonstrating that 80 per cent of black female pupils wished to continue in full-time education after the age of 16. These findings contrasted with the responses of the white girls, only 65 per cent of whom stated their preference for staying on. It was also found that the majority of young black women in the sixth forms were doing GCSE level resits rather than A levels in order to get the grades and subjects they had previously been unable to attain. The motivation for achievement through educational qualifications is, for young black women, reflected in their choice of social work jobs. The occupations they chose always required a course or several courses of rigorous professional training. Thus when we consider the reasons why the girls aspired to high-status, caring jobs, they were in effect expressing their meritocratic orientation within the constraints of a racially and sexually divisive educational and economic system.

In the example of Dianne, it becomes clear as to what is the nature of and mechanism by which this 'rationale' operates. She explains:

> I have chosen to go to college at the end of the year because the job I want to do only happens at college and not at school. The course I want to do is social care and lasts up to two years. At my age now I would not go into a job because the payment at 16 is disgraceful so if I go to college for two years then I would leave and get a job after I know that I am qualified.
>
> (Dianne, aged 17; father: welder; mother: cook; ability range high)

Dianne's statement clearly shows that her decision to do social care is based largely on the fact that for her it offers the opportunity to go on and enhance her financial status by virtue of increasing her occupational mobility. Educational qualifications are seen as part of that process and for black women social work is a known and safe option in which to strive for such a goal. Similarly, office jobs were regarded as upwardly mobile choices for young women whose migrant parents had been, or still were, located in the often unpleasant, badly paid sector of unskilled/semi-skilled manual labour in the UK. These jobs were pragmatic choices, since not only did they present attractive prospects to the girls as far as pay and conditions were concerned but they were also attainable in terms of the necessary qualifications.

While the majority of black women do opt for what may be described as the more traditional 'gendered' black women's careers, there was some evidence that black girls were far more likely than their white peers to move willingly into traditionally male occupational preserves. Their desire to do woodwork and other conventionally defined 'male' subjects at school is often cited as evidence of this uniquely black female tendency (Griffin 1985; Riley 1985). Their relatively higher uptake and enrolment on 'trade' and access courses, leading to plumbing, electrical and carpentry training, is also used to indicate this trend. Why should this be so? To date the explanation for this 'phenomenon' has centred around an argument which suggests that this willingness is a form of resistance; a conscious statement of 'black-womanhood'. However, in my opinion, the willingness of young black women to undertake traditionally male work is the outcome of two aspects that are related to their orientation to education and work.

First, all the evidence so far suggests that young black women are primarily motivated in their career aspirations by the prospect of upward mobility. A job, therefore, is an expression of the desire to move ahead by means of the educational process. The belief in the promise of a meritocracy and the rewards of credentalism spur black women on to take up whatever opportunities may become available and accessible to them, especially opportunities that entail a chance to increase their further educational qualifications.

Second, there was no evidence of any cultural constraint that inhibited a woman from aspiring to any occupation that she felt competent to train and undertake, an aspect of enquiry to which I now turn.

The social construction of blackwomanhood: challenging the myth of the superwoman

Within the subcultural model the central dynamic for black female motivation is the strong role model of the mother figure, and in particular their 'unique' orientation to motherhood. However, in an assessment of the cultural construction of gender among young African Caribbean women, which I undertake here, there was little evidence to support the notion of the 'strong black mother'. The 'strong black mother' as constructed in educational research is not unlike its better known counterpart, the 'black superwoman'; a popular image with the press.[10] Despite its dubious merits, the media myth of the dynamic black superwoman busy outstripping her male partner in terms of achievements in education and work has been uncritically adopted as a social reality in the public mind. Employing a similar rationale, the academic notion of the 'strong black mother' suggests that black women possess internal and natural strengths that account for their endurance and ability to overcome the structural racism and sexism they face in the workplace and in the home.

Although on the surface the notion of intergenerational maternal support appears a logical and positive interpretation of black female motivation, it nevertheless presents many problems for the development of educational and social policy with regard to black women. Because black women are seen to be able to motivate themselves by drawing on their inner strengths and cultural resources, it engenders a complacency towards them. Young black women, who are seen as the beneficiaries of special maternal encouragement, and enjoy the advantage of positive role models, are considered part of a privileged and select club. In contrast, young black men, whom it is deemed are marginal within the family structure and therefore do not receive any special maternal support, remain subject to the injustices of racism and discrimination. It is clear, however, that the positive intention of this account of differential achievement has conservative implications. Our attention is subtly turned away from the importance of racial and sexual discrimination, highlighting instead cultural determinants to economic success or failure.[11]

There is little evidence to suggest that black women succeed at the expense of their male partners. The asymmetrical pattern of attainment in education and the labour market is not a reflection of cultural favouritism within the family. The findings of this study suggest that among young black men and women a situation of relative autonomy between the sexes prevailed. Within this particular definition of masculinity and femininity few distinctions were made between male and female abilities and attributes with regard to work and the labour market. It is this, and not the positive role model of the strong black mother, that has resulted in the positive female orientation to work and education. In the interview data provided by the young black women, strong feelings about the need to work were evident. In their expression of this desire, these women located the essential role of their mothers (or female guardian or relative) as an important inspiration, as the following statements show:

I want to be like my mother, well liked, sociable, outgoing and most of all successful.

(Joanna, aspiration: teacher; mother: secretary)

My mother has had to work hard to bring us up, and she brings us up in the West Indian ways. She's had to take shit at work, but I think she's brave.

(Anita, aspiration: social work; mother: cook)

However, the young women also stated that while they wanted to work, they did not wish for a repetition of their mothers' experiences. They often spoke of their mothers' work, which was discussed invariably in terms of hardship and sacrifice. They always gave a unanimous 'no' to the question 'would you like to be like your mum and do the same sort of work?' The key to why this situation of positive orientation and commitment to work should prevail was provided by the girls themselves. While the statements they made showed that they expected to work just as their sisters, mothers, aunts and grandmothers had done for generations before them, they (and this is the important point) expected to do so without the encumbrance of male dissent. This meant that the young women did not regard their male relationships, whether within the institution of marriage or not, as inhibiting their right to work in any way.

Studies have persistently attributed the relatively high proportion of black women in the economy to the absence of a male provider or his inability to fulfil his role.[12] This pathological explanation of the black family that has come about from the belief that it is 'culturally stripped', essentially a hybrid of Western culture, has failed to acknowledge that in the Caribbean what has evolved is an essentially egalitarian ideology with regard to work, an ideology that, as Sutton and Makiesky-Barrow (1977: 323) observe, 'emphasises the effectiveness of the individual regardless of gender'. The study revealed a notable lack of sexual distinctions about work among second-generation African Caribbean youth. Many girls said that they did not see any difference between themselves and their male counterparts in terms of their capacity to work and the type of work they were capable of, as these two African Caribbean young women articulate:

> I think men and women have the same opportunities, it is just up to you to take it.
>
> Men should do the jobs women do and women the jobs that men do. There's nothing wrong with men midwives, I think all men should find out what it is like to have a child, it's the nearest they can get to it.

Similarly, the African Caribbean boys in the study had no objections to their future partners working.[13] They were in full support of their womenfolk being gainfully employed, as the following statements illustrate:

> My mum, she's a cook and she looks after me and my brother . . . I think if I got married, I don't see no difference, I don't see it any other way really.
>
> (Davis, aged 16, aspiration: armed forces)

Ironically, the dynamic that has produced this equality between the sexes within the Caribbean social structure has been the external imposition of oppression and brutality. Davis (1982) documents the evolution of this egalitarian ideology. She argues that under the conditions of slavery egalitarianism characterised the social relations between male and female slaves in their domestic quarters. Here the sexual division of labour did not appear to be hierarchically organised. Both male and female tasks, whether cooking or hunting, were deemed equally necessary and therefore considered neither inferior nor superior to each other.

Sutton and Makiesky-Barrow (1977: 307), in their study of Barbadian society, make this comment about the Caribbean female orientation to work:

> Women are expected not only to contribute to their own and their children's support but also to acquire and build separate economic resources, control their own earnings and use them as they see fit. Men readily accept the idea of their wives working; in fact a man might boast of his wife's position and earnings.

This attitude to work, marriage and motherhood among black women has been misinterpreted by white socialist feminists.

While they have argued that for white women, marriage is a 'psychologically and materially oppressive institution' (Barrett and McIntosh 1982), they state that for the West Indian, marriage is 'no more than a prestige conferring act' (Phizacklea 1982: 100; see also Sharpe 1987: 234). This suggestion appears to imply that black people 'mimic' the social institutions of the dominant white society. The effect of this 'commonsense' assumption has been that marriage, the family and male relationships in the African Caribbean context are dismissed as unimportant in the lives of black women.

However, Caribbean feminists provide evidence to the contrary. For example, Powell (1986) suggests that Caribbean women are strongly marriage oriented, though there seems to be little urgency regarding its timing. While conjugal relationships, motherhood and child-rearing were important dimensions in the lives of black women, they did not perceive their unions as presenting barriers to the things they wished to do. In support of Powell's findings it was not uncommon to find among the young women in the study statements such as this:

> Work is as equally important in marriage, or your relationship. I don't care if it's marriage or not, whatever, I think it's important.
>   (Floya, aged 16, aspiration: data processor)

This did not mean, as Riley (1985: 69) seems to suggest in her analysis of similar types of statements, that young black girls were pursuing a course of aggressive assertion of their femininity (which in the case of black girls is interpreted as female dominance) at the expense of all else, especially permanent male relationships. Nor, as Fuller (1982 : 96) suggests, was this the manifestation of a 'going it alone' strategy.

In my opinion what the young women were articulating was a much more subtle ideological orientation than either of these two authors suggest. Unlike their white peers, who appear to have inculcated the dominant ideology that women only take on major economic roles when circumstances prevent their menfolk from doing so, the black girls held no such belief about the marginality of their economic participation and commitment to the family. Providing for the children and the household was regarded as a joint responsibility, as the following statement illustrates:

> I think it is important for a woman and man to work, to both provide for your family is an important thing to do.
>   (Karen, aged 16, aspiration: computer programmer)

The existence of joint responsibility is more widespread than most sociological commentators of both radical and conservative ideological persuasions care to acknowledge. Providing evidence of joint economic responsibility, there are high proportions of black women in the labour market relative to black men. While 80 per cent of black men work in Britain, so do 75 per cent of black women (*Employment Gazette* 1993; Jones 1993).

The issue of relative economic and social autonomy between the sexes should not be confused with the matter of the sharing of domestic labour or the permanency of male/female relationships, as is so often the case. That African Caribbean men do not participate equally in household tasks is well documented, as is the tendency towards instability of consensual relationships (Besson 1993; Justus 1985; Momsen 1993; Moses 1985; Powell 1986). These facts, however, do not impair the matter of joint responsibility towards consanguineal offspring or children within a consensual relationship. Relationships where joint responsibility towards the household within the context of relative autonomy between the sexes are a common feature of African Caribbean life.

Clearly the evidence does suggest that African Caribbean women do have different relationships within their families and, in particular, with the males in these families, that contribute to a unique orientation to work. Explanations as to why this may be so point to the central concept of an ideology of meritocracy in African Caribbean working-class life, in which both men and women appear to participate equally. As Sutton and Makiesky-Barrow (1977: 302) observe,

> The position a woman acquires often results from her own achievements rather than her spouse and women tend to be individually ranked even if they are married. . . . Women as well as men are pre-occupied with finding a way of 'rising' a notch above within the social hierarchy, and both look to the occupational system of doing so.

Lee (1982: 10) makes the following interesting observation with regard to the ideology of meritocracy and its effects on the equality of opportunity between the sexes. He writes with regard to the Irish situation:

> The less a culture emphasises merit, the more resistant to equality are the males likely to be . . . if only because the supremacy of the dominant males does not depend on superior merit. They are therefore likely to feel vulnerable to what they perceive as a threat posed not so much by women, as by ability in women.

In a culture that places a value on merit, such as the African Caribbean working-class culture in Britain, this syndrome that Lee describes in the Irish situation does not appear to arise in the black British context. It would seem from the evidence given by the males in the study that female labour market participation is not perceived as a threat to their own economic and social status.

Acknowledging that there is a specific form of black femininity among young black women, characterised by an egalitarian ideology with regard to appropriate male and female roles, allows us to move towards a more satisfactory understanding of the persistence of young black women's pursuit of educational qualifications than that provided by the idealised notion of the 'strong black female'.

Conclusion: positive strategies in a negative climate

As a theoretical tool for analysing black female educational experience, the subcultural model obscures our understanding of the black female positive orientation to education. With its emphasis on 'cultures of resistance', subcultural analysis has romanticised the classroom experience, suggesting that young black women overcome disadvantage through their identification with their 'strong black mothers'. British black women Bryan, Dadzie and Scafe explain that such well-intentioned accounts by social scientists:

> portray black women in a somewhat romantic light, emphasising our innate capacity to cope with brutality and deprivation, and perpetuating the myth that we are somehow better equipped than others for suffering. While the patient, long-suffering victim of triple oppression may have some heroic appeal, she does not convey our collective experience.
>
> (Bryan *et al.* 1985: 1–2)

Revealing the true rather than the assumed nature of the black female 'collective experience' has been my concern here. My findings show that black women engage in a dynamic rationalisation of the education system. They strategically employ every means at their disposal in the educational system and classroom in order to negotiate the institutional practices and impoverished resources that limit their educational opportunities.

This was clearly illustrated by their desire to 'stay on' into post-compulsory schooling, and also through the career choices they made. Many young women 'stayed on' longer in order to redress the unsatisfactory outcome of their schooling in terms of educational qualifications. Similarly, the black girls chose caring or office occupations, not so much because of the nature of the job, but they used the stated educational requirements as a vehicle for obtaining more or better qualifications. This they did in order to enhance their career prospects and satisfy their desire for credentials often denied them at the secondary level.

Thus young black women 'resist domination' not by way of their subcultural stance at the classroom level, but through the influence of the African Caribbean working-class migrant orientation towards the meritocratic ideal. This they expressed through their overwhelming desire for personal academic qualifications. Such a desire was reflected not only among the young black women in my study, but is mirrored on a national level. The Labour Force Survey indicates that 77 per cent of young black women aged 16 to 24 have achieved a recognised qualification at GCSE A level or equivalent or lower (*Employment Gazette* 1993). It could be argued that this quiet but persistent 'collective action', aimed at obtaining social mobility through credentials, takes the form of a contemporary social movement, the ultimate outcome of which is the subtle 'resistance to domination.'

In the recent climate of educational reform the creative and dynamic rationalisation strategies of black, working-class young women are now being tested to their limits. There has never been any pretence that educational reform has been for the benefit of the ethnic minorities. In fact, as Gilroy (1990) makes quite clear, the reverse is true. The attack on the anti-racist/multicultural classroom is central to the ideology of the New Right. Anti-racism and multiculturalism, identified as an assault on traditional 'good old-fashioned British education', has been seen as responsible for the decline in educational standards (Palmer 1987). Tomlinson (1993) provides further evidence of the lack of commitment to issues of equity in recent educational reform. In the political struggle over the National Curriculum, she reveals, firsthand, the process which led to the official disbanding of the Multi Cultural Task Group.

Radical ideological education reform in Britain, with its opposing twin planks of strong centralisation and more parental choice, was popularised on the premise of the decline in standards (Lawton 1992). In 1988 with the inception of the Education Reform Act, it was predicted that, without any significant financial investment, far from raising standards these reforms will herald 'a new victorian era in education' (Ainley 1988). In the mid-1990s this had already begun to happen.

A disturbing report on the effect of educational reform on urban schools concludes, 'The rising tide of educational change is not lifting these boats' (OFSTED 1993: 45). The report found that in urban schools,[14] their effectiveness was significantly below the national average in attainment and entrance at GCSE level. Schools were immersed in day-to-day crises, leaving no time for strategic planning or good management. Standards of work were appallingly inadequate and the quality of teaching was superficial and unchallenging to the pupils.

Most significantly, for the young black women who have been discussed here, the report found that post-16 opportunities were seriously limited for young people who did not perform well in GCSE examinations. The extent of breakdown in coordination and information in adult and post-16 education services effectively boycotts the systems these young women have evolved in their struggle to strategically overcome the odds of their already impoverished educational career; odds which are now increasing with an intensity.

Chapter 2

Mapping race, class and gender[1]

The White Paper *Excellence in Schools* set the tone for the main thrust of education reforms in Britian in the late 1990s and into the twenty-first century. In his Foreword the Secretary of State for Education and Employment described the government's core commitment as 'equality of opportunity and high standards for all' (DfEE 1997: 3). The White Paper also recognised that inequality of educational attainment is a key factor placing young people at risk of isolation, non-participation and social exclusion later in life. A second document, The Stephen Lawrence Inquiry, set up in the aftermath of the shocking racist killing of a young black man in London, generated a widespread commitment to racial equality and also made recommendations to develop an educational agenda with regard to tackling racism in schools.[2] However, the educational recommendations of the Lawrence Inquiry have been met by concern about institutional racism on one hand, and confusion as to the way forward on the other. The report, *Raising the Attainment of Minority Ethnic Pupils*, published by the Office for Standards in Education (OFSTED) shortly after the Lawrence Inquiry suggested that most Local Education Authorities (LEAs) and schools lacked clarity and direction when it came to addressing inequalities of attainment between different ethnic groups (OFSTED 1999: 7–8).

It is within this context that this study to map race, class and gender inequalities in education was commissioned. Drawing on new evidence, much of it never previously published, this analysis seeks to place ethnic inequalities within a wider discussion of educational inequality. The aim is to establish, on the basis of the best available evidence, the relative significance of 'race' and ethnicity alongside other factors, especially gender and social class background, so as to clarify the issues to take forward an agenda for racial equality in education. This study examines how different groups share in the rising levels of attainment at the end of compulsory schooling. It also draws on the best available evidence in the field, including analyses of official data supplied by the Department for Education and Employment (DfEE) such as LEA submissions to the Ethnic Minority Achievement Grant (EMAG)[3] and material based on the ongoing Youth Cohort Study of England and Wales

(YCS). It is hoped that by clarifying the facts in this particular area this review will contribute to progressing the debate on race, class, gender and educational inequality.

As with the previous OFSTED review in this area (Gillborn and Gipps 1996), the focus of this study is on the principal minority ethnic groups as defined in the last census: Black Caribbean, Black African, Black other, Indian, Pakistani and Bangladeshi. Together, these groups account for around 80 per cent of Britain's minority ethnic population (ONS 1996). Children from Gypsy and Traveller communities are not included here because, at the time of commissioning, a separate project was out for tender on this group.[4] Chinese children are also not included. This is because the number of Chinese pupils in any one locality is generally low and so prone to rapid fluctuations in attainment statistics, where such data are presented as percentages based on small populations.[5]

The ethnic group names that are used in this study are those most commonly adopted in official statistics and relevant academic research in the UK.[6] There is also a recognition of terms that would be acknowledged and supported by the people so labelled. Consequently, the term 'African Caribbean' is used as a general signifier for people of Black African and/or Black Caribbean heritage. This term is also used where statistics sum together the various black groups identified in official data.

Raising standards for all?

The 1990s saw a dramatic improvement in the proportion of pupils completing their compulsory schooling with five or more GCSE higher grade (A*–C) passes or their equivalent. However, the national statistics are not broken down by ethnic origin and the DfEE collects national data on attainment in relation to gender but not ethnicity. In the absence of comprehensive national data, the best available estimate is provided by the Youth Cohort Study (YCS) of England and Wales, a long-established research project funded by the DfEE.[7] A striking finding of the YCS is that, in keeping with rising national standards, members of each principal ethnic group are now more likely to attain five higher grade GCSE passes than ever before. This is an important achievement which demonstrates that levels of attainment can be improved for every ethnic group. However, as the data in Figure 2.1 reveal, there are still considerable differences in attainment between different ethnic groups. The data show that not all ethnic groups have shared equally in the overall improvements in attainment at the five A*–C benchmark level. African Caribbean (black) Pakistani and Bangladeshi pupils are markedly less likely to attain five higher grade GCSEs than their white and Indian peers nationally. This suggests that pupils of different ethnic origins do not experience equal educational opportunities.

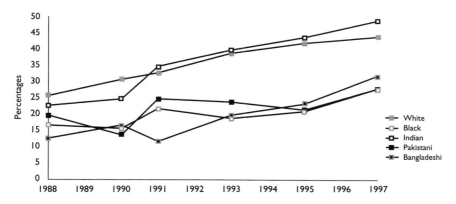

Figure 2.1 GCSE attainment by ethnic origin, England and Wales 1988 to 1997 (five or more higher grade (A* to −C) passes)

Source: Youth Cohort Study (state schools only): DfEE and Demack *et al.* (2000).

The term 'underachievement' is often used to describe these differences in attainment and there has been confusion about the meaning of the term.[8] It is often assumed, for example, that the reason for 'underachievement' must lie with the pupils and/or their families rather than with the education system itself (Mirza 1992; Wright 1987). It has also been argued that the notion of 'underachievement' undermines ethnic minority efforts to succeed and desire to do well, masking their true achievements and alternative educational practice (Mirza 1998). As several writers have emphasized, the notion of 'underachievement' has too often become a stereotype (Troyna 1984). What began life as a useful concept, meant to identify an inequality of opportunity, has sometimes slipped into a pervasive 'discourse of despair' among and about ethnic minorities. Differences in average achievement between racial, gendered or social groups raise cause for concern but do not, in themselves, prove anything about the potential of those groups. The reasons for such relative 'underachievement' are multiple and patterns of inequality are not fixed. For example, here and in the previous OFSTED review of the field (Gillborn and Gipps 1996) evidence shows that any one group, say, African Caribbeans, may be ranked poorly in national measures of achievement (such as the proportion attaining five higher grades (A*–Cs) in their GCSE examinations), but the same group may be doing relatively well in some schools and in some LEAs.

Emphasising difference in attainment between groups can be part of a necessary analysis of inequalities in educational outcomes. However, care should be taken that such an approach does not lead to a hierarchy of ethnic minorities based on assumptions of inherent ability and innate ability. In our desire to celebrate multiple identities and diversity, a 'postmodern construction of difference' has emerged which has the potential to embed creeping forms of benign racialisation. A 'new racism' is evolving where groups defined in terms of their race and sex are hierarchically compared and contrasted with each other on the basis of their inherent cultural capacities, 'natural' talent, genetic ability and IQ (Mirza 1998; Gillborn and Youdell 2000). Such racialised constructions of comparative difference among different ethnic and cultural groups dominate common-sense political thinking. For example, qualitative research shows how accounts of educational success and failure become 'racialised' through culturalist explanations.

African Caribbean girls who do relatively well in comparison to their white male and female peers within the locality of their schools have been much cited as evidence of gendered strategies to resist oppression and overcome racism. These strategies are simplistically located in fixed essentialist constructions of 'the strong black female role model'. Unlike black males, it is believed that black females can overcome disadvantage by drawing on their 'matriarchal roots'. This culturalist explanation of black female success ignores the wider structural context of gendered and racialised patterns of migration, labour market opportunities, and patterns of sexualised racism in the educational system. Given these explanations, the relative success of black girls has generally been misinterpreted to mean that it is only black boys and not black girls that face inequality. Hence the key issue in the DfES is the 'inclusion' of black boys against a background of their educational underachievement, high rates of truancy and disproportionate levels of exclusion.

Just as black African Caribbean girls' educational success is culturally constructed, so too are Indian girls' achievements nearly always explained in culturalist terms. Whereas for black girls explanations are framed in terms of their 'maternal role models', for Indian girls it is their parents' 'positive orientation to educational values' that are valorised. Cultural orientation is expressed as a racial fact. Educational success is constructed as inherent to that gendered/racialised group. Little account is given of the educational capital and social class background of the majority of this migrant group. Little is said about the geographical areas where pockets of working-class Indian pupils do the least well in terms of not achieving five or more higher grade GCSEs (Gillborn and Gipps 1996). In contrast to other minorities who 'fail', Indians are deemed a 'model minority' held up as an example to us all of the power of personal and cultural transcendence and the impossibility of there being any institutional racism.

Social class and educational attainment

There is a strong direct association between social class background and success in education: put simply, the higher a child's social class, the greater their attainments on average.[9] According to DfEE figures, children from the most advantaged backgrounds (classified as 'managerial/professional' in the YCS) were more than three times as likely to attain five or more higher grade GCSEs than their peers at the other end of the class spectrum (in the 'unskilled manual' group) (DfEE 1999b: 9). This is one of the longest established trends in British education but the association is not static. Indeed, there is evidence that the inequality of attainment between social classes has grown since the late 1980s. For example, in relation to the five higher grade benchmark GCSEs between 1988 and 1997, the gap between children from 'managerial/professional' backgrounds and 'unskilled manual' groups grew from 40 to 49 percentage points.[10]

Social class background is both difficult and costly to categorise. There is, for example, no single scale that enjoys universal support. Although almost all measures include information about parents' employment status, there are differences in how occupations are categorised and disputes about additional factors that are sometimes included, such as parental education (Bonney 1998; Compton 1998; and Marshall 1997). Another problem is that gathering reliable data from pupils can be difficult. This information must then be translated into a form that can be manipulated statistically and, unlike most items on questionnaires, social class codings cannot be routinely computerised in any simple automated way. Many academic writers draw a simple distinction between 'manual' and 'non-manual' backgrounds (where the former is taken as roughly equivalent to 'working class' and the latter 'middle class'). A great deal of work in education uses whether or not a child is eligible for free school meals (FSMs) as an indicator of social disadvantage. This is a convenient measure because the necessary raw data are routinely available within the education system. However, receipt of FSMs is really an indicator of family poverty, not a measure of social class in the sense that the term is usually understood.[11]

Before examining new data on the interaction of 'race' and social class, it is important to acknowledge that statistics which reveal an association between certain factors do not necessarily indicate a direct causal relationship. It might be assumed, for example, that because working-class pupils have historically lagged behind their more economically advantaged peers, the explanation must lie within working-class pupils themselves, their families and/or communities. Clearly there are many ways in which children from relatively prosperous backgrounds are advantaged. However, it should not be assumed that all (or most) of the reasons for differences in attainment lie outside the school. Research in both the USA and Britain overwhelmingly concludes that black pupils and their working-class white peers are likely to be over represented in lower ranked teaching groups (for example, where schools adopt 'setting by ability' or other forms of selective grouping).[12] Their disproportionate concentration can be mapped by tracing the process of selection inside schools. Research has documented how these processes are significantly influenced by differential teacher expectations, which tend to be markedly lower for these groups of pupils (see above). The pupils' subsequent placement in lower ranked teaching groups, in both primary and secondary schools, institutionalises these differences and can create additional barriers to achievement. Even in schools that do not embrace setting, some form of selection is increasingly common (Hallam 1999). The structure of the GCSE examination itself now requires most subject areas to enter pupils for one of two different 'tiers' of exam, where the highest grades are only available to pupils in the top tier.[13]

Class, 'race' and attainment inequalities

The previous OFSTED review of research in this area indicated that differences in attainment between certain ethnic groups remained significant even when taking social class into account (Gillborn and Gipps 1996: 16–18). The authors warned, however, that the available data were old and the ethnic categories relatively crude. We now have access to more sophisticated and up-to-date material. In general, however, the same trends are still apparent.

Figure 2.2 shows the proportion of pupils attaining five or more higher grade GCSEs, distinguished by social class and ethnic origin, between 1988 and 1997.[14] This is the first time that it has been possible to trace differences in attainment by class and ethnicity for such a long time period and many important issues are highlighted. When interpreting the data, however, we must remember the caution urged previously: although the YCS uses a large

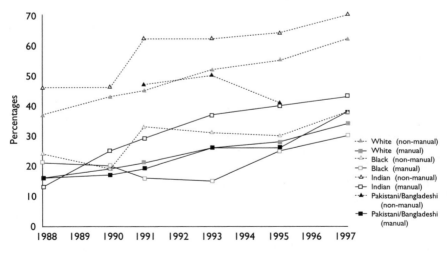

Figure 2.2 GCSE attainment by social class and ethnic origin, England and Wales 1988 to 1997 (five or more higher grade (A* to –C) passes)

Source: Youth Cohort Study (state schools only): DfEE and Demack *et al.* (2000).

and nationally representative sample, some of the subsamples can become quite small whenever researchers try simultaneously to analyse several factors. In Figure 2.2, for example, cases have been excluded where the sample was fewer than 30 pupils. Consequently, the combined Pakistani/Bangladeshi category (which has already been created owing to small sample sizes) does not appear for non-manual pupils in three of the six cohorts.

One of the most striking findings is that generally pupils from non-manual backgrounds have significantly higher attainments, as a group, than do their peers of the same ethnic origin but from manual households. The familiar association between class and attainment may be seen to operate within each of the main ethnic groups. This confirms the strong association between class and educational achievement. However, in the case of African Caribbean pupils the social class difference is much less pronounced; indeed, the pattern is actually reversed in one of the cohorts.[15] The data suggest that even when controlling for social class, there remain significant inequalities of attainment between different ethnic groups. For example, only white pupils improved year on year regardless of their class background.[16] During the research period there were points of relative decline in the attainment of African Caribbean and Pakistani/Bangladeshi pupils from both manual and non-manual backgrounds.

Comparing like with like in terms of their class background, clear inequalities of attainment are evident for Pakistani/Bangladeshi and African Caribbean pupils. For most of the period in question, black pupils were less likely to attain five higher grade passes than were peers of the same social class in any other ethnic group. This has not always been the case: at the beginning of the research period, in 1988, black pupils were the most successful of the groups from manual backgrounds. The relative decline of working-class black pupils has therefore been marked. The gap is also particularly striking between African Caribbean pupils from non-manual backgrounds and peers of the same social class in different ethnic groups. Indeed, in the most recent data, Indian and Pakistani/Bangladeshi pupils from manual backgrounds were at least as successful as black pupils from non-manual homes (with white manual pupils only four percentage points behind).

These new data clearly establish that ethnic inequalities persist even when class differences are taken into account. Two clear patterns emerge when considering the interaction of ethnic origin and social class. First, the familiar difference in attainment between pupils from non-manual and manual backgrounds is replicated within each ethnic group. Second, social class factors do not override the influence of ethnic inequality: when comparing pupils with similar class backgrounds there are still marked inequalities of attainment between different ethnic groups. Indeed, in some respects the analysis reveals new inequalities; showing that black pupils from relatively advantaged backgrounds are little better placed, as a group, than white peers from manual backgrounds. This suggests that while targeting class disadvantage is clearly necessary, in isolation such action may have only a limited effect in closing the gap between particular ethnic groups. As the data demonstrate, new areas of concern are emerging where expected social class differentials are mitigated by the effects of 'race' inequality.

The 'gender gap'

In recent years there has been a great deal of discussion about the growing gap between the average attainments of boys and girls in GCSE examinations. Data supplied by the DfEE confirm that the gap is increasing. In 1989, 29.8 per cent of boys and 35.8 per cent of girls attained five or more higher grade GCSE passes, a gap of six percentage points; by 1999, however, the gap had increased to more than ten points, with 42.8 per cent of boys and 53.4 per cent of girls attaining five higher grades.[17] In explaining these changes researchers have pointed to a range of factors, including: new approaches to assessment, teaching and learning; the introduction of comprehensive schooling; and the positive impact of targeted equal opportunities policies (Arnot *et al.* 1998; David and Weiner 1997; Epstein *et al.* 1998a, 1998b: Weiner *et al.* 1997; Wragg 1997). Some have sought to explain boys' lower attainments in relation to changing notions of masculinity and new attitudes to school and work (Mac an Ghaill 1994, 1996; Steinberg *et al.* 1997). It should be remembered, however, that the phenomenon of boys' under-achievement is not consistent across subject areas. There are considerable differences in entry and attainment patterns between the sexes in some curriculum areas, with the relative gains made at GCSE sometimes being reversed later in A level attainment (Arnot *et al.* 1998; Murphy and Elwood 1998). Studies also show that girls face a range of additional barriers in fulfilling their potential.[18] Despite these complexities, notions of a 'new gender gap' (with boys lagging behind) have captured the popular imagination. In this context it is useful to try to contextualise this aspect of educational disparity. Figure 2.3 attempts to set the scale of the gender gap in context by showing differences in attainment between boys and girls alongside examples of ethnic and social class inequalities.[19]

In this illustration the horizontal axis represents the proportion of pupils nationally who attained five or more higher grade GCSE passes and their equivalent. Hence, in 1997 (the most recent year for which YCS data are available), five or more higher grades were attained nationally by 45 per cent of pupils overall: this included 51 per cent of girls (six percentage points above the national average) and 42 per cent of boys (three points below). Consequently, in the illustration, boys' attainment is positioned three points below the national average, and girls appear six points above the axis. The illustration shows that the gender gap is considerably smaller than those associated with 'race' and class. In the latest figures the black/white gap is twice the size of the gender gap.[20] In relation to the national average it is clear

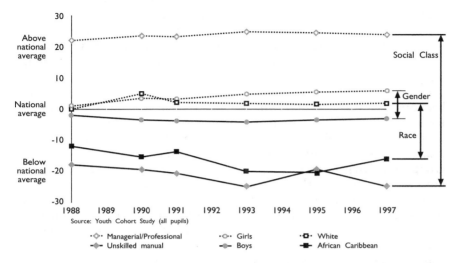

Figure 2.3 Attainment inequalities by race, class and gender, England and Wales 1988 to 1997 (five or more higher grade GCSEs relative to the national average)

Source: Youth Cohort Study (all pupils).

that black pupils and their peers from unskilled manual homes experience the greatest disadvantage. Figure 2.3 is, of course, only a relatively crude comparison: as already shown, patterns of attainment vary by social class background within ethnic groups (see above). Nevertheless, the illustration is helpful because it characterises something of the relative scale of these inequalities. Indeed, this analysis suggests that, of the three best-known dimensions of inequality ('race', class and gender) the latter, gender, and in particular boys' underperformance, represents the narrowest disparity. In contrast to the disproportionate media attention, these data show gender to be a less problematic issue than the significant disadvantage of 'race', and the even greater inequality of class. The intention here is to contextualise these relative disadvantages: it is important not to fall into the trap of simply arguing between various inequalities. All pupils have a gender, class and ethnic identity – the factors do not operate in isolation.

'Race' and gender

Qualitative research showing African Caribbean girls doing relatively well in comparison to their white male and female peers within the locality of their schools has been much cited as evidence of gender-specific strategies to resist racism and overcome disadvantage (Fuller 1980; Mac an Ghaill 1988;

Mirza 1992). This has generally been misinterpreted to mean that it is only black boys, and not girls, who face inequalities. However, these data from the Youth Cohort Study suggest that while the gender gap is now established within each of the principal minority ethnic groups, there are nevertheless consistent and significant inequalities of attainment between ethnic groups regardless of pupils' gender.

Figure 2.4 presents data on GCSE attainments by ethnic origin and gender, between 1988 and 1995, which indicate that by 1991 girls in the Pakistani/Bangladeshi group had emulated girls in other ethnic groups by overtaking their male peers.[21] By 1995 a pattern was established with a gender gap of similar proportions within each ethnic group (with girls in each group about ten percentage points ahead of boys).[22] As Figure 2.4 illustrates, however, throughout this period there have also been consistent and significant inequalities of attainment between ethnic groups regardless of pupils' gender. Since 1991 white girls and Indian girls have attained five higher grade passes in roughly similar proportions with a considerable gap between them and Pakistani/Bangladeshi and African Caribbean girls. As with findings noted previously in this report (e.g. in relation to unequal shares in the benefits of change) the data highlight a particular disadvantage experienced by Pakistani/Bangladeshi and African Caribbean pupils. Here the girls attain rather higher than their male peers but the gender gap within their groups is insufficient to close the pronounced inequality of attainment associated with their ethnic group as a whole. The inequalities of attainment of Bangladeshi/Pakistani and African Caribbean girls not only mean that they do less well than white and Indian girls, they are also less likely to attain five higher grade GCSEs than white and Indian boys.

These data must be treated with caution. When controlling for multiple background factors (such as ethnic origin and gender) the sample sizes in the

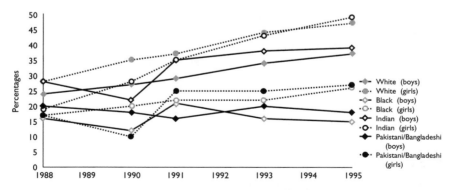

Figure 2.4 GCSE attainment by gender and ethnic origin, England and Wales 1988 to 1995 (five or more higher grade (A* to −C) passes)

Source: Youth Cohort Study (state schools only): DfEE and Demack et al. (2000).

YCS begin to shrink dramatically.[23] It is worth noting, however, that several of the LEA applications for funding under the Ethnic Minority Achievement Grant include data that support the same general trends. In one especially large metropolitan authority, for example, 28 per cent of African Caribbean girls attained five or more higher grade GCSEs: a rate of success higher than African Caribbean boys (13 per cent) but lower than white and Indian pupils irrespective of gender. The same pattern is true for Pakistani girls in the LEA (see Figure 2.5). As we have already seen, there is a range of variation at the local level: nevertheless, data such as this (both from one of the country's biggest LEAs and from a nationally representative survey) suggest that ethnic inequalities of attainment are not confined to any particular gender. Thus it may be concluded that when controlling for ethnic origin and gender, the data reveal similar patterns to when they were subjected to controls by social class (above). 'Race' and ethnicity remain key defining factors in both cases.

'Race', class and gender

While there are many studies that look at the separate effects of 'race' or class or gender there is a dearth of research that addresses these three variables together. The Youth Cohort Study provides a unique opportunity to analyse the three variables of 'race', class and gender simultaneously: we are fortunate here in being able to draw on the most up-to-date analyses of relevant YCS data. Figures 2.6 and 2.7 illustrate the proportion of pupils attaining at least five higher grade GCSEs in relation to their gender, social class and ethnic origin.[24] Because of small sample sizes it has again been necessary to combine the Pakistani and Bangladeshi groups and to use a twofold model of social class (comparing non-manual and manual backgrounds). Even so there are

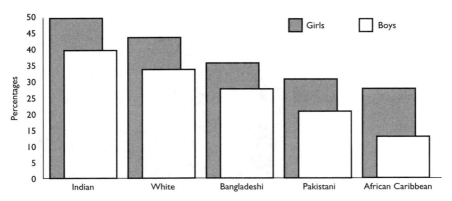

Figure 2.5 GCSE attainment by gender and ethnic origin for one LEA in 1998 (five or more higher grade (A* to −C) passes)

Source: EMAG submission (1999).

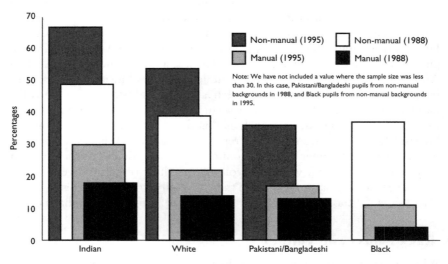

Figure 2.6 GCSE attainment in England and Wales 1988 and 1995: boys by social class and ethnic origin (five or more higher grade (A* to –C) passes)

Source: Youth Cohort Study: Demack *et al.* (1999, 2000).

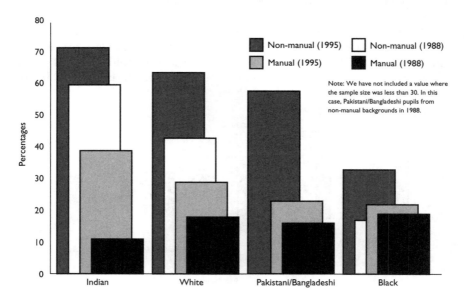

Figure 2.7 GCSE attainment in England and Wales 1988 and 1995: girls by social class and ethnic origin (five or more higher grade (A* to –C) passes)

Source: Youth Cohort Study: Demack *et al.* (1999, 2000).

still cases where individual values would represent less than 30 pupils and, in these cases, the values have not been shown in the relevant illustration.

As would be predicted on the basis of the findings established up until this point, pupils in each category (comparing like with like in terms of gender, social class and ethnic origin) were more likely to attain five high-grade GCSEs in 1995 than they were in 1988. The significance of this finding should not be overlooked: it means that every group has drawn some benefit from the general improvements in attainment over the past decade or so. However, the emerging pattern of ethnic inequalities (noted in earlier sections of this chapter) is also present and in both the 1988 and 1995 cohorts. Comparing pupils of the same gender and social class background there are five groups for whom we have a value for each ethnic group in the research: in four of these cases Indian pupils did best, followed by white, Pakistani/Bangladeshi and black pupils respectively.[25] Bearing in mind the limitations of the data, the conclusions here are tentative. Nevertheless, the available evidence points to the following: the gender gap is present within each ethnic group regardless of social class background; ethnic inequalities persist even when simultaneously controlling for gender and class; when comparing like with like in terms of gender, class and ethnic origin, consistent and significant ethnic inequalities of attainment remain clear.

Conclusion

A number of broad conclusions may be drawn from this review concerning education inequalities in relation to 'race', class and gender. First, ethnic inequalities of attainment vary from one area to another but, despite this variability, distinct patterns of inequality are consistently visible. Second, inequalities of attainment in GCSE examinations place African Caribbean, Pakistani and Bangladeshi pupils in a disadvantaged position in the youth education, labour and training markets, and increase the likelihood of social and economic exclusion in later life. Third, social class and gender differences are also associated with differences in attainment but neither can account for persistent underlying ethnic inequalities: comparing like with like, African-Caribbean, Pakistani and Bangladeshi pupils do not enjoy equal opportunities. Finally, ethnic inequalities are not new but neither are they static. Evidence shows that in some cases the inequalities have increased in recent years. African-Caribbean and Pakistani pupils, for example, have not shared equally in the rising levels of GCSE attainment.

In the context of an inclusive educational agenda that seeks to raise standards for all, this evidence indicates a need for clarity and guidance in translating the commitment to equality and inclusion (so often expressed at the national level) into policy proposals and practice at the local/school level. Since the last OFSTED review of research on the achievements of minority ethnic pupils, several studies have added to the attempt to identify school and local education (LEA)-based strategies for raising minority attainment.[26] Certain factors repeatedly emerge as significant, including:

- strong leadership on equal opportunities and social justice (from the LEA and the headteacher in particular);
- seeking and using pupil and parent perspectives;
- designing and enacting clear procedures for recording and acting on racist incidents;
- generating and sustaining an ethos that is open and vigilant, which enables pupils to discuss 'race' issues and share concerns;
- developing and communicating high expectations accompanied by a clear view that under-performance by any group is unacceptable;
- reviewing curricular and pastoral approaches to ensure their sensitivity and appropriateness;
- using ethnic monitoring as a routine and rigorous part of the school's/ LEA's self-evaluation and management.

Schools and LEAs require support and encouragement in their attempts to develop and sustain good practice in this area. It is evident from our analysis of the EMAG submissions that there is no clear consensus about how the inclusion agenda, prominent in some official policy statements, should be translated into real change at the school and LEA level. In keeping with existing approaches to inclusion and equal opportunities in education, and in view of new legislation which places a positive duty on the public sector, including schools, to promote racial equality, the development of more inclusive strategies presents a clear way forward.

Part 2

Theorising race and gender differences

Chapter 3

Race, gender and IQ[1]

Issues of differential intelligence among racial and gendered groups in society seem to still capture the popular imagination even now, 150 years since the rise of social Darwinism. Press reports of black people as less intelligent have been aroused in the UK by the publication of *The Bell Curve* in the USA. Similarly, reports that girls may be outperforming boys in examination results has invoked much media attention, reviving issues of differential genetic capacities between the sexes. This chapter, based on the Lister Lecture presented at the British Association for the Advancement of Science, aims to ask, 'Why does IQ, as an explanation for differential educational performance between the races and sexes, remain so popular?' Despite its controversial empiricism, suspect methodology and inconclusive claims, the appeal of this pseudoscientific discourse remains intact. Its logical presentation of 'facts' and simple causal explanations heralds a 'new post-biological discourse' on 'difference'. In the new millenium, ideas about innate, genetic, scientifically provable difference are still at the heart of our thinking about race and gender.

A natural state of affairs?

Why does the visible matter so much in this world? Why does everything seem to come down to what we see, to what is skin-deep, to what is on the surface? No matter what anti-racist science says, and it currently says we are all the same, from the same common ancestor 'out of Africa', young black people in Britain, those marked by physical, phenotypical, external, visible difference – those with dark skin, curly hair, almond eyes, full lips, proud noses – do not enjoy the same opportunities as young white people.

I know this because research shows that 30 per cent of young black and Asian people are unemployed compared to 12 per cent of white youth – and when they do get a job 20 to 50 per cent earn below the minimum wage (CRE 1997a). I know this because it is three times harder to get a job interview if you are Asian, and five times harder if you are black (CRE 1997b). I know that even though ethnic minorities are more likely to have a higher educational qualification than their white peers, the unemployment rate is twice as much for them (9 per cent) than among similarly qualified whites (4 per cent) (*Guardian*, 4 February 1997).

And the list goes on. Young black people are four times more likely to be excluded from school (Gillborn and Gipps 1996). They are two and a half times more likely to be stopped by police (*Guardian*, 4 February 1997: CRE 1997c). Asians are 50 times and African Caribbeans are 36 times more likely than whites to be the victims of racial violence (Kirby *et al.* 1997: 200; CRE 1997d).

Is this a natural state of affairs? Is this just the way things are? We say we live in a free and equal society, we say we are fair-minded, open. We have noble ideas of equality, that we are all the same, or even, if different, that at the very least we are all equal. . . . If this is the case, why does this belief in equality not match the facts of inequality? I am confused by this contradiction, this tension in the difference between what we say and what we do. How do I explain the daily racism that floods my senses when I go about my business of researching in schools or teaching at university? Where does it come from?

I need to understand the origin of the words of a teacher when they tell me, 'These black girls have absolutely no motivation . . . most of them will never succeed . . . they are just unable to remember. They can't make it at this level never mind what is demanded in higher education.' I need to understand the origin of the thoughts of a university professor who says, 'Black men take up so much space, I'm not being racist – I mean no offence . . . but they are so big, when we are all in the same room I can't possibly tell them what to do . . . they might react.'

What does it mean when a woman of God, a Catholic nun, a teacher in a school, says, 'You can't have a sports day, things just wouldn't be fair. All the blacks will win the prizes and that would cause trouble.' What propels a well-known 'African expert', an anthropologist, to say to me, 'Africans haven't reached our levels of education yet . . . their writing isn't as good, so I make allowances in publishing their work. I don't apply the same standards.'

How do I explain the motivation of a primary teacher who says to a young black child that she has been cheating when she gets all her sums right? Where do the monkey noises come from when a black boy enters a classroom? Who ignites the fire of hatred which burns in the letter-box of an Asian pensioner? Who ties the laces of the boot that chases a young black mother and child down a dark alley? I need to know.

The racial discourse in which we are so deeply embedded is a confusing moral maze. On the one hand there is colour-blindness, a deracialisation of the discourse. No one wants to speak of difference, though it is one of the most observable phenomena in our global, fast, mixing-and-matching world. Colour-blindness is the polite language of race (Williams 1997). It is not polite to see the physical differences. In its well-meaning false optimism it proclaims, 'we're all the same under the skin'. It says, 'some of my best friends are'. It hears all our children sing, 'we are the world, we are the children' as they hold hands and float up to the sky in a cloud of peace and love. 'We're all human', it says, ignoring the realities of racism and social divisions.

Shit through a letter box, 'it's only youthful high spirits'.

Sorry we have no seats left, 'you're being over-sensitive'.

They won't give me a job, 'you're imagining it my dear'.

But when I look there is no chip on my shoulder.

But the catch-22 of colour-blindness is that while it wants to distance itself from biological essentialist racism – that overt racism which preys on physical difference – it does not challenge racism. In so doing it maintains the status quo, it validates inequalities, which in turn fuels the arguments of biological racism.

On the other hand we are told we are all different. We are encouraged to celebrate our differences, to revel in our multicultural diversity, to be ethnic and interesting, to be tolerant of our differences, to put on our saris, and dance the dance of the exotic and desirable, because in this melting-pot, in this world of colour and spice, are we not after all different but equal? But when we celebrate these differences, when our backs are turned in pleasure, the worm crawls out from under the stone. The voice of racism whispers, 'Of course you are different, culturally different, nationally different, inherently different, essentially different. Difference is in the blood. Being British is in the blood. Blacks can't be British – we know, we've given them the "cricket test." '[2]

In the postmodern world of difference we talk of foreigners, Englishness, aliens. Cultural boundaries are drawn around who belongs or not. The way you speak, the way you look, the way you dress – it is in the blood. It is obvious, you cannot learn to become what you are intrinsically not. In these boundaries, within these paper walls of difference, racial hatred breeds – harassment flourishes. What Gayatri Spivak calls chromatism (Fuss 1989: 92), and Franz Fanon epidermalisation (Hall 1996: 20) – the inscription of race on the skin – lingers under the cloak of culture. Both black and white are caught in the drama.

But where does the drama start? I need to know. The question I want to ask is this:

Why is there a lingering desire among us to name racial and cultural difference as in the blood, in the genes, as natural? I want to know if the dangerous words of the marginal racist pseudoscientists with their biological theories keep alive popular arguments of innate sexual and racial inferiority. I want to know if their accessible commonsense explanations of social difference reflect or play on public ideas and beliefs about racial difference.

Ruth Frankenberg in her excellent book *White Women, Race Matters* (1993) – a book about the social construction of whiteness, that invisible but powerful position of normative race privilege – argues that ontological, essential biological difference, a discourse that dominated race thinking for more than 500 years, is still an absent presence. She explains that, because biological racism marked the inauguration of race as meaningful difference, contemporary commonsense articulations about racial identity, whether culturally constructed or not, still have to engage with it. She writes:

> Essentialist racism has left a legacy that continues to mark discourses on race and difference in a range of ways. First precisely because it proposed race as a significant axis of difference, essentialist racism remains the benchmark against which other discourses on race are articulated.
> (Frankenberg 1993: 139)

I would agree, but would like to take this one stage further. I want to argue that biological racism is more than a term of reference for the manifestations of our contemporary racial discourse – manifestations such as anti-racism, colour-blindness or cultural racism. Because biological racism has not been exorcised from our vocabulary, from our mental maps, our ideas of 'them and us', essentialist notions of race – those notions of innate inherent difference – remain intact. I want to suggest that essentialist thinking actually occupies a far more central and sinister place in our social understanding of difference than our polite, civilised sensibilities would like to acknowledge. Thus despite the apparent 'writing out' of essentialism in the new postmodern academic discourse on identity and difference as a fiction, I would argue that good old-fashioned biological racism is alive and well and living in a place near you.

Science fiction; social fact

It is no accident that gender and race, two visible differences, two physical ways in which we are marked as different, have become two characteristics that are firmly linked in the equation of modern inequality. When we crack open the sinister box of the pseudoscience of race and gender the picture is disturbing; we see a tangled mass of contradictions where cultural prejudice is shaped and honed into scientific fact.

From the mid-nineteenth century evolutionary biology built fictions, which were woven into narratives of scientific fact (Haraway 1992; Young 1995). At the heart of fictions of empire, of racial superiority and inferiority were analogies. Such analogies were made between the criminal and shiftless poor, childlike, uncivilised savages and infantile, sexually promiscuous women. Nancy Leys Stephan (1990: 40) tells us of a German scholar of race, who in 1864 claimed:

> the female skull approached in many respects that of the infant, and in still further respects that of the lower races, whereas the mature male of many of the lower races resembled in his 'pendulous belly' a Caucasian woman who had many children, and in his thin calves and flat thighs the ape.

Racial inferiority was attributed to the lower orders of society – the 'dangerous classes'. The racialisation of social and class differences within European society was transposed on to exotic different 'other' populations external to European society. Such 'races apart' symbolised all that the white, civilised male feared he was as not. Powerful metaphors which likened the so-called lower races and women to anthropoid apes or children seeped into the logic of science. In an effort to construct human nature, choices were made in the study of human differences. Brains of women were deemed smaller, selectively ignoring that their body weight was also less. The African similarity to apes through measuring the jaw was asserted, ignoring white men's similarity to the animal on the basis of thin lips. In the selective construction of physical data, commonsense analogies were confirmed. Arbitrary relationships were made to seem as 'natural phenomena'. In this way unconscious representations were turned into self-conscious theory. During this time, 150 years ago, Frederick Douglas, the African American philosopher, observed:

> When men oppress their fellow men the oppressor finds, in the character of the oppressed, a full justification for his oppression . . . by making the enslaved a character fit only for slavery, they excuse themselves for refusing to make the slave a free man.
>
> (quoted in Gates 1995: 94)

But this was 150 years ago. Surely we don't think like this now? Let us consider how these myths of rationalised racism are given form and shape in twentieth-century racist and sexist pseudoscience. In *The Bell Curve* (Herrnstein and Murray 1994), a bestselling book on race and intelligence in America, we have a prime example of the social construction of a pseudoscientific discourse. Here, like their nineteenth-century counterparts, myths, intuition and social prejudice are all laid into the bedrock of so-called scientific method.

Three years ago Herrnstein and Murray, two hereditarian psychologists, unleashed *The Bell Curve*, a 800-page tome of statistical and social analysis.

They claimed that high levels of hereditary genetic intelligence correlates with success in school, ultimate job status and therefore high IQ naturally lead to membership within the 'cognitively entitled' establishment. Logically it follows, in their argument, that low intelligence is the cause of America's immediate and observable social problems, the underclass, those who, because of their culturally deficient behaviour and low IQ, would besmirch the social fabric with their poverty, educational failure, unemployment, illegitimacy, chronic welfare dependency and crime.

In a mass of what has since become publicly denounced as statistically unsound and misleading data (Drew *et al.* 1995; Fischer *et al.* 1996; Fraser 1995), Herrnstein and Murray produce a bell curve – the graphical illustration of the normal distribution of intelligence. It is in there, in the curve, that we find the racial subtext that fuels their agenda. The authors argue that African Americans score on average 15 points lower than whites on IQ tests and that one in five blacks score below 75, the borderline of mental retardation.

Women, poor women of both races, are particularly demonised. The authors write: 'going on welfare really is a dumb idea, and that is why women who are low in cognitive ability end up there' (Herrnstein and Murray 1994: 201). In their analysis unwed mothers are the root cause of everything that plagues the nation. They argue that these women produce low-birthweight babies with low IQs who will themselves grow up to become chronic welfare recipients and abusive parents: a natural causal cycle, a cycle of poverty, a cycle of deprivation. Their message is plain and simple: don't waste taxpayers' money on affirmative action or educational initiatives, welfare handouts or anti-discrimination legislation – these folks are dumb, culturally and intellectually predetermined and social spending will make no difference.

For them, differences in intelligence and therefore differences in attainment are natural, genetic, ordained by God – each is in its appointed place. Given this natural state of affairs they conclude with the advice that 'It is time for America once again to try living with inequality, as life is lived' (ibid.: 551). In this unstoppable 'cognitively partitioned society', the poor and dispossessed will naturally be driven to inhabit a different world from the rich, cognitive elite. In their second-class world, Herrnstein and Murray benignly argue that these wretched citizens can create a valued place for themselves in spite of their meagre intellectual gifts.

But in classic pseudoscientific tradition *The Bell Curve*'s argument confuses observation with explanation; it muddles selective correlation with purposeful causation. Here in the world of pseudoscience, socially constructed difference becomes hardened into ideological fact from which biological truths are then exacted. Like their nineteenth-century counterparts, Herrnstein and Murray take commonsense observation and culturally, racially biased intuition as a so-called self-evident truth and then seek to statistically verify their beliefs. Social prejudice becomes scientifically legitimated. The narratives of 'truth' they weave appear organic, natural, until fiction becomes fact. However, like their nineteenth-century counterparts what Herrnstein and Murray choose to leave out is more telling than what they choose to put in.

In Herrnstein and Murray's racist pseudoscience they choose to tell us that intelligence is more important than socioeconomic status in determining jobs. But they choose not to tell us that IQ rises with educational opportunities, nutrition and environment (Fischer *et al.* 1996). Herrnstein and Murray choose not to tell us that IQ and eventual social success appear to go together because both are consequences of other causes. For example, family background rather than IQ is the overwhelming reason why an individual ends up with a higher than average income. Strong performance on IQ is simply a reflection of a certain kind of family environment and access to certain types of schooling. Thus a correlation may appear near perfect intuitively, such as IQ and social success, but have little or no causal relation. In an effort to show that statistical correlation is not the same as causation, Stephen Jay Gould, author of *The Mismeasure of Man* (1981), a relentless critique of pseudoscientific claims on intelligence, gives an example of a near-perfect correlation between his age and the expansion of the universe, demonstrating that correlations can be made between anything (see also Kohn 1996: 92).

In racist pseudoscience they choose not to tell us that IQ tests are culturally loaded to measure specialised skills (Rose *et al.* 1984: 89). Tests measure culturally specific vocabulary. They measure culturally specific class judgements. They measure socially acceptable behaviour. They also embody racial assumptions. In the IQ test I was given and failed when I was 10, I even remember being asked which doll was prettier when given a choice between a black doll and a white doll.

High IQ scores have a strong correlation with whether individuals were raised in a setting which habituated them to the kinds of mental processes the tests assess (Hacker 1995). One-a-minute multiple choice demands you have a matrix in your mind that mirrors a multiple-choice format. The very design of the test determines who will do well. IQ tests are not an independent predictor of social success. The varied tests have been standardised to correlate well with school performance. They measure acquired knowledge, not innate intelligence. The notion that they measure intelligence as a fixed potential is simply a justification to validate them.

In racist pseudoscience they tell us that there are greater differences between racial groups than within any one particular racial group (Eysenck 1973; Jensen 1973; Herrnstein and Murray 1994). However, Rose *et al.* in their superb and now classic book *Not in our Genes* (1984), demonstrate convincingly that geneticists have shown that 85 per cent of all genetic variation is between individuals within the same local population. Just 7 per cent of genetic variation is between the major races. Similarly, as Marek Kohn in his book *The Race Gallery* (1996) – a meticulous unveiling of racist biological determinism – explains, in any one population the range of differences is so great that no common assumptions can be drawn about the innate capacities of a race. In considering the arguments for African sporting prowess he explains:

> Africans are not all alike . . . Africa encompasses the greatest variability in its human populations. To take visible characteristics alone, the tallest and the shortest people on Earth are found there; as are people with the thickest and the thinnest lips.
>
> (Kohn 1996: 82)

In racist pseudoscience they choose to tell us that there is such a thing as innate hereditary general intelligence, g; g, they tell us, is the general factor of cognitive ability on which humans differ as measured by IQ tests. In fact the whole credibility of racist pseudoscience depends on the very existence of g. But g is no more than a statistical artefact, meaning that it is made up out of thin air (Kohn 1996). g is derived from the factor analysis of dubious IQ test scores. It has been shown to appear and disappear according to manipulation of the data (Gould 1995). Thus pseudoscientific race studies follow all the apparent precepts of scientific investigation, but here's the catch: the object of their study, g, doesn't exist, it has no external reality. Quite simply general intelligence upon which their entire science of social and racial difference is based is not a verifiable immutable thing in the head.

Herrnstein and Murray warn that governments should wake up and recognise the correlation between race and IQ as a 'smoking gun', a social time-bomb in their midst. They argue that America will soon have a custodial state on their hands, one that will resemble 'a high tech more lavish version of the Indian Reservation' (Herrnstein and Murray 1994: 526). But the relationship between race, IQ and social difference is just a pack of cards, a confidence trick, a house of straw, a puff of smoke, poof!

Popular persuasion

If racist pseudoscience is so clearly the work of the crackpot fringe whose scientific claims have been globally denounced, why is it so popular? *The Bell Curve* made the front cover of *Newsweek*. It was on the *New York Times* bestseller list for 30 weeks (Drew *et al.* 1995). Why were 400,000 copies printed in two months? Why do we morbidly crave biological explanations for social phenomena? Why do we yearn to quantify and qualify our differences in essential terms? Why do we still say, 'it is all in our genes'?

We live in a climate where the public love affair with genetic determinism – easy, televisable, reportable, bizarre, almost paranormal explanations – seizes the public imagination. We like to hear the anecdotal tales of the

Minnesota Study of twins, who though genetically similar but raised apart, end up sharing the same habit of flushing the toilet before as well as after using it (see Kohn 1996: 103). It would seem that this new age of gene science appears to be able to accommodate a new, popular version of biological determinism. Our physical visible differences have become popular public spectacle.

On the front page of our newspapers, we can read that by extracting the DNA from ancient bones, as the *Guardian* headline announces, 'We're African, No bones about it' (*Guardian*, 11 July 1997). We are drawn into the unfolding racial drama that this finding has triggered. We can read the counter-claim by racial scientists that this still does not mean that we are equal. Pseudoscience has an Ice Age theory that whites have a higher IQ because they had to adapt to the cold. It would appear from their theory that Native Americans and Innuit Indians did not get quite cold enough (*The Times*, 10 August 1997). DNA testing just is no match for pseudoscientific logic.

We can read more socially acceptable racial theory about the possibility of genes for sporting prowess in headlines about Linford Christie proclaiming 'Can Blacks Run Faster than Whites?' (*Sun*, 17 August 1993). The racial drama is played out, images are captured in our minds as we can see that with the right cultural opportunities and personal dedication 'white men can also jump' (Kohn 1996: 82–83). Turn on the TV, open a newspaper. In a time of Aids, when public fears are heightened, the public is reassured that there is a gay gene – so don't worry: homosexuality is not contagious. In an age of stress, depression and Prozac, the papers reassure us that there is a gene for happiness. In a time of a crisis of family values, we are even told there is now a gene for divorce (*Guardian*, 17 June 1997).

In public discourse the search for the 'truth' about the issue of innate gender differences is recurring front-page news. The received wisdom of sex differences is that cerebrally, females live with language in the left hemisphere and males live in the visual-spatial in the right hemisphere. This, we are told, explains why boys are mathematically skilled and more aggressive and hence more successful than girls. In a free society, we are told, gendered job choices are merely a reflection of this innate psychology, a natural ability. When this 'safe' commonsense wisdom is challenged by the current awareness of female success in schools, it sends the press into a feeding frenzy. It's news! Over the past four years headlines report the panic: 'Male Brian Rattled by Curriculum Oestrogen' (*The Times Education Supplement*, 14 March 1997); 'Go Ahead Girls Leave Experts with a Mystery' (*Sunday Times*, 22 May 1994). The cause of the fuss is that examination results for GCSE show that girls are outperforming boys in nearly every subject. Girls do well especially in English, which is up by 15 per cent, but not maths, where the gap is closing but still stands at 2 per cent.

The safe parameters of the natural social order are upset by the statistical research showing a closing of the gender gap in educational performance.

Research by the Equal Opportunities Commission (Arnot *et al.* 1996), the Institute of Education (Elwood 1995; Elwood and Comber 1996) and South Bank University (Weiner *et al.* 1997) shows that the difference is due to a complex range of factors that bring girls back into the classroom picture. Changes in exam technique, the move towards more coursework, and preference and confidence in subject choices all affect educational performance of the different sexes. Changes in school culture together with equal opportunities is making a difference. Thus it is not so much that the boys are failing, as the panicked headlines exclaim, but rather that the girls are beginning, for the first time, to have access to learning experiences previously not available to them socially and materially.

On the surface, in the public discourse on gender differences, the evidence of the influence of policy changes should suggest that biological determinism should be in retreat. But you quickly learn that there are never winners. In the cultural war of difference biological reductionism always finds a new path. It would appear that in this age of genetic technology the old gender nature/nurture debate lives on, only now it is a case of old wine in new test tubes. Here the backlash can be witnessed in recent sensational headlines which read, 'X Certificate Behaviour' (*Guardian*, 12 July 1997); 'Genes Say Boys will be Boys and Girls will be Sensitive' (*Guardian*, 14 July 1997). This front-page news reports the latest piece of sexist pseudoscience. Here the universal evidence for women's intuition and social deftness, and men's oafishness and lack of social skills, was deduced from a sample of 80 children with a rare disease, Turners Syndrome. With Turners Syndrome the children inherit only one X chromosome rather than the usual XX for girls and XY for boys.

What the headline never told us is that this so-called genetic result was deduced from inconclusive test scores calculated from questionnaire data. The questionnaire data included responses from parents who were asked questions like, 'Does your child lack an awareness of other people's feelings?'; and 'Is your child difficult to reason with when upset?' Quite simply the researchers assert the existence of the physical presence of genes for gender differences from a process of commonsense social deduction from personality questionnaires. Shades of IQ testing: can we call this science?

It would seem that the persistence of racist and sexist pseudoscience is the outcome of a deep underlying tension that marks contemporary society, namely the tension between the ideology of equality and universal humanity – the foundation of our liberal right-minded thinking – and the continued persistence of material, economic social inequality. Kenan Malik in his masterful and challenging analysis of racial discourse echoes this line of thinking in his book *The Meaning of Race* (1996: 225) when he argues:

> The discourse on race did not arise out of the categories of Enlightenment discourse but out of the relationship between Enlightenment thought and

the social organisation of capitalism. The disparity between the abstract belief in equality and the reality of an unequal society slowly gave rise to the idea that differences were natural, not social.

I would argue further that this contradiction – an ideology of equality and the social reality of inequality – has opened up a space in the discourse, a festering wound, which has allowed for the continued thinking that differences, whether cultural or physical, are innate, fixed and immutable. The 'New Right' have set up shop in this intellectual vacuum, this space of irreconcilable tension. They claim they carry the banner of good sense; they are the courageous vanguards of sensible thinking who are brave enough to speak the unspeakable truth about social difference. Like Herrnstein and Murray they proclaim, 'the truth will out'. They inform us, albeit regrettably, and with deep pathos, that the pseudo-facts of their pseudo-findings propel them to tell the pseudo-truth no matter how much they are beaten back by the waves of political correctness and loony left censorship. Thus the focus on inherent, heritable difference has become a quick fix, an easy explanation, a way of 'blaming the victim' when faced with the material reality of privilege and wealth, and racially structured political and economic inequality.

The underclass 'litmus test'

If we were to employ the logic of commonsense pseudoscientific assumptions about race and gender, let them arrive at their 'natural conclusion', then we would be compelled to find that black females, those marked by double inferiority of skin and sex, should hardly even register on the intelligence scale. These gendered and racialised nitwits, these wretched beings, who as Herrnstein and Murray suggest are 'really dumb' owing to their cultural and social predication to be unwed, single, teenage mothers, should, in their reckoning, be relegated to the dustbin of society.

But you don't have to be a member of the 'crackpot racist fringe' to believe the female-centred pathology of what is considered to be the mainly black underclass. The unredeeming picture of black women in Britain and America is that of the unmarried lone mother scrounging on the welfare, and having babies to manipulate and bribe their way into council accommodation. Man haters, man lovers, trying their best, but oh so many babies, not very clever, a drain on society. Such pervasive images seep into our minds when we pass through the decrepid, seething, inner city. We pity the poor women trapped in their council flats, those harassed souls who stuff their screaming, ungrateful children into very expensive pushchairs (how *do* they afford those? we ask).

We need a 'War on Poverty' we are told (*The Times Educational Supplement*, 22 July 1997). And as fast as lightning the government's solution is a unified crusade to get single mothers back to work. But haven't they heard that the 'War on Poverty' is not a very novel idea? It has been the rhetoric of empty government vessels in America for years. In 1989 Murray even came to England on a messianic mission to seek out the underclass (Murray 1994). After a few hours on a council estate in Peckham, he declared to *The Sunday Times* that like the plague the disease of the underclass has spread from America and will, in five years' time, overrun the UK. I understand he has been back periodically in a blaze of New Right publicity to check on his failing prophecy (Lister 1996).

If I didn't know better, if I was not one of 'them', one of those dumb and hopeless women, I may even be persuaded by the fear produced by the rhetoric of the underclass cancer in our midst. But I was one of them. I did and still do live in the inner city, I went to school in Brixton, I was a teenage mum, I am a lone mother – hey, I must be stupid, of course I am; remember: I failed my IQ test! But this is just anecdotal evidence, not real research. Anyway, as I am always reminded by those who do not want to upset the comfortable parameters of their social order, 'you are an exception to the rule, not like the others, the one that got away'. But I am not different. It is the myths that structure our ideas of social reality that are the problem. Myths about teenage mothers, who become lone mothers. Lone mothers who cannot read and write, who are themselves poor parents and whose children without love and care go on to join the ranks of the educational under-achievers. That is the unabiding logic, the mythical cyclical causation that lies at the heart of the black underclass debate.

We need to apply the 'litmus test' to test the salience of these myths. The underclass myths grounded and fuelled by the common sense of racist and sexist pseudoscience. These paper myths construct a social problem until we all believe it, even though it isn't really there. The litmus test I propose lies in the disclosure of the facts about the black female condition in Britain. Seeing the world from a different perspective, a black feminist perspective rather than the dominant political perspective, can produce a very different picture. Let us dip the blood-red paper of the racist pseudoscience claims into the cauldron of the black underclass debate and see what happens. If the paper turns transparent, if it becomes invisible, vanishes into thin air, then there is no truth in their claims.

First, let us litmus test the issue of black teenage mothers. Teenage mothers both black and white make up less than 5 per cent of lone mothers in Britain (Phoenix 1991). And if lone mothers make up only 14 per cent of all mothers (Reynolds 1997) this leaves the numbers of black teenage mothers so small that it is hardly calculable. Research by Ann Phoenix, in her authoritative book on the subject *Young Mothers?*, shows that teen mothers are not necessarily lone mothers, and many are married. In addition, teenage mothers are not a breed apart; they make highly rational choices which are not dissimilar from older mothers. They do not get pregnant to get on to welfare. Poverty is not an aspiration of young people. The litmus paper vanishes in a cloud of dust.

Second, we need to litmus test the myth of the black lone mother. To begin with, we need to put the numbers of black lone mothers into perspective. Surprisingly, only 7 per cent of lone mothers in Britain are black (Reynolds 1997). Again, if lone mothers make up only 14 per cent of all households in the UK we are talking about a very small group of women. So why does the image of the black lone mother have a larger-than-life presence? Why do politicians, newspapers and TV all ride upon their breaking backs? What the last census shows us is that the black community (African Caribbean) suffers from a disproportionate number of lone mothers. Black women are three-and-a-half times more likely than white women to be in a female-headed household (Reynolds 1997). This phenomenon has caused an outcry concerning the crisis of the black family. The failing black family, we are told, is classically dysfunctional. The weak and marginal male is absent, feckless, lazy and emasculated. He is left to dwindle on the fringes of family life while the domineering matriarch, that insatiable workhorse, that larger-than-life 'superwoman', heads the household, pushing all aside in her single-minded, determined quest for self-satisfaction. What a classic pathology. But oh, what good news for the papers! It has been a central obsession of the black and white press for some time. It has led to stories of love, hate, rejection, blame, and even, God forbid, mixed marriage.

But the current census figure of 49 per cent of lone mothers within the black community does not tell us the whole story (Reynolds 1997). Considering the life cycle of relationships, at any one time a significant proportion of these women (in fact 79 per cent) actually have a male partner and live in a stable conjugal union (Mirza 1992). In my book *Young, Female and Black* (Mirza 1992) I suggest that the progressive and alternative ideology of seeking compatibility between partners rather than economic security through marriage explains the high incidence of lone mothers among black families in Britain. In what I have called the relative autonomy between the sexes in black African Caribbean families, a woman is allowed a great deal of independence and freedom to determine her own circumstances of work and mothering. Such relative autonomy can only be seen as a crisis of family values if female self-determination is viewed from the seat of a fragile patriarchal familial structure under siege.

I want to make one last point with regard to black lone mothers. There has been a somewhat shameful silence concerning an important phenomenon associated with the disproportionate number of black female-headed households – that is, the disproportionate incarceration of black males in prison. Although black men make up only 5 per cent of the British population (Mason 2000) they constitute 18.5 per cent of the prison population (Kirby et al. 1997: 200). What has come to be called black male absenteeism needs careful analysis before cries of dysfunction fall from the lips of the moral majority. Thus in the matter of the mythical construction of lone mothers, pseudoscientists fail the litmus test again.

The third myth propelled by popular pseudoscience, the one that completes the circle of deprivation and dysfunction within the underclass, is the myth of black underachievement. Here, in the analysis of black underachievement, we find the *piece de résistance*, the triumph of all triumphs, the ultimate litmus test against pseudoscientific claims of a deficit black IQ. Young black women are relatively successful in education. In my own research I found that black girls did approximately 6 per cent better than any of their working-class white male and female peers in the same school at GCSE level (Mirza 1992). National statistics show that 47 per cent of young black women (aged 16 to 24) are in full-time education compared to 32 per cent of young white women (CRE 1997c); and overall a greater proportion of these young women have further and higher qualifications (53 per cent) than their white counterparts (43 per cent) (Modood *et al.* 1997). I feel excited, elated, as I search but cannot find those the pseudoscientists promise me I will. Those with low genetic cognitive ability, those racially and sexually predetermined dumb folk. The pseudoscience litmus test on black and gendered IQ has failed yet again.

The reason why so little is known about young black women's success is that black women fall between two discourses that valorise visible difference separately. On the one hand, there is the feminist discourse with its focus on white women, femininity, marriage and reproduction. On the other, there is the race discourse with its focus on black males, aggression, masculinity and exclusions. This dichotomy explains the blind spot, the invisible location that leaves the complex messy and untidy issue of black women's success unaddressed. Black female success upsets established clean-cut ways of thinking about race on the one hand, and gender on the other. But let us rupture the fixity of these discourses and sing a new song. It's about time. Black female success must be understood as a process of transcendence, resistance and survival. It must be understood in the context of racism, discrimination and poor conditions. These young women do well compared to their peers in their run-down, poorly staffed, chaotic, failing schools. They strive to do well.

In *Young, Female and Black* I show how it happens (Mirza 1992). I argue that the young women employ a range of strategic acts which enables them to rationalise their restricted opportunities. Classrooms were no places to learn. Much of the education was custodial, to keep them in and off the streets. But the girls worked on their own, at the back of the chaotic classrooms, at home in crowded rooms. Teachers had had enough, 'they have no motivation; they can't learn; send them back', were some of the things I was told by those charged with the responsibility for their minds. But the young women learned to avoid subjects taught by racist teachers and, within those constraints and without support, they carefully chose subjects that would allow them access to further and higher education.

They would accept the 'realistic careers' they were guided towards as carers, nurses and office workers only because, at the end of it all, it meant a chance of going to college. They would tell me that it was not that they wanted to be a nurse and clean bedpans like their mums, but that it meant that maybe this would lead to learning, real learning, in an atmosphere of trust and respect. Perhaps an access course in social studies, then a diploma in social work, and then, several years down the road the ultimate goal, a university degree. They had ingeniously worked out a system of 'backdoor entry' into further and higher education. It was a sad indictment of the pervasiveness of their circumstances that it had become an unspoken norm among these young women that racism would not allow them the normal route into university. Unlike their black male counterparts, young black women could move ahead by rationalising the racist and sexist assumptions of the labour market which, at the moment, has opportunities for low-paid women's work in caring and adminstration for them to fit into and work their way out of.

The story of the black struggle to gain access to educational privilege that others take for granted can be told at many levels. Recent statistics for university entrance show that in relation to population size ethnic minorities are over-represented in the new universities compared to the white population. For example, African Caribbean students are over-represented by 42 per cent, Asians by 162 per cent and Africans by 223 per cent. This compared to the white population which is under-represented by 7 per cent (Modood and Shiner 1994).

I have also been involved with documenting the growing phenomena of black African-Caribbean community schools (Reay and Mirza 1997). Run by volunteers, and funded by the black community itself, these schools are mushrooming in churches, empty classrooms, and even people's front rooms. We know of 60 such schools in inner London where over 50 per cent of the black community lives. In their relentless effort to side-step the perpetual hum of racism that marks their lives, black parents are involved in a covert educational movement for change.

The irony is that no matter what successes are achieved, our sensibilities are swamped daily by talk of black underachievement. Young black people are pulled down and sucked under in the air of pessimism and hopelessness it produces. Teachers, politicians and parents are all caught up in a web of trying to find the cause. In the 1960s, experts said underachievement was caused by low IQ. In the 1970s, the explanation was the need for ethnic minorities to assimilate and lose cultural and linguistic markers. In the 1980s, the multicultural programmes stressed that underachievement was caused by low self-esteem, and feelings of negative self-worth among black pupils.

In the 1990s, OFSTED's latest report on the subject, entitled *Recent Research on Ethnic Minority Pupils*, articulates a new take on the debate (Gillborn and Gipps 1996). Underachievement now wears the new clothes of anti-racist postmodern difference. We are told that schools have been colour-blind, differences and diversity must be addressed, racism is to ignore differences. It sounds right, it sounds good. But then, I worry, I think to myself, 'differences . . . making distinctions between groups, was that not the cause of all of our problems in the first place?' How can we progress out of this moral maze?

Conclusion: The new post-biological syndrome

We call the current way we talk about race the 'cultural discourse on race'. In this discourse, using film, text and autobiography, we focus on identity, representation, subjectivity and the 'discursive effects' of cultural racism. But I want to rethink the cultural discourse on race as a 'new post-biological discourse' on race. I do this because I believe ideas about innate, genetic, scientifically provable difference are still at the heart of our thinking about race. We need to come back from identity construction and look the ugly face of scientific thinking straight in the eyes, because that is where commonsense everyday race hatred breeds; the kind of hate that cold-bloodily stabbed Stephen Lawrence, brutally stomped on Quddus Ali, and cowardly suffocated Joy Gardner.[3]

In the late twentieth century it is just the words of the discourse on race that have changed, not the deeds. Culture has become 'biologised', the process being ably assisted by the popular and pervasive work of racial pseudoscientists, who thrive on turning social inequality into respectable scientific difference. In our polite and civilised way, we no longer talk of Negroids, Caucasoids and Mongoloids. Now in the new culturally acceptable language of race we talk of Asians, Chinese, Africans, Arabs. Sometimes we talk of Muslims, Hindus and Jews. Sometimes we talk of Pakistanis, Somalis, the English, Scottish and Welsh. We give these geographical, regional, religious, national, cultural and ethnic categories meanings – clever at maths, good at sport, 'love' family life, likely to commit crime, fervently irrationally religious, breed like rabbits, downright lazy, sneaky and sly, noble and generous, mean and murderous. And through our systems of classification, official surveys and ethnic monitoring – which ironically we now need to ensure social justice – our differences nevertheless become qualified, quantified, measured and ascertained. Our academic failures, familial patterns and working habits become scientific fact.

In the new post-biological discourse on race, we talk of the inner city poor and the underclass, welfare mothers, the illiterate and marginal, the dispossessed and the alienated, and mean those who are different – behaviourly, culturally and socially innately different from us – us the moral majority. In the new post-biological discourse on race our civilised sensibilities tell us, 'but surely we don't believe in innate inferiority now, not now, not among us anyway, not here in this room, now that we are approaching the twenty-first century. Not now in this age of science and progress when we can clone a sheep from a single cell,[4] extract DNA from bone 200,000 years old.[5] Not when we have the Human Genome Project[6] and the Adam and Eve Project[7] to preserve and protect us from extinction and disease in the future. Not now when nanotechnology can take us on journeys beneath the skin – where we can see that we are all the same, under the skin!' Or perhaps that is why we need biological reassurance more than ever – to reassure us that we are not all the same under the skin.

The spectacle of biological pseudoscience plays out before our very eyes. On the stage we are all the players . . . and whiteness, that silent pervasive, place of power and privilege – 'The Thing' that propels us to dwell on visible cultural blackness – quietly directs the show. The performance is kept alive by our innermost fears about who we really are. We must be ever vigilant. The logic of racist and sexist pseudoscience has spread through our social bodies like a poison in the blood. It has seeped into our veins, and we can hear it on our lips – it whispers . . . 'boys are logical, girls are emotional, blacks are physical'. And while it is not a new discourse on difference it remains omnipresent. Like a vicious dog its teeth are sunk into the haunches of our minds . . . it clings on to the fabric of our society. I know: I've heard it in the classroom, in the supermarket, on the bus, in the tube, I've read it in the tabloids. The possibilities of biological determinism still waft through our minds, limiting possibilities for us all, black and white, male and female, to achieve our potential.

Chapter 4

A genealogy of black British feminism[1]

In a time when your 'belonging', who you *really* are, is judged by the colour of your skin, the shape of your nose, the texture of your hair, the curve of your body – your perceived genetic and physical presence; to be black (not white), female and 'over here', in Scotland, England or Wales, is to disrupt all the safe closed categories of what it means to be British: that is, to be white and British. Black British feminism as a body of scholarship is located in that space of British whiteness, that unchallenged hegemonic patriarchal discourse of colonial and now postcolonial times which quietly embraces our commonsense and academic ways of thinking. Whiteness: that powerful place that makes invisible, or reappropriates things, people and places it does not want to see or hear, and then through misnaming, renaming or not naming at all, invents the truth – what we are told is 'normal', neutral, universal, simply becomes the way it is ((charles) 1992; Wong 1994).

To be black and British is to be unnamed in official discourse. The construction of a national British identity is built upon a notion of a racial belonging, upon a hegemonic white ethnicity that never speaks its presence. We are told you can be either one or the other, black or British, but not both. But we live here, many are born here, all three million of us 'ethnic minority' people, as we are collectively called in the official Census surveys (Mason 2000). What defines us as Pacific, Asian, Eastern, African, Caribbean, Latina, Native, and 'mixed race' 'others' is not our imposed 'minority' status, but our self-defining presence as people of the postcolonial diaspora. At only 5.5 per cent of the population we still stand out, we are visibly different and that is what makes us 'black'. Thus being 'black' in Britain is about a state of 'becoming' (racialised); a process of consciousness, when colour becomes the defining factor about who you are. Located through your 'otherness' a 'conscious coalition' emerges: a self-consciously constructed space where identity is not inscribed by a natural identification but by a political kinship (Sandoval 1991). Now living submerged in whiteness, physical difference becomes a defining issue, a signifier, a mark of whether or not one belongs. Thus to be black in Britain is to share a common structural location; a racial location (Hall 1992).

In Britain in the 1980s, this shared sense of objectification was articulated when the racialised disempowered and fragmented sought empowerment in a gesture of politicised collective action. In naming the shared space of marginalisation as 'black', postcolonial migrants of different languages, religions, cultures and classes consciously constructed a political identity shaped by the shared experience of racialisation and its consequences. As a political articulation it appeared strategic, but in terms of community and personal identity 'black' remains a contested space. Localised, personalised struggles for who could or should be named as 'black' (i.e. Asians, Chinese, 'mixed race') characterised the political terrain of multicultural Britain for over a decade. It was argued that such a reductionist notion of blackness erased religious and ethnic difference (Anthias and Yuval-Davis 1992; Modood 1994). The desire to be named according to (cultural) difference and not (racial) sameness demonstrated the need for recognising the meaning of hair, skin and colour, the importance of shared history and religion, in the construction of identity and belonging. The translation of such need into fictions of essential racial and cultural origins among Britain's black and ethnic populations represented the desire for 'a place called home' (Rutherford 1990). It is the desire for a 'place' that anchors us in the strategic battle for cultural preservation in the continuous war of hegemonic cultural reappropriation of difference (Fusco 1995; hooks 1992).

In this context, then, black feminism as a spontaneous yet conscious coalition is a meaningful act of identification. In this 'place called home' named black feminism, we as racialised, gendered subjects can collectively mark our presence in a world where black women have for so long been denied the privilege to speak; to have a 'valid' identity of our own, a space to 'name' ourselves. Challenging our conscious negation from discourse – what Gayatri Spivak calls 'epistemic violence' (Spivak 1988) – we as black British women invoke our agency; we speak of our difference, our uniqueness, our 'otherness'. In a submerged and hidden world where there is no official language, words or narratives about that world – except those held in our hearts and minds – black women inhabit a third space (Bhabha 1990). It is a space which, because it overlaps the margins of the race, gender and class discourse and occupies the empty spaces in between, exists in a vacuum of erasure and contradiction. It is a space maintained by the polarisation of the world into blacks on one side and women on the other (Crenshaw 1993; Higginbotham 1992). The invisibility of black women speaks of the separate narrative constructions of race, gender and class: in a racial discourse, where the subject is male; in a gendered discourse, where the subject is white; and in a class discourse, where race has no place. It is because of these ideological blind spots that black women occupy a most critical place – a location whose very nature resists telling. In this critical space we can imagine questions that could not have been imagined before; we can ask questions that might not have been asked before (Christian 1990).

But this is not a claim to theoretical legitimacy through authentic voice. To simply 'have a place' in the academic discourse is not the project of black British feminism. Black women do not want just to voice their experiences, to shout from the roof-tops 'we have arrived! . . . listen to me . . . this is my story'. We do not claim to have a special knowledge, a privileged standpoint, a valorised subjectivity, a unique consciousness, borne out of our collective experience of marginalisation and the mere 'living life as a black woman' (Collins 1991). Such a claim to epistemic privilege would be to assume a naive essentialist universal notion of a homogeneous black womanhood, no better in its conception of the self and the nature of power than that embodied in the authoritative discourses we seek to challenge (Bar On 1993; Suleri 1993). We are engaged in a far more subtle project, a project in which we have attempted to invoke some measure of critical race/gender reflexivity into mainstream academic thinking. In telling our different story, in exposing our personal pain and pleasures, black British feminists reveal *other ways of knowing* that challenge the normative discourse. In our particular world shaped by processes of migration, nationalism, racism, popular culture and the media, black British women, from multiple positions of difference, reveal the distorted ways in which the dominant groups construct their assumptions. As black women we watch from the sidelines, from our space of unlocation, the unfolding project of domination.

Genealogy offers us a way into revealing the project of domination. The Foucauldian method of genealogy attempts a critique of dominant discourses. It draws on knowledges and ways of thinking that are marginalised and stand outside the mainstream (Dean 1994:138). The retrieval of counter-memories, of subjugated knowledges, which are thought to lack a history, functions as a challenge to the taken-for-granted normative assumptions of prevailing discourses. Thus genealogies operate not so much as theories but as mechanisms for criticising theories (Sawicki 1991: 53). For black feminists this provides a means to interrogate the discourses which embrace and so wish to structure our very being – the racial discourse, with its obsession with black (male) desire and fear (West 1993); the discourse of gender, dominated with the (white) feminist project of truth-seeking (Weedon 1987); and the discourse of class, that central structural discourse of our time, with its privileging of the universal and exclusion of agency and reduction of all things to the economic (Hall and Jacques 1989).

It could be argued that mapping the counter-history of black feminism can be no more than a mapping of the history of the objectively assigned and dialectically constructed subject positions as written and spoken for black women by others. True, if the black woman is traced in history what we see is how she is permitted to appear. We see glimpses of her as she is produced and created for the sustenance of the patriarchal colonial and now postcolonial discourse (Mani 1992; McClintock 1995). She appears and disappears as she is needed, as the dutiful wife and daughter, the hard (but happy and grateful!) worker, the sexually available exotic other, the controlling asexual mother, or simply homogenised as the 'third world' woman (Mohanty 1988). In her representation she is without agency, without self-determination, a passive victim, waiting to be inscribed with meaning by those who wish to gaze upon her and name her. She is an object, not the subject of her story. However, the project of black feminism asserts and reclaims our agency in the telling of who we are. Our voice, our being, and our very presence within the patriarchal imperial project of sexualised racialisation, is to actively contest the system of which we form a part.

However, if genealogies span centuries, can we undertake a genealogy of black British feminism when the immediate history of concerted black feminist activity in Britain reaches back only over the past 60 years, over the relatively short time of postcolonial migration and settlement here? West (1993) talks of a micro-institutional or localised analysis, which is part of a bigger genealogical, macro-institutional, materialist inquiry of racism. Black British feminism with its location – and with its critical project to reveal the mechanisms that promote, contest and resist racist logics and practices in the everyday lives of black people – may be seen as such a micro-institutional genealogical project; it is to the mapping of this project that I now turn:

Journeys to the 'motherland': 1940s–1970s

Using a broad notion of the project of black British feminism as a critical social force, it may be argued that a genealogy of black British feminism as a theoretical and intellectual movement has its genesis in the activism and struggles of black women migrants from the postcolonial Caribbean, African and Indian subcontinent. These women came to Great Britain during the post-World War II recruitment drive for cheap labour. Official statistics and texts written about and documenting the main period of postcolonial migration from the 1940s to the 1960s writes out the female story of postcolonial migration. What remains for us to gather are the snippets of black women's stories as they emerge to challenge their negation and disrupt the neat telling of those times. Among these are the narratives of black women soldiers in World War II; the writing and campaigns of Una Marson for the League of Coloured People in the 1940s; the internationally recognised political activism of Claudia Jones in the 1950s; and the sustained collective organising of Olive Morris and the trade unionist Jayaben Desai in the 1970s – all have been kept alive by black women writers and narrators.[2]

But these stories of black female activism and engagement are in contrast to the picture that is commonly painted of black women in Britain. In the British government's conscious drive to recruit cheap labour from the newly independent colonies in the early 1950s, it was simply assumed that migrant workers, like their own workers, are always male. The colonial violence of enslavement and economic plunder that structured black female work as a necessity was, of course, unenunciated in the assumption, erased from official logic. Women in the colonial patriarchal discourse were invisible nonentities. Immigration law and welfare policy reinforced this assumption. Women, it was believed, came as either wives or children, dependants. However, the majority of Caribbean women came independently and in almost equal numbers to men (Foner 1979; Fryer 1984) – a fact erased from the telling. Migrant women could only claim rights on the grounds of marriage: that is, through their association with men. Women emerged in the official patriarchal, neo-imperialist discourse only as subjects for sexual and racist humiliation. In the construction of women as objects of male ownership the British government invoked a twisted cultural legitimacy to harass and deter male migrants. They used the ultimate transgression of power, the forcible and violent entering and defiling of the bodies of the invisible. Unbelievably, they tested Asian women to see if they were bone fide 'virgin' wives.[3] Crude, overt racist brutality has been the hallmark of immigration and asylum policies in the declining embattled British state (James and Harris 1993).

The pervasive image of the invisible or passive black woman was rudely interrupted by the labour struggles that exploded in the 1970s exposing the British sweat shops. Amrit Wilson in *Finding a Voice: Asian Women in Britain* (1978) gives a first-person account of the conditions and struggles of Asian women workers on the picket line in the Grunwick photo-processing dispute. The narrative speaks of the agency of these women in their sustained, organised class struggles in the workplace. The women themselves tell of the historically specific nature of their class and cultural consciousness which was embedded in material relations of capitalist production. On the one hand, the women were positioned in a cultural context as Asian women, and were exploited and harassed on those grounds. On the other hand, the women's socio-awareness of their objective class status meant that they sought collective action and trade union affiliation; a strategy that ultimately led to their defeat. The complex cultural identities and social subject positioning that were manifest in the struggle for social justice are articulated by the women themselves in their narratives of everyday life on the picket line. While Asian women were largely located in the private sector in factory and production, Caribbean and African women were situated in the public service and caring industries. Amina Mama in 'Black Women, the Economic Crisis and the British State' (1984) maps the clear-sighted, lucid project of a restructuring postcolonial capitalist state rationalising its logic through the active production of a disenfranchised and thus contingent and disposable workforce. Black women, in large numbers compared to the white female population, were (and are) disproportionately employed in low-paid, low-status work (Bhavnani 1994; Lewis 1993). The insidious erosion of rights emphasises black women's shared social and material conditions in a highly structured, gendered and racialised labour market. Race, in the context of the globalisation of capital, places gender at the centre of the new working class (Brewer 1993; Ong 1987).

The struggle for black feminist identity: 1980s

In the early 1980s black women collectively organised not only to protect their rights in the workplace, but also to engage with the sustained fascist and racist onslaughts of white British politicians, the police and the white street mobs which inhabited the heightened racialised terrain of late twentieth-century Britain.[4] In the official racial discourse where black men are the valorised racialised agents, named and feared through their visible acts of riots and rebellion, women are permitted only to appear (if at all) as mothers of sons and carers of husbands. In this context, Bryan, Dadzie and Scafe reveal the political agency of black women in *The Heart of the Race: Black Women's Lives in Britain* (1985). The story of OWAAD (the Organisation of Women of African and Asian Descent), set up in 1978, is about black women's collective politics of engagement. The grassroots black women's movement became important to an emerging black British feminist consciousness. Their struggles reveal the political agency of black women of different languages, religions, cultures and classes who consciously constructed a politically based 'black' identity in response to the exclusion of women's experiences of racism within the anti-racist movement. The call to Afro-Asian unity by OWAAD demonstrated the emergence of an organic racialised consciousness. It was an empowering act in an empowering time, but one that did not last.[5] While Afro-Asian unity appeared to be a strategic political articulation at the time, OWAAD folded under pressure from internal tensions within the organisation to assert heterogeneous identities. It became increasingly difficult for women to subsume their diverse ethnic and political identities within a single movement. Ironically the legacy of that reductionist naming of 'blackness' was to shift the racial discourse on to new ground, away from confrontational struggle in the political and economic domain towards the struggle to be heard among ourselves in the social and cultural domain. The desire for visibility through celebrating cultural, religious and sexual difference characterised the struggle for a claim on the racialised terrain in the 1980s. Seduced by this opening, a space in which to express our hidden subjugated selves, identity politics appeared superficially to empower marginal groups.

Identity politics, a political ideology that consumed the 1980s, was based on the premise that the more marginal the group the more complete the knowledge. In a literal appropriation of standpoint theory, the claim to authenticity through oppressive subjecthood produced a simplistic hierarchy of oppression. The outcome was the cliché-ridden discourse which embodied the Holy Trinity of 'race, class and gender' (Appiah and Gates 1995), within which black women, being the victims of 'triple oppression', were the keepers of the holy grail. The solution within this conceptualisation of oppression was to change personal behaviour rather than challenge wider structures. In a time when what should be *done* was replaced by who we *are* (Bourne 1987: 1), the freedom to *have* was replaced by the freedom *to be* (Melucci 1989: 177). Identity politics offered no radical way forward in the critical project of revealing how we come to be located in the racialised and sexualised space where we reside. Whiteness, that silent, pervasive, patriarchal discourse, the father of identity politics, with its complementary discourse on anti-racism and New Right anti-anti-racism, was never named (see Bonnett 1996; Gilroy 1990).

Just as the political arena witnessed a backlash to the reductionism of identity politics, so too was there a reaction to the reductionism inherent within white feminist theory in the 1980s. The desire for equality, the struggle for social justice, and the vision of universal sisterhood was the consuming unidirectional project of white (socialist) feminism throughout the 1970s and early 1980s. Patriarchal power, its manifestation in terms of female invisibility, and the inevitable psychic social and economic oppression it engendered across the globe, was the central logic driving the feminist discourse. However, racial power within the white feminist production of knowledge about gender relations was never problematised. Whiteness was a 'given' social position. Ironically it meant that an epistemology that rests on inclusion and equality was itself excluding and unequitable. The explanation as to why feminism should be locked into such an untenable position lay in revealing the foundations of a feminist epistemology which was embedded in the project of modernity, its premise being rational universal humanism.[6]

In feminist theory knowledge about social relations was experiential. The central drive of the feminist project was to reveal hitherto obscured realities, other worlds – the 'woman's' world, a world silenced by the privileging of masculinity. But if the 'woman's' standpoint was embedded in that given unproblematised space of whiteness – and it was – then how could feminism claim universal legitimacy? Black women's experience was invisible, or if made visible spoken for and constructed through the authoritative, imperial voice of whiteness (Mohanty 1988; Ware 1992). The call to recognise difference and diversity in the feminist project was incompatible with the notion of an essential, universal 'woman' subject.

The struggle of black women to claim a space within the modernist feminist discourse, and at the same time to engender critical racial reflexivity among white feminists, consumed the black feminist project for more than a decade. The writings of Hazel Carby, Valerie Amos and Pratibha Parmar exemplify the height of this critical time. Hazel Carby, in 'White Woman Listen! Black Feminism and the Boundaries of Sisterhood' (1982a), embodies the classic black British feminist response to exclusion and white feminist authority. Centring her argument around the key areas of feminist discourse – the family, patriarchy and reproduction – she interrogates the contradiction of the white feminist theoretical claim to universal womanhood on the one hand, but the practice of exclusion of women who are different on the other. Similarly, Valerie Amos and Pratibha Parmar in 'Challenging Imperial Feminism' (1984) focus on white feminism's subversion of the discourse around the family, sexuality and the peace movement in its unconcious attempt to valorise and represent nothing more than white women's own cultural experience as global.

White feminists were reluctant to relinquish the authority to name the social reality of the gendered subject, a reluctance manifest in a particular white feminist appropriation of the black feminist critique. While black feminists called for the recognition of racism in white feminist theorising, white socialist feminists strategically responded with a recognition of their ethnocentrism (the valorising of the white cultural perspective). In an article in *Feminist Review* Barrett and McIntosh (1985) suggested that the solution to the problem of black female invisibility was to simply insert an appreciation of black cultural difference into the analysis of the family, work and reproduction. Racism, the acknowledgement of which is central to developing a truly critical position in relation to the discourse on whiteness, was not up for debate in the work of white feminists, as Kum-Kum Bhavnani and Margaret Coulson argue in 'Transforming Socialist Feminism' (1986). It opened out a heated but necessary and productive debate between black and white feminists. The focus on the centrality of an open reflexive appreciation of racism in the production of an ethical feminist discourse was continued and kept alive in the constructive dialogue between black feminists (Kazi 1986; Mirza 1986) and white feminists (Lees 1986; Ramazanoglu 1986) in a special section in the journal *Feminist Review* entitled 'Feedback: Feminism and Racism'.

Throughout the 1980s black feminists in Britain responded and resisted the overarching imperial mission of white feminism by refusing to be 'named'. They invoked their agency by challenging stereotypical images of black women as passive victims through studies, research and writing that revealed the hidden world of migrant and black British women. In that world, women were brave, proud and strong. They wrote of Asian girls' resistance in schools and at work; they told of the African Caribbean experience of schooling; they revealed black women's struggle against domestic violence, immigration and the police. They engaged in black lesbian activism, and spoke of enriching, empowering but complex alternative family forms and other ways of living and being.[7]

A feminism of difference: 1990s

By the end of the 1980s, the black feminist critical project to excavate the dynamics of racial power and the silences it produces within white feminist discourse left black feminists exhausted and in need of self-recovery. The flattening out and reduction of difference and diversity which had been assigned to interrogate whiteness within the feminist movement had outlived its purpose. The homogenising of black women, that empowering act of collectivity rooted in racism, began to erode black feminist theoretical legitimacy. Black feminism, it was now being said, was a politically limited project. It undermined its own position as a critical discourse by exclusionary practices which did not recognise the ethnic, religious, political and class differences among women (Anthias and Yuval Davis 1992; Brah 1994). Now the call was for black feminists to enter into the diversionary discourse of anti-racism. Anti-racism appeared to offer a form of inclusive, strategic, engaged political activism which (superficially at least) could cut across difference by initiating black/white or local alliances articulated around the unified struggle against the racist practices of the state.[8] The emphasis on the manifestation of racism(s) and not the deeper underlying structures of what constitutes 'race' in the British context meant that anti-racism as a political ideology could only ever put a 'coat of paint' on the problem of black inequality (Gilroy 1990).

Sensitive to the limitations of reductionism, and a desire to explore our difference, the black feminist theorists turned to locating black female identity at the centre of their analysis. By opening up a critical inquiry into theories of social reproduction and class inequality, black feminists decentred the authority of such established theories to speak about and on behalf of all marginalised groups (Mirza 1992). Ann Phoenix, in 'Theories of Gender and Black Families', (1987), articulates the complex levels of gender difference from a race and class position. Gender is not experienced in the same way when you are positioned as working class or black, or both. Children learn these differences and reproduce them in their knowledge about the social world. Ann Phoenix shows that specificity and difference are important.

A sense of reflexivity and renegotiation within the black feminist critical space is articulated by Pratibha Parmar in 'Other Kinds of Dreams' (1989). Autobiographical reflections of black women emerge during this time that speak of a desire to claim a space and so enable the healing processes of self-discovery necessary after the long journeys through migration, work, identity politics, racism and feminist exclusion of the 1980s (Grewal et al. 1988). The explosion of black women's literature and poetry also makes possible new contexts for creativity. Sharing their pain and pleasures, these black women writers living in Britain give strength and wisdom to others.[9] Photography, art, film and performance produce images and acts that, in celebrating diversity, reflect, deflect and destabilise the white gaze.[10] Black women gained a space to write about the body and mind in terms of colonial appropriation (Kanneh 1995: Mama 1995) and in terms of disability and exclusion (Begum 1992). They explored possibilities of new social movements in Europe (*Feminist Review* 1993), organised against religious fundamentalism (Sahgal and Yuval-Davis 1992), and campaigned for lesbian sexual politics (Mason-John 1995).

Even though black women demonstrate their undeniable presence, the theoretical inclusion of their difference still appears illusive. Whereas 1970s and 1980s feminism centred its struggle on 'the right to be equal', postmodern feminism in 1990s turned to a celebration for the 'right to be different'. The black feminist critique makes visible the inherent contradiction of such relative pluralism. As black women we ask: Is it possible to achieve equality within difference? Interrogating the concept of difference we find it analytically weak and unclearly defined.[11] The discursive terrain is unsure: Are we talking about difference in relation to sexual difference (men/ women); difference in relation to 'race' (black/ white); or difference in relation to subjectivities (between women – class/ ethnicity/ age/ religion)? However it is defined, difference is plagued by some central philosophical problems. First, it could be argued that celebrating and valorising difference of any sort depoliticises feminism. It effectively dissipates the basis for collective activism as we look inward to the self with claims to relatively oppressed status, deflecting attention away from power which is still materially located (Bordo 1990; Bourne 1987). Thus, ironically, the discourse on difference obscures how we come to give meanings to our differences. Second, the discourse on difference privileges whiteness (Spelman 1990). Razia Aziz takes up this point in 'Feminism and the Challenge of Racism: Deviance or Difference?' (1992). The very notion of difference is relational; you are always positioned in relation to the norm, which is whiteness. In such a politicised construction, other differences of class, age, ethnicity, religion have been subdued in the selective valorising of black/ white difference. A postmodern black feminist identity, Aziz suggests, is not just based on racism and oppression but on recognising the fluidity and fragmented nature of racialised and gendered identities. In this sense we can reclaim subjectivity from the cul-de-sac of identity politics and reinstate it in terms of a powerful, conscious form of political agency. This is the task facing black feminism today.

Finding the spaces in between: black female representation

In the space opened up by the discourse on difference, black women continue the critical task of genealogical enquiry: to excavate and so reveal the seemingly imperceptible, the smallest of the small ways in which we are absorbed into the resistance of that which we are expected to be, while we live trying to be what we want to be. Oriented around issues of difference, essentialism, representation and cultural hybridity the collective project of black feminism is now concerned with mapping our experience. But this is not a simple mapping of experience to uncover the 'truth', but rather an engagement with experience; a placing of the self in theory so as to understand the constructions and manifestations of power in relation to the self (Griffin 1996). A critical black feminist theory is grounded in relation to practice, it cannot be not separate: praxis is central to our survival (Christian 1994, 1995).

It is argued that the new cultural racism that marks this postmodern era is legitimated thorough dominant regimes of representation (Hall 1992). But are we what we are expected to be or are we much more? In '(Mis)Representing the Black (Super)Woman' (1997) Tracey Reynolds takes on the unchallenged discourse of the black superwoman; that powerful, indomitable work-horse; that matriarchal giant that pushes aside men and climbs on up the career ladder; that single-minded calculating woman who has babies alone; that untrustworthy woman who even consorts with white men when she achieves. Does she really exist beyond representation? Whatever the evidence – and Tracey Reynolds shows there is very little in terms of substantive research on motherhood, work and education – everyone still believes she does exist. She is valorised and reproduced in white academic and social policy discourse. Reinforced in the black press, the superwoman has even become a celebrated empowering notion among black women themselves. The call is to refuse voyeuristic reception of the 'other' and to imagine the self differently in order to act otherwise.

Racialised, sexualised meanings seem to have engulfed our very ways of thinking and knowing ourselves. Debbie Weekes, in 'Shades of Blackness: Young Black Female Constructions of Beauty' (1997), explores black female assertions of black female identity through the lived reality of fixed biologically verifiable notions of blackness. Black women erect boundaries of what counts as blackness based on skin colour and hair texture which they then police. This is how identity is experienced – on the streets, on the bus, in the classroom, at home. That is how young black women talk, think and walk. We may wish to dismiss such ugly, 'racist' unpleasantries in an effort to cool out what does not fit. But such essentialising is not a 'fiction', an imagining, a misinformed, unsound, politically incorrect, false consciousness. It *is* these young women's reality. If it is ugly, then it is only as ugly as the racial discourse from which it is honed. Lived, essentialised blackness is a mirror of pervasive unenunciated whiteness – the 'Thing', as Weekes calls it. The perverse nature of this reinscription of power and agency through becoming a self-defined, essential racial subject needs to be understood not dismissed (hooks 1992).

For a black woman to be different is to be what she is not expected to be. To be different, as Bibi Bakare-Yusuf reveals in 'Raregrooves and Raregroovers: A Matter of Taste, Difference and Identity' (1997), is to subvert the restricted codes of a narrowly defined racialised essence and acceptable feminity. If young black women do not behave as 'black' in the narrow cultural sense of a Jamaican underclass, then does that mean they are not 'black'? The rare groove scene is a space of re-invention, where young women appropriate black female identity; rescue it from fixed essentialised constructions of the way they 'should be'. Aspirational, middle-class young women express difference in terms of their taste and style, choice of leisure and pleasure. They are engaged in the risky business of strategic tactical cultural reinscription which makes the hegemonic discourse of race, class and gender imperceptible.

But the pervasive use of essentialist definitions of blackness has a price. In the racialised terrain, dominated by fixed racialised beliefs, those who are defined as neither black nor white carry the pain of erasure. In 'Diaspora's Daughters, Africa's Orphans? On Lineage, Authenticity and "Mixed Race" Identity' (1997), Jayne Ifekwunigwe reveals the lives of the *metissage*, those who are neither considered black nor white, those who exist everywhere but belong nowhere. Through their construction of self, *metisse*, or 'mixed race' women illuminate the contradictions and logic of an impoverished racialised discourse, a discourse grounded in crude culturalist notions of 'race', nation and culture. The *metissage* are thus the product of racialised discourse. They occupy a critical position, an orphan consciousness, creating their own space in the recalling of their English-African-diasporic histories. By assuming visibility in their role as *griotte* (story-tellers), these *metissage* narrate what is 'real' (as lived) and fictitious (as constructed) in racial discourse. The critical place that *metisse* women occupy is interrogated by Sara Ahmed in ' "It's a Sun Tan, Isn't It?": Auto-biography as an Identificatory Practice' (1997). Memories and reflections, which are always selective, can only tell us about the way one is seen, and hence addressed, within the dominant categories of the social world. When asked, with a wink, if her colour was just a sun-tan by predatory white police in Australia, multiple levels of identification and disidentification in the incident illuminate the instability, temporality and negotiation of racialised, gendered, classed meaning. The incident shows the impossibility of being fixed by a single name or gaze in the process of identification, when you are a racially marked, gendered subject. Modes of address that attempt to fix the subject are riddled with contradictions and social antagonisms. The process of identifying with the collective term 'black women' makes visible the clash between two regimes of identification: gender and race. By invoking the generalisable category 'black woman', Sara Ahmed shows the impossibility yet necessity of the politically affirming gesture of naming the self as 'black woman'.

Disrupting diaspora: new identities and new meanings

Is the notion of a 'black woman' a viable concept? Identity politics, that ideological policing of who counts as *'black'*, *Black or black*, that has invaded our thinking and being, has, without doubt, closed down our possibilities for self-definition and political engagement. Magdalene Ang-Lygate in

'Charting Spaces of (Un)location: On Theorising Diaspora' (1997) explores, through the invisibility of Filipina and Chinese women living in Britain, the enclosures and erasure inherent in the racialised discourse of identity politics. The political concept of blackness does not convey belonging and community, but instils a false sense of national identity that sets those with dark black skin colour apart, while silencing those who are lighter than black. She argues that it consorts with the colonialist imperialist categorisation of immigrant as outsiders, alien, different. Constructions of unidimensional black identity can only reinforce white supremacy by the logics of duality. To refuse such limited racialised constructions and create over and over again our difference is to disrupt and so subvert neocolonialist paradigms.

Naz Rassool in 'Fractured or Flexible Identities? Life Histories of "Black" Diasporic Women in Britain' (1997) explores how a conscious black identity evolves among women coming from very different socioeconomic, historical and geographical places and now living in Britain. Life histories of women as diverse as African Caribbean, Iraqi Kurd, black South African and an African Indian Kenyan reveal the organic, complex interweaving of past-present experience in the recovery of diasporic subjectivity. In the search for the self in traces of memory, what may seem on the outside to be the fragmented and alienating social experience of migration and dislocation has an inner coherence and continuity. Cultural hybridity, the fusion of cultures and coming together of difference, the 'border crossing' that marks diasporic survival, signifies change, hope of newness, and space for creativity. However, in the search for rootedness – a 'place called home' – these women, in the process of self-identification, disidentify with an excluding, racist British colonising culture. They articulate instead a multifaceted discontinuous black identity that marks their difference.

The desire to belong, the search for a 'place called home' is interrogated by Nalini Persram in 'In My Father's House There are Many Mansions: The Nation and Postcolonial Desire' (1997). Through a personal narrative she takes us on a journey of unbelonging, of changing colour codings and shifting gender roles. She unmasks the hegemonic masculinist discourse of national identity that structures and informs our search for who we are. The search for our authentic self rooted in a time, a place, with a history and a culture, is reproduced in the diasporic, migrant counter-discourse on 'home'. The compensatory narrative of 'home' – 'that there is a *there* there' – with its myth of unitary origin, is produced through the masculinist discourse of 'lack'. If you lack a nation, as diasporic travellers do, then how do you celebrate who you *are*? Reknowing identity is to remake a space that valorises movement not location, that is determined by migrancy and not being a migrant. It is a personal journey towards belonging.

Reclaiming and recentring our bodies

To take the inner journey to 'self' reveals different ways of knowing. In 'Two Stories, Three Lovers and the Creation of Meaning in a Black Lesbian Autobiography' (1997), Consuelo Rivera Fuentes transforms herself to a site of resistance. In her reading of Audre Lorde's *Zami* she creates and re-creates her identity in and out of the text. In her diary she shares with us Lorde's bodily geographical journey towards self-construction which changes reality from within the body. Consuelo reveals a place inside which plays with language and makes love to poetry. It is a sensual inner space that is not determined by the dominant discourse of being black and lesbian. In this place, her many selves – the writer, the reader, the autobiographer – passionately engage with each other, until the boundaries between each identity disappears. In the end no one knows where one identity starts and where another one finishes. It is possible to create an identity with new layers of meanings, to have multiple subjectivities without separating the self into different speaking subjects: to be one with many parts. Identity is a living process; though it is temporal, spatial and shifting, it can be transformative through risk, desire, decision and struggle.

There is an assumption that theories (and hence facts) come from our heads and feelings (and hence fictions) come from our bodies. In 'My Body Myself: How Does a Black Woman do Sociology?' (1997) Felly Nkweto Simmonds makes the point that sociology labours under the fiction that social reality has nothing to do with the body. However, for black women, social theory has fed on their embodied experiences. Black bodies are killed, displayed, watched, analysed, stroked, desired because of their embodied 'otherness'. Anthropology's fascination for the anatomical landmarks of different races has fed the fantasises of the Western imagination which fuelled the desiring machine of capital. Black women cannot be dispassionate, disembodied theorists. Their social reality, their habitus, is to be black, gendered subjects in a white world. For Simmonds, cancer gave her a new relationship with her body which allowed her to rethink her place in the social. For the black woman, revealing certain 'private information' is necessary in order to understand how others see her and her experience as a 'curiosity'.

The one thing we do know as black women is that our eroticised, exoticised bodies have become objects of desire. They preoccupy and obsess the white gaze. Gargi Bhattacharyya, in 'The Fabulous Adventures of the Mahogany Princesses' (1997), weaves a tale in the oral tradition of her parents, and parents' parents. It is a tale that tells of the violence of colonial exploitation which has reduced us all to looking at skin colour as a way of being, defining and living. Locked into a racialised, sexualised discourse, represented as exotic others, we have forgotten other ways of imagining who we are. Gargi's folk narrative enables the reader/listener to find wisdom and meaning in sagas made up of endless episodes without having to hear the whole thing. The unfolding narrative's central logic asks: Does studying our representation in pictures, books and films reveal how gender and race really work? The postmodern preoccupation of studying the effects – our action and reaction to how we are pictured – has locked us into a distracting cycle of reflecting on how we are perceived, and then believing how we are perceived is who we are. What we see as mahogany princesses does not come into it at all. The story of the mahogany princesses is part dream fantasy, part bedtime story, and part twelve-step self-help programme, which is disciplined in another way – other than what is expected in 'power-tripping, name-dropping' academia. It can allow us to escape our mental confines, use our knowledge, and to think differently about who we are.

Changing the future: black feminism and political engagement

For black feminists, a politics of difference is a politics of engagement, which operates from a site of critical location (hooks 1991). As 'critical organic catalysts' (West 1990) we desire neither acceptance, transgression nor transcendence with regard to the mainstream. What we are involved in is active insurgency through conscious alliances, critical dialogue and intellectual rigor in our task to reveal the operations of power in which we are implicated. Our hope is that if we change the way we think and speak about things, then we might change the way we live. Pragna Patel, in 'Third Wave Feminism and Black Women's Activism' (1997), tells of the struggle of Southall Black Sisters (SBS) and Women Against Fundamentalism (WAF) to uphold women's status through legal rights. SBS and WAF struggle in the twilight zone of the dominant patriarchal discourses of anti-racism, multiculturalism and religious fundamentalism. Cases of domestic violence, sexual abuse and forced marriage illuminate the alliances between the state and patriarchal authority by legitimating the rhetoric of Asian male community leaders who seek to maintain the sanctity of the family for ideological empowerment. SBS and WAF are involved in campaigns to redefine the relationship of women to the criminal justice system. In so doing they work to change the language and so the meaning of the law to embrace an understanding of transgressions against women (such as rape) as violations of human rights. The sites of engagement, the locations for our insurgency are not always in the political domain where they are expected. In 'Black Women in Education: A Collective Movement for Social Change' (Mirza 1997) I ask the question: Is the desire to do well and succeed in education a subversive act? The positive orientation of black women to education is significant. They may appear on the surface to be engaged in instrumental, seemingly conservative acts of buying into the system, but this is an illusion. Black women, without access to power and privilege, redefine what education is for. The analysis of female collective action offers a new direction for thinking about new social movements, challenging masculine assumptions of social change through confrontation. Ultimately, to do well in a racist society is a radical act. Given the parameters of the world we live in, we must think about transformative struggle through inclusive acts.

Coming full circle, this genealogy of black British feminist thought ends on a note of hope, for an inclusive feminism that can embrace our class, race, sexual and (dis)ability differences. Terminology constructs boundaries and meaning. If excluded from meaning, as black women were from the meaning associated with feminism, then they become invisible. Helen (charles), in 'The Language of Womanism: Rethinking Difference' (1997), asks if an inclusive universal feminism is both possible and desirable. The organic nature of terming means that a word must come from its value to those who use it. 'Womanism' as a self-conscious, black-based term stopped short of popular appeal. Naming the self as 'black feminist' comes from a demand to be recognised by those in power. But to focus on terminology rather than a critique of the race-sexism of white feminism leads to no change. The black feminist critique engendered a guilty paralysis among white feminists for over 20 years, and this needs to be intercepted if feminism is to move forward. Feminism as a term, and as a movement, is not static, it is not impervious to change. If feminism changes to embrace differences, rather than to be preoccupied with difference, then its meaning will change and strengthen black and white feminist activism through a unified cohesive and strategic identity.

Conclusion: Towards black British feminism(s)

Postmodern theory has allowed the celebration of difference, the recognition of otherness, the presence of multiple and changeable subjectivities. Black women, previously negated and rendered invisible by the inherent universalising tendency of modernity, finally have a voice. We appear to have 'arrived'. Here we are, afforded the status of *black British feminism*. Postmodernity has opened up the possibility of a new 'feminism of difference'. Such a feminism now allows black women the legitimation to do what we have been doing for a long time, in our own way; we have now been afforded an intellectual space to valorise our agency, redefine our place on the margins. But in a genealogy of black British feminism, we need to ask: How do we appear in the emerging postmodern discourse on difference? How are we being produced, and implicated in that production? The answer is, through ourselves. In writing about our world, our place on the margins, black feminists take the risk of what happens when we expose ourselves as an object of study. Laid bare by our unveiling, our innermost life stories become objects for public gaze; our resistance is known. We engage in naming our subjectivity, telling our story. We undertake journeys of self-discovery, which are then appropriated and recorded as objective knowledge, 'original context' and 'specificities'. The dominant culture achieves hegemony precisely by its capacity to convert and recode for the authoritive other (Grossberg 1996).

In this so-called fragmented, dislocated, experiential reality that is postmodern Britain, to valorise our 'different' experience means we have to locate that experience in materiality. Holding on to the struggle against inequality and for social justice anchors the black feminist project. For it seems that whatever the project of postmodern theorising, black women remain subject to discrimination and exclusion. Black women remain preoccupied with their struggles against low pay, ill-health and incarceration, and for access to care, welfare and education. In spite of postmodernism, little has changed for the majority of black women globally and nationally. For them power is not diffuse, localised and particular. Power is as centralised and secure as it has always been, excluding, defining and self-legitimating.

In our efforts to theorise our position, we speak of black feminism, not black feminism(s). This is because the political project has a single purpose: to excavate the silences and pathological appearances of a collectivity of women assigned as the 'other' and produced in a gendered, sexualised, wholly racialised discourse. Black feminism has many ways of doing this. As has been revealed in this genealogy, there have been many sites of struggle: migration, work, white feminist theory, and now identity and difference. Strategic multiplicity and contingency is a hallmark of black British feminism. If anything, what our struggles demonstrate is that you can have difference (polyvocality) within a conscious construction of sameness (i.e. black feminism). As long as there is exclusion, both in academic discourse and in materiality, there will be a black feminism. It is in this sense contingent. As long as such exclusion is produced spatially in regions, nations and places, there will be a black *British* feminism.

Chapter 5

Intersectionality and the marginal black woman[1]

Why is it that in twenty-first-century multicultural Britain black and minority ethnic women[2] are still not part of the race equality picture? Even though there is an awareness of multiple discrimination, there is still a pervasive assumption in everyday policy and practice that racial inequality and social exclusion are gender-neutral experiences. Evidence shows us that ethnicised women suffer disproportionately in terms of gender rights and their marginal position in the workforce means they are economically disadvantaged, with poorer health and educational opportunities (Fawcett 2005: Mirza 2003). Yet these women are largely invisible in both the race and the gender equality discourses that inform our legislative and policy plans.

I begin by asking why black and minority ethnic women are invisible in mainstream studies and debates on gender and race, yet highly visible in negative ways when they are included, such as the media spotlight on Muslim women wearing the veil. I argue that black and minority ethnic women are caught up in a collision of invisibility and visibility that means they slip through the cracks of everyday policy and politics. I explain how it is only by understanding how the intersectionality of patriarchy and power operates to maintain disadvantage and mask privilege that we can begin to get to the root causes of the persistent multiple discrimination they suffer. I conclude that black and minority ethnic women can teach policy-makers a great deal about citizenship and social action. In the face of growing inequality gaps, black and minority ethnic women have shaped their communities and their own lives through determined activism and social commitment – showing us what a feminised prospectus for a multicultural future could look like.

Mind the gap: slipping through the race and gender equality cracks

For years I have had to start my writing with the cliché that black and minority ethnic women have been 'left out', 'could not be found', or 'could not be incorporated' in reports and studies. While there are patterns of *visibility* that concern us in the analysis of black and minority ethnic women, there are also patterns of *invisibility* that characterise our representation. Indeed it has been argued that research on black women has been characterised by a *'normalised absence/pathologised presence'* approach (Phoenix 1996). This means that if they are included they are constructed as problematic, but for the most part they are either marginalised or left out when normalised mainstream race or gender issues are discussed. In the 1970s an African American women's chant summed this up: 'all the women are white, all the blacks are men, but some of us are brave' (Hull *et al.* 1982). This saying seems still to hold true – gender is still seen as a white women's issue, while it is taken for granted that 'race' is a black male issue. Black women appear to fall into the cracks between the two. They are often invisible, occupying a 'blind spot' in mainstream policy and research studies which talk about women on the one hand or ethnic minorities on the other.

Public campaigns such as those on 'work-life balance' which aims to better the working conditions of parents and carers are predicated on the notion of a generic un-raced and un-classed woman. However, as the Equal Opportunity Commission's (EOC) *Moving On Up?* study of black and minority ethnic women shows, pay and conditions at work are deeply racialised (EOC 2006; Fawcett 2005). Success in education is not proving to be a guarantee of wider job opportunities or higher earnings for second- and third-generation Pakistani, Bangladeshi and Black Caribbean young women (Platt 2007). Young black and minority ethnic women aged 16 to 24 are more than twice as likely to be unemployed as white women, with Pakistani female graduates under 24 over four times more likely than white female graduates to be unemployed. Over one in five young Pakistani, Bangladeshi or Black Caribbean women have had to take a job below the level of their qualifications because no one would employ them at the level they were qualified for, compared to only one in 20 young white women employees. Over all, despite their high educational achievements and positive aspirations (Bhavnani & PTI 2006: Botcherby 2006), black and minority ethnic women disproportionately face lower pay (Platt 2006) and fewer prospects for promotion and are more likely to be found in a narrow range of jobs and segmented in certain sectors of the economy such as health, social care and retail.

However, such distinctive differences and disadvantages are not integrated into mainstream British labour market reforms for women. They are dealt with as special case scenarios, in specially commissioned separate ethnic minority studies. The 'soft' remedial policy implications of these non-mainstream studies are aimed at educating employers about cultural attitudes that lead to discrimination or suggest weak non-statutory compliance measures such as equality proofing and benchmarking as solutions. While discrimination and disadvantage remain the focus of government action, the more fundamental issue of segmented labour markets underscored by structural racism and sexism remains intact. Thus the root cause of the inequality, namely that ethnicised women are locked into certain gendered and raced sectors of the labour market, such as homeworking, cleaning or caring, remains secondary to the analysis.

It is important to recognise that racial equality is a deeply gendered issue and there are many racialised barriers preventing the equitable inclusion of black and minority ethnic women in the workforce. For example, there is a great deal of rhetoric in the public sector about a commitment to racial equality through meeting recruitment targets, being flexible and working in partnership with different groups. However, the 'tools of the race equality trade' such as audit and evaluation, which are the key mechanisms of organisational change, are not gender neutral and complement a masculine approach to social change in a still largely male working environment. For black and Asian women to get into any level yet alone senior levels in the public sector requires recognition of their particular needs as carers. Pakistani, Bangladeshi and Black Caribbean women have their first child on average earlier than white women, and Pakistani and Bangladeshi women are likely to have a larger number of children, while black and Caribbean women are more likely to be lone parents. These family patterns mean that the availability of childcare and flexible working have a major impact on the women's employment options, as release from family commitments is a real issue for all black and minority ethnic women who want to work.

However, racial equality action plans rarely include the specific recognition of this gendered predicament and gender duty schemes rarely recognise the cultural contexts of different childcare needs. Furthermore, neither tends to include the gendered context of racial discrimination experienced by these women within their organisations. It is clear that racism, sexism and discrimination are part of the everyday experience of black and minority ethnic women who are up to three times more likely to be asked about their plans for marriage, children and family at job interview than white women (EOC 2006). This is ironic, seeing that Pakistani and Bangladeshi young women fly in the face of stereotyped expectations by expressing higher aspirations and commitment to the labour market than their white counterparts. They are more likely to want to pursue self-employment and professional careers and also show no more desire to get married than any other group. Nevertheless, one in six black and minority ethnic women experiences racist or sexist comments at work, and one in five Pakistani and Bangladeshi women experiences negative attitudes towards her because of religious dress.

Changing the rules: legislation, intersectionality and black feminism

It could be argued that persistent inequalities and patterns of social exclusion among black and minority ethnic communities are being addressed universally through new and far-reaching anti-discrimination and equalities legislation. Protection now can cover direct and indirect discrimination based on sex, race, colour, language, religion, political or other opinion, national or social origin, association with a national minority, property, birth, racial or ethnic origin, religion or belief, disability, age and sexual orientation. Yet such extensive protection needs to be accessible to the most marginal and excluded in society if it is to be credible. The covert nature of the process of exclusion experienced by ethnicised women challenges the context of these legal and institutional mechanisms for redressing inequalities.

In spite of progressive equality legislation which includes establishing a single equality body, the Equality and Human Rights Commission, in 2007, it has been demonstrated that black and minority ethnic women are still categorised in unmeaningful ways in the application of the legislation (Lester and Clapinska 2005). Ethnicised women are often simplistically defined in universal terms using preconceived political and social categories which underpin social policy and equalities thinking. For example, women's life experiences of poverty, neglect, marginalisation and discrimination are often disaggregated (and hence disappear) in official equalities documentation and statistics as they are classified in terms of being either women, and hence 'gendered', or ethnic minorities, and hence 'raced'. Similarly, the official equalities terminology divides and cuts across women's natural multiple identities in terms of the intersection of their age, sexuality, disability, religious and class and cultural differences. For example, an older working-class South Asian widowed woman who has worked in the family business and may have no pension will have a very different identity and face different equality issues compared with a younger professional South Asian woman doctor in an NHS hospital who may have to deal with domestic violence issues in the family. Just as their experiences are different, so too have multiple definitions evolved in terms of their everyday lived experience of gendered and racialised social relations. However, the 'intersectionality' which characterises these women's lives is not reflected in the equality discourse which artificially dichotomises racial, gendered and other identities when, in effect, each one is experienced through the other. As Maynard explains, 'racism and sexism are interlocking systems of domination that uphold each other. It does not make sense to analyse "race" and gender as if they constitute discrete systems of power' (Maynard 1994: 21).

Black, postcolonial and anti-racist feminists have long called for an understanding of the value of an intersectional analysis which aims to reveal the importance of the multiple identities of black and minority ethnic women.[3] Intersectionality not only centralises the complex multiple social positions that characterise lived social reality, it also seeks to explain the way in which power, ideology and identity intersect to maintain patterns and processes of inequality and discrimination which both structure and are reflected in black and minority ethnic women's lives. Women, who are collectively defined as 'ethnic minority', have different multiple experiences in terms of their age, sexuality, disability, religion or culture. Thus it is argued that racism, patriarchy, social class and other systems of oppression simultaneously structure the relative position of these women at any one time creating specific, and varied, patterns of inequality and discrimination. It is the cultural and historical specificity of inequality that black, postcolonial and anti-racist feminists stress as important in developing a more holistic approach to mainstream feminist analysis of women's social disadvantage. As Nira Yuval-Davis (2006) argues, we need studies that separate out the different levels in which social divisions are constructed and analyse how they are intermeshed with each other in specific historical situations.

As a consequence of a lack of an intersectional analysis, black and minority ethnic women fall between the scope of the separate legislative provision for race, sex and disability discrimination. Ethnicised minority women who experience complex interacting levels of discrimination have been found to suffer 'double' (if race and gender are factors) or even 'triple' jeopardy (if, say, disability, sexuality, age or religion is also a conflicting factor). They are very rarely able to make multiple discrimination claims based on the holistic nature of their racialised and sexualised experience. Lord Lester among others has been long arguing for a Single Equality Act, since Britain's complex equality code is 'a tangled thicket of inconsistent and incomplete legislation in urgent need of coherent reform' (Lester and Clapinska 2005: 175). The Discrimination Law Review is currently addressing long-held concerns about the state of current anti-discrimination legislation (DCLG 2007b). Hopefully its conclusion will achieve parity across the equality strands with reformed legislation that provides a levelling up so that all different forms of discrimination will receive an equal level of protection. The value of having a single equality commission and a proposed Single Equality Act is that in the future it will hopefully provide a 'one-stop shop' – if coherently applied and resourced – for people who have been discriminated on more than one ground.

However, to achieve a truly intersectional appreciation of the dynamics of inequality and to combat the persistent and structural disadvantage black and minority ethnic women face, the Equality and Human Rights Commission (EHRC) needs to move beyond simply recognising that discrimination can be based on more than one ground or strand of equality. Responses to the government's Green Paper consultation on the proposed Single Equality Act suggests legislation should be guided by a 'purpose clause' (GLA 2007; O'Cinneide 2007). Such a clause would set out the essential purpose, principles and overall objectives and set the tone and spirit of the legislation.

From a black feminist standpoint, such a clause should be about more than ensuring equal opportunity through alleviating discrimination and pursuing effective remedies in law. Eliminating discrimination and disadvantage after the fact is like closing the door after the inequality horse has bolted. The clause should embrace the reality of the intersectional experience at a more fundamental root cause level. First, this would include a complex understanding of the sites of 'elite' intersectional discrimination where power, privilege and patriarchy intersect (Bhavnani *et al.* 2005). This would mean a determined and resolute commitment to target the lack of mainstream economic and political will for reform in areas that would empower black and minority ethnic women, such as democratic representation and pay and conditions in the workplace, especially the private sector.

Second, there needs to be an 'honest' incorporation of a holistic understanding of identity that can flexibly respond to new and emerging situations that lead to gendered and raced inequality and disadvantage. This would mean being vigilant in areas in which women are vulnerable in relation to the law, such as women at risk of domestic violence and sexual exploitation. It should be able to link their situation to other factors such as immigration status and poor access to services. It would also include women as carers and the relationship this has with disability, finances and age-related issues. Third, such a clause would need to be absolutely resolute about facilitating women's access to justice, dignity and fair treatment. There is no point in having legislation if it is not accessible and the powers of enforcement are weak. As the Equalities Review has shown, black and minority ethnic women are still one of the most disadvantaged in society across all levels of work, education and health (DCLG 2007a). Over 40 years of equality legislation has not turned this fact around in terms of embedding any true social change, and inequality gaps are growing. The question EHRC needs to ask and answer is: 'What is it about intersectional positioning and multiple discrimination that remains so illusive to and resistant to remedy?'

The Muslim menace: ethnicised women in the spotlight

While there are patterns of *invisibility* that concern us in the analysis of black and minority ethnic women, there are also patterns of *visibility* that characterise our representation. In a 'normalised absence/pathologised presence' approach ethnicised women are either marginalised or left out when mainstream race or gender issues are discussed. When they are included they are constructed as problematic and 'exceptional'. This heightened visibility in particular contexts such as the veil debates leads me to ask the question, 'What is behind this growing concern for the hitherto invisible and marginalised "ethnic woman" and why are they the focus of our attention now?'

Since 9/11, and more recently the 7/7 bombings by young British Muslim men in the UK, there has been an overwhelming preoccupation with Muslim women in the press. As Gayatri Spivak, an eminent black feminist academic, tells us, it is the work of the postcolonial feminist to ask the simple question 'What does this mean? – and begin to plot a history' (Spivak 1988: 297). When black and minority ethnic women have been highlighted, what is revealed is a long-standing pathological pattern of visibility that characterises the 'ethnicised woman'. This pattern is underpinned on the one hand by a Eurocentric universalism, which reduces the complexity and individuality of these women's lives to a single objectified category – which in this case is the ubiquitous, stereotypical 'Muslim woman'. On the other, this visibility is also characterised by a particular form of cultural relativism that highlights only specific cultural issues to do with these 'othered' women. Anne Phillips explains how culture is now widely employed in the discourse on multi-culturalism in ways that deny the human agency of minority or non-Western groups who (unlike their Western counterparts) are seen to be 'driven' by their cultural traditions and practices compelling them to behave in particular kinds of ways (Phillips 2007). Thus while South Asian women are seen to suffer 'death by culture' when they are subject to honour killings or dowry murder (Meetoo & Mirza 2007a), white British or American women who are associated with societies characterised by freedom, democracy and mobility are deemed immune from an analysis where culture has any explana-tory power, even when they are victims of culturally specific forms of patriarchal violence such as gun crime or domestic violence.

The dual pattern of visible representation experienced by ethnicised women is not new, it has its roots in imperial times (McClintock 1992; Simmonds 1997). Then (as now) Black African, Caribbean and Asian women have been depicted as 'mute visible objects', voiceless victims of their cultural practices in need of rescue. The civilising mission of the Empire was often underpinned by so-called masculine heroic acts of 'white men saving brown women from brown men' (Spivak 1988: 297) as in the case of the British banning of Sati (widow burning) in India. However, historically the ethnicised woman was also sexualised as the exotic other. Here she was constructed as the erotic temptress – a manipulative, self-serving 'jezebel' slave who is thus implicated in her own rape and humiliation (hooks 1981). In the absence of her own voice there has been a powerful reappropriation of her agency and she becomes the object (to be 'named' and studied) rather than the subject (who tells her own story).

Over the past 50 years, since postwar migration to the UK, there has been a continuous postcolonial preoccupation with the ethnicised woman's victimhood and sexuality. When we think of Asian or African women they are synonymous with patriarchal backward practices such as forced marriage and honour killings or genital mutilation and rape. If they have agency they are often depicted as manipulative, scrounging refugees and asylum seekers or overbearing black female matriarchs who marginalise and emasculate their menfolk (Reynolds 1997). If they are victims they are portrayed as disem-powered, sexually exploited mail order brides or sold into sexual trafficking. Clearly the social and economic realities of exploitation and oppression need to be addressed; however, my point here is that it is hard to escape and move beyond the racialised and gendered stereotypes that mainstream society has of us. Such stereotypes are powerful forms of knowledge, which shape our possibilities and identities and so construct our lived experience as ethnicised women.

The shift in this focus towards Muslim women which we are witnessing in the new millennium follows a similar pattern of visibility and representation. As before, black and postcolonial feminists have taken issue with the cultural superiority and simplistic, sensationalised cultural constructions of Muslim women in the media that negate black and minority ethnic female identity and agency, and depoliticise her (embodied) struggles for self-determination. A clear example of this is the heated public media debate triggered by Labour Minister Jack Straw who, after 25 years in office, expressed his personal discomfort with Muslim women wearing the face veil in his constituency surgery in Blackburn (Bunting 2006). As the media hysteria grew over several weeks, stories of 'the Muslim woman' appeared on the front pages of the papers every day. Her body became a battlefield in the symbolic war against Islam, the barbaric 'other', and the Muslim enemy 'within'. Her complex dress was given symbolic meaning over and above its religious and social status (Dywer 1999). Her private reasons for wearing the hijab (the headscarf) or niqab (the full face veil) became public property: a 'weapon' used by many different competing interests from male politicians to white feminists to argue their case for and against assimilation, multiculturalism and human rights. In what Chandra Talpade Mohanty has called the 'latent ethnocentrism' of the West, Muslim women are presented as voiceless, stereotyped, racialised victims rather than active agents working to determine and engage their rights as individuals (Mohanty 1988). Articulate Muslim women were hardly heard in the cacophony of competing interests for her agenda (Fawcett 2006). Those who stepped outside the paradigm and showed self-determination were vilified (as in the case of the Muslim teacher who refused to remove the veil).

While patriarchal atrocities, acts of violence and backward cultural practices in any society should be challenged in no uncertain terms, from the point of view of Muslim women it could be argued that what they are experiencing is not so much a concern with their human rights and social conditions, but a postmodern reworking of the heroic colonial stance of 'being saved', as in the past. Now in a new era of colonial appropriation we have 'white men and women saving Muslim women from Muslim men'. This was no more evident than when Afghanistan was invaded in response to 9/11. Cherie Blair and Laura Bush, the wives of the UK Prime Minister and USA President, came together to champion against the Taliban oppression of women and children in Afghanistan. They held special meetings in 10 Downing Street to highlight the women's 'shocking and inspiring stories and give back voice to Afghani women'.[4] But such concerned action after years of women's oppression in Afghanistan begs the question, 'Why now and why these women?' As previously suggested the work of the black and postcolonial feminist is to ask the simple question

'What does this mean? – and begin to plot a history'. I continue this task of mapping our representation in an effort to seek clarity on our complex condition.

Women are doing it for themselves: activism and the multicultural challenge

Women, it is argued, are the 'bearers of the races' and 'guardians of culture' (Yuval-Davis 1997). They are deemed central to the ideological construction and reproduction of national identity and hence the (multicultural) state. While black feminists[5] have long argued that race and gender matters in the way it affects social divisions, the new multicultural vision of 'Britishness' as described by Tony Blair and Gordon Brown[6] is made up of gender-neutral ethnic communities that (despite a few recent remedial meetings with Muslim women[7]) privileges male minority leaders. The inclusive 'national story' they propose writes out the complexities of the black and minority ethnic woman's struggle for a place in the postcolonial national picture. Black feminism as a political and social movement in Britain is often overlooked, but has its roots in the postcolonial activism and struggles of black women migrants from the Caribbean, Africa and the Indian subcontinent who came over during the post-World War II recruitment drive for cheap labour (Mirza 1997a). As a theoretical and intellectual movement black British feminism questions the racial and gendered subtext of British national identity, its unspoken assumption of whiteness, and assertion of the importance of class or gender over all other axes of differentiation such as 'race' in mainstream explanations for inequality and oppression.

Although rarely recognised, black women's groups have since the 1970s contributed to placing their issues on the agenda themselves. They have been central in raising awareness and tackling problems within specific communities and groups, including the thorny issue of religious conservatism. Ranu Samantrai argues that black British feminist activism has been more than just about accessing rights and services. Black women's activist groups are a contingent and politically destabilising force, in constant state of flux, where neither allies nor enemies are readily identifiable and where even their own campaigns and activists may become obsolete when gains are made. But more importantly, she argues, they play a central role in challenging the fundamental core of British identity. As she explains, black British feminists are 'a *privileged interlocutor of the similitudes and differences that constitute postimperial Englishness*' (Samantrai 2002: 2). By challenging the racial subtext of British majority and minority identities, black and minority ethnic women are engaged in the very radical project of refining the 'we' of the nation – in effect 'who are the British'.

Lynn Savery points to the significant impact feminist campaigning groups have had on changing the behaviour of the state with regard to women's rights. She explains, 'advocates struggling for change at the domestic level need to be aware that discursively challenging political elites' ideas of proper and appropriate gender roles and relations in society contributes to generating State behavioural change' (Savery 2002: 111). In the same way it could be argued that black feminists have had a significant impact on the multicultural state by slowly instigating state behavioural change with regard to gendered human rights issues for women. Black feminists have used international and domestic law to challenge the patriarchal alliance between white and black minority ethnic male leaders – an alliance that (despite state racism) remains secure at the heart of the liberal democratic state in Britain. Gains and losses made at the constitutional level do contribute to the state's image of itself as a progressive and civilised society – a society that has an egalitarian and humanitarian collective identity upholding principles of gender and racial equality.

For example, as Hannana Siddiqui (2006) discusses, though marginalised in mainstream politics and poorly represented in public life, Southall Black Sisters successfully secured an amendment to the discriminatory One Year Rule which stated that immigrant women would have to stay with their husbands for at least one year or face deportation. This effectively trapped women experiencing domestic violence as they would lose their right to stay in the UK if they left their spouse. Such victories can irrevocability shift the image and identity of the state as it is forced to make adjustments that embrace broader concepts of gendered rights and the challenges this means to British citizenship, British justice and the underpinning principle of so called British 'fair play'.

Clearly black and minority ethnic women are involved in new and strategic forms of engagement. In this sense they offer up a challenging vision. Although largely defined and excluded through their marginal status as women on one hand and ethnic minorities on the other, they adjust their strategies to accommodate a changing variety of racially contested public and private spaces. They negotiate better schooling for themselves and their children, form the backbone of their communities and neighbourhoods, and work and campaign for better health conditions.

These 'acts of citizenship' which require 'other ways of knowing' are rarely given legitimacy in the classical political and social discourse on citizenship and belonging that underpin the current debates on social exclusion. As mothers, wives and workers, their agency and activism sheds new light on traditional conceptualisations of citizenship. In their gendered/ racialised version of citizenship the women combine their social capital and emotional capital skills of resourcefulness and networking to enable them to become collective transformative agents. Their activism and radical forms of 'giving back' open up a 'third space' of strategic engagement (Mirza and Reay 2000a). This third space has hitherto remained invisible as the traditional gaze on the public (male) and private (female) dichotomy in current citizenship theorising has obscured 'other ways of knowing' and thus 'other ways of being' a truly British citizen.

Conclusion: Black women – a prospectus for the future

What can the lives of black and minority ethnic women tell us about the dynamics of inequality and discrimination? Why do they slip through the cracks of mainstream analysis on race and gender equality? How have they come to be represented in particular ways, as either the dangerous sexualised 'other' or voiceless victims in the media? What can policies and legislation based on an intersectional analysis look like? What lessons does black women's activism have for understandings of citizenship and civic participation?

While these questions have framed our explanation for the continued marginality of black and minority ethnic women, the key to moving forward lies in an analysis that places at its core the intrinsic value and contribution of these women. A prospectus for the future is about understanding the fundamental challenge these women bring to the 'equality table'. We have reached a critical point in the equality arena. There is a new Equality Act and a new Equality and Human Rights Commission, and more is to come with proposals for a Single Equality Act, yet inequality for this group remains entrenched. Now more than ever we need to raise our level of analysis and understanding of the issues. We need to move beyond the construction of gendered and racial stereotypes which inform our commonsense understanding of these women. This means seeing them not simply as problematic subjects who suffer multiple discrimination and who pose a remedial challenge to policy and legislative inclusion. Rather, it means appreciating the significance of their multiple identity and their position as privileged critical citizens who are also key players changing the face of British society. It is a vision of the future that I for one will be looking forward to.

Chapter 6

Multiculturalism and the gender trap[1]

> Multiculturalism does not cause domestic violence, but it does facilitate its continuation through its creed of respect for cultural differences, its emphasis on non-interference in minority lifestyles and its insistence on community consultation (with male self defined community leaders). This has resulted in women being invisibilised, their needs ignored and their voices silenced.
>
> (Beckett and Macey 2001: 311)

Socially responsible educators in multicultural Britain need to address the issue of gendered risk which young 'ethnicised'[2] women can face within their own communities and families. Young women growing up in minority ethnic communities who are subject to specific forms of cultural domestic violence, such as honour killings and forced marriage, are caught up in the contradictions of the cultural relativism of British multiculturalism on the one hand, and the private/public divide which characterises our approach to domestic violence on the other. Liberal multiculturalism is popularly conceived as celebrating diversity and 'tolerating' different cultural and religious values between groups. However, in this model the notion of mutual tolerance is fragile. One way in which multiculturalism negotiates this fragility is to maintain a *laissez-faire* approach to gendered cultural difference. This chapter looks at some of the tensions and confusions involved in dealing with the hard and sensitive issues of gendered human rights violations which can become issues in our multicultural schools.

Heshu Yones, a young Kurdish woman, was just 16 when she was brutally beaten and murdered by her father in 2004. He slashed her throat in the bath when he discovered that she was trading love letters with a boy in her class in her London school. His 'cultural defense',[3] which was supported by dozens of men from the Kurdish community, was that she had become too westernised and had brought her death upon herself.[4] In Great Britain, a police review of 22 domestic homicides in 2005 resulted in 18 being reclassified as 'murder in the name of so-called "honor".'[5] While such extreme violence upon a woman for breaking an honour code of the community is an abuse of human rights, there have been many attempts to justify it on religious or cultural grounds. This is also the case for forced marriage, a practice among certain minority ethnic communities living in the UK. A forced marriage, unlike an arranged marriage, is when the young person is coerced under either physical or emotional duress into a marriage against his or her will in the name of family honour.[6] The Forced Marriage Unit (FMU) deals with approximately 300 cases annually of marriage conducted without freely given consent.[7] Many of the cases involve young women under the age of 18. It is often younger women in their late teens and early twenties who are victims of these 'dishonourable' crimes when their emerging sexuality comes under increasing regulation and control by the family and wider community. It is the young woman's sexual purity and 'honour' that is seen to define the status and regard with which the family is held in the community. The opposite to honour is shame, and this emotive combination is a powerful means of social control. Jasvinder Sanghera who founded Karma Nirvana, an Asian women's project which provides confidential emotional and physical support for vulnerable women facing domestic violence, explains, 'every woman who comes to us has a problem with shame. It is a form of social control which oppresses Asian women and suppresses their ability to speak'.[8]

We may be incredulous when we read the sensationalised press reports[9] that a father and other close relatives, including women, can inflict such brutality on their own children in the name of honour or 'izzat', but many young women facing familial domestic violence of forced marriage and honour killings are being educated under our watch, within our school and college walls. As socially responsible educators we need to ask: How do we understand and act on the gendered risk faced by many of these young 'ethnicised' women in their own communities in the name of 'honour'? In this chapter I attempt to unravel some of the tensions and confusions that surround approaching the hard and sensitive issues of human rights violations in our multicultural schools.

Gendering multiculturalism: understanding the dynamics of sexism, racism and domestic violence

It could be argued that these extreme forms of domestic violence involve only a small number of young women of Asian, African and Middle Eastern origin, but the persistence of such female-centred crimes in Britain raises many issues about cultural sensitivity and the gendered nature of multi-culturalism in the UK. Multiculturalism is a much disputed term, but it has evolved in the British context to mean respecting diversity and valuing cultural difference in the context of core shared values (Hall 2000; Runnymede Trust 2000; Blair 2006; Brown 2006). It is often used loosely in political discourse to affirm the distinctness, uniqueness and individual validity of different religions, cultures, groups or communities, and recognises the importance of acknowledging and accommodating these differences and distinctness. Reporting at the turn of the new millennium, the Commission on the Future of Multi-ethnic Britain (Runnymede Trust 2000) highlighted a need to move towards a multicultural post-nation in which Britain would be a 'community of communities'. In such a 'community' we may have shared values, but we also have the autonomy of cultural expression, so we may wear the Muslim hijab headscarf or eat Halal meat. As Hall (2000) has argued, state intervention in policy and professional discourse in the UK has been predicated upon a loose and historically haphazard notion of 'multicultural drift'. Here multicultural policies have been piecemeal and based on concessions, extensions and exemptions such as scheduling exams to avoid key festivals for various religious groups, Sikhs being exempt from wearing helmets, and slaughterhouses for Jewish and Muslims. These concessions have been won or lost through the struggles of postwar migrant communities living in Britain.

However, multiculturalism as it has evolved in the British context is also deeply racialised (Hesse 2000). While liberal multiculturalism is popularly and politically conceived as celebrating diversity and 'tolerating' different cultural and religious values between groups, the notion of mutual tolerance is fragile. Multiculturalism in this sense is 'skin-deep', and it works only if the demands of visible and distinct ethnic groups are not too 'different' and not too rejecting of the welcoming embrace of the 'host' society (Ahmed 2004). This fragility was tested when the Commission on the Future of Multi-ethnic Britain report suggested Britishness had unspoken racial connotations linked to Empire. This was met with a hostile media backlash against multiculturalism as it was seen to challenge the homogeneity of an exclusive imaginary 'white' Britishness (McLaughlin and Neal 2004). In the face of growing racist political rhetoric and anti-asylum and immigration policies in the UK, we are witnessing a retreat from multiculturalism and a move towards 'civic integration' (Wetherell et al. 2007). As part of the civic integration agenda newcomers have to swear an oath at ceremonies, the toughening of the English language requirement when acquiring British citizenship, and mandatory citizenship and democracy education at English schools. In the context of racial unrest and ethnic segregation in the northern towns in Britain in 2001, 'social cohesion' and 'civic integration' has reframed the discourse on multiculturalism (Bhavnani et al. 2005). Social cohesion emphasises 'building bridges' between segregated communities through inter-faith and cultural understanding, legitimating the link between citizenship and nationhood as essential for multicultural coexistence. Integration and active citizenship are now seen as the solution to economic inequality, political representation and structural segregation in housing and education which are and remain the core issues of racial unrest. However, as a consequence of culturalist tendencies in mainstream political discourse, the exclusion of ethnic minorities is often legitimated through specific multi-cultural policies (such as social cohesion) which locates ethnic communities in marginal spaces, on the periphery of decision-making both politically and in terms of policy.

However, gender differences within multicultural societies now and in the past have yet to be recognised (Okin 1999). Liberal multiculturalism in its many and shifting manifestations has consistently functioned to privilege 'race' and ethnicity over gender (Samantrai 2002; Mirza 2003). In the Commission on the Future of Multi Ethnic Britain women get a three-page mention in the 314-page report (Runnymede Trust 2000). Similarly, Community Cohesion reports fail to look at the specificity of gendered social action (Bhavnani et al. 2005). Multiculturalism deals with problems *between* communities, but rarely with problems *within* communities, failing to recognise the gendered power divisions within ethnic groups. A gender-blind multiculturalism has consequences for 'ethnicised' young women who have remained to a large extent invisible, locked into the private sphere of the home where gender-oppressive cultural and religious practices are still played out. In this regard young women growing up in minority ethnic communities are caught up in the contradictions of the cultural relativism of British multiculturalism on one hand, and the private/public divide which characterises our approach to domestic violence on the other.

To understand the invisibility of gender and violence in our construction of multiculturalism we need to look at the way in which ethnicity has become reified and fixed in terms of our understanding of the inherent qualities of ethnic minority groups. This process of reification, when ethnic group identity becomes defensive and cultural and religious practices are constructed within imagined but rigid and fixed boundaries, is called 'ethnic fundamentalism' (Yuval-Davis 1997). Migration whether forced or planned often brings with it the breakdown of traditional certainties structuring life courses and heightening anxieties of loss and belonging. For migrant women who are seen as the upholders of traditional values, patriarchal practices can be amplified when they are estranged and separated from their homeland. Under threat, certain aspects of culture can ossify, become romanticised or even perversely preserved – what I call 'pickled in aspic'.[10] When this happens, as we can see in the context of the negative discourse on Islamophobia, we witness a resurgence and persistence of fixed and regressive notions of ethnicity and nationalism as a primary basis for the elaboration of traditional beliefs. Such 'ethnic fundamentalism' is reflected in our multiculturalist discourse. In our everyday talk we not only often assume cultural homogeneity among local communities, with each one spatially segregated, but it also means that we often do not talk about difference within cultures as it is seen to be divisive and could lead to offence.

Focusing on culturally specific forms of domestic violence is often seen as very controversial ground. It is generally disputed that culture can explain how and why particular practices happen. By highlighting domestic violence issues in specific cultural and religious ethnic communities in the UK are we at risk of stereotyping these communities as backward and barbaric? Does this place a disproportionate emphasis on the 'ethnicised' woman – racialising her by separating out these forms of domestic violence as a special cultural phenomenon needing special cultural sensitivity? These questions lie at the heart of understanding the tensions between recognising gender oppression and preserving multicultural difference. This debate has been raised in relationship to gendered sexualised practices in particular cultures such as female genital mutilation, forced marriages and honour killings where the sanctity of (male) community rights is privileged over the bodily rights of individual (female) victims. I now turn to address some of the broader issues that frame this tension.

The 'new risk': Islamophobia and the ethnicised woman

Mary Douglas (1992) argues that we are living in a 'risk society' and that some risks are constructed and legitimated for public attention at particular times. In the case of familial and community violence to young ethnicised, and in particular Muslim women, the question arises as to why their risks are selected for attention over others right now? It is ironic that while multiculturalism invisiblises ethnic women, the discourse on Islamophobia visiblises them in negative and reactive ways. Post 9/11 and the 7/7 bombing in London, it could be argued that the increased attention given to honour killings and forced marriage in the media has had a positive effect in that it has opened up the issue of individual human rights for these young women. However, it has also had the negative effect of exacerbating Islamophobia and 'fear of the other'. The increased focus on 'honour'-based crimes in Muslim communities needs to be seen within the current climate of Islamophobia. When such crimes are reported in the British press, the young women are constructed as either romantic heroine, struggling for the benefits of the 'West' against her cruel and inhuman father and family, or victim, succumbing to her backward and traditional 'Eastern' culture (Ahmad 2003; Puwar 2003). As the heated public debate triggered by Labour Minister Jack Straw on the matter of Muslim women wearing the face veil demonstrates,[11] the Muslim woman's vulnerable yet 'over-determined' body has become symbolic in the battle against Islam and the barbaric 'other' (Dwyer 1999). The visibility of community and group cultural practices conveniently contributes to the construction of the 'other's' barbaric customs and cultures. Thus while certain forms of ethnicised, cultural violence are real in *effect* in that the young women are brutally treated, the crimes are also constructed as an ethnicised phenomenon within the racialised multicultural discourse, and are as such also an *affect* or product of this discourse. In this regard heightened media reports have a real consequence. They contribute to putting women at risk by sensationalising these crimes through their style and content of reporting resulting in voyeuristic spectacle (cries of 'how dreadful'!) followed by multicultural paralysis and inaction ('nothing to do with us! It is part of their culture'). In the discourses of multiculturalism and Islamophobia women are presented as voiceless, stereotyped, racialised victims rather than as active agents working to determine and engage their rights as individuals. Such sexualised objectification of ethnicised women disavows the relationship of gender, power and patriarchy within the negative social constructions of Islamophobia and multiculturalism.

However, black and Asian feminists do seek to address the issues of power and patriarchy in their own communities by raising difficult issues of sexism and domestic violence. As African American writer Toni Morrison asserts, we must raise difficult issues of sexism and domestic violence within our own (black) communities (Morrison 1993). In vulnerable and racialised communities there are tensions between protecting men from the racism of state agencies and negative media representation on the one hand, and the need to raise the issue of gendered violence and protect women's rights in these communities on the other (Crenshaw 1991). As Salim explains in the Kurdish community there is a fear among some that putting honour crimes on the public agenda might cause a dangerous backlash in the immigration debate and heighten xenophobic sentiments against asylum seekers (Salim 2003). As a counter to the racist assertion that black and Asian men are more barbaric, Gupta (2003) argues that we must take a global perspective on domestic violence and see honour killing and forced marriage as part of a wider global patriarchal phenomenon of violence. Women are beaten and murdered across the globe for similar reasons and it is not particular to one culture or religious group or community. She argues that domestic violence cuts across race, class, religion and age. Patriarchal structures use violence extensively to subjugate women in different forms in relation to class, race and ethnicity. Domestic violence is not an issue of racial or ethnic differences, it is a question of the economic, political and social development of a society and the levels of democracy and devolution of power within communities. She suggests research shows that low-violence cultures have female power and autonomy outside the home, strong sanctions against interpersonal violence, a definition of masculinity that is not linked to male dominance or honour, and equality in decision-making and resources within the family. These progressive qualities are absent from societies in which female sexual purity is still linked to familial and community dignity and social status, where the male is the custodian of that honour (Gill 2003).

Negotiating risk: dealing with gender difference in multicultural settings

How can professionals working with young people approach the issue of domestic violence and gendered human rights violations in the multicultural school? With the government's *Every Child Matters* agenda schools are now key actors in identifying a young person deemed at risk. *Every Child Matters* is comprehensive in its scope, stating, 'organizations involved with providing services to children – from hospitals and schools, to police and voluntary groups – will be teaming up in new ways . . . to protect children and young people from harm and help them achieve what they want in life'.[12] Within this discourse professionals in schools are now seen as part of the 'new class intellectuals' with privileged access to young people and therefore instrumental in monitoring who is 'at risk' (Kelly 2007). In this climate of increasing accountability and risk assessment individuals and organisations are charged with getting risk right and are often required to defend decisions from litigation and assessment. The tendency to individualisation and accountability in the discourse on risk, along with a *laissez-faire* multicultural approach to dealing with violent gendered cultural practices within the private domestic sphere of the family, can easily lead to a situation of non-interventionism or what I call 'multicultural paralysis' in cases of domestic violence.

This was particularly apparent in the recent case of Banaz Mahmod, a 20-year-old Kurdish woman who was sexually brutalized then murdered by her father and uncle because her boyfriend was not a strict Muslim and not from their immediate community. She was found strangled with a shoe lace and stuffed in a suitcase. The police did not respond to her repeated cries for help and she was described by one police officer in a gendered and racist stereotypical way as 'melodramatic and manipulative'.[13] Yasmin, a 19-year-old Asian woman, had a similar experience. At 15, her parents told her she was going abroad to get married. She explains, 'My step-father, he beat me up so badly because he always used to punch me. Once he punched me in the jaw and I couldn't open it for two weeks.' But when Yasmin tried to tell her teacher she said, 'My teacher just laughed it off. She didn't believe it was happening to me. The teacher, the school should have at least said something, done something. Or Social Services could've at least visited me to see if I was OK . . . but no one bothered'.[14]

On the other hand It may be difficult to tackle the issue of domestic violence as young women wish to protect their families' honour and divert attention away from the abuse. For example, 'S', a 14-year-old young British woman of Bangladeshi origin,[15] was a bright pupil with a good school record. By age 16 she was withdrawn and began to truant, and while marks on her wrists and back raised concerns for teachers, she blamed the marks convincingly on 'intergenerational tensions'. After her GCSEs she disappeared, having being drugged and sent to Bangladesh to be forcibly married. Although her teacher called the FMU and she was made a ward of the High Court, 'S' did not complain, as she did not want to bring shame on her parents, and so no action was taken. However, on her return to the UK she ran away from home and sought shelter in a refuge as she was raped by her husband. Although there was intervention on her behalf the agencies and services tasked with her protection still failed to protect her.

While an overly sensitive multicultural approach can lead to negative action or inaction, it can also replicate structures of oppression within communities. Karma Nirvana, a voluntary organisation which helps young women flee forced marriage situations, reported that they have experienced problems disseminating information through schools due to schools being concerned about damaging their relationships with the parents.[16] As recent BBC research shows, schools are at the centre of the debate on domestic violence as they have the potential to recognise that a forced marriage may take place when a female pupil is taken out of school and should report this to the appropriate authorities.[17] However, while the Forced Marriage Unit and DfES provide schools with guidelines on forced marriage,[18] over half of councils who should have oversight of the issues in their locality do not know how many cases, if at all, are occurring, nor do they have any guidelines on the issue.

Black and minority ethnic women's groups have been central in raising awareness and tackling problems related to domestic violence, sexuality and cultural and religious conservatism within specific communities, and groups have contributed to placing minority ethnic women's issues on the agenda; thus various services have been developed as a result of struggle by these groups.[19] In their evidence to the Working Party on Forced Marriage, Southall Black Sisters (SBS) were concerned about the failure of service providers to address the needs of women and girls at risk of forced marriages and honour killings (CIMEL/Interights 2001). Such service providers may cite cultural grounds for this failure, on the assumption that minority communities are self-policing, and they therefore do not have to intervene on behalf of these women. According to Siddiqui (2003) many community leaders who were consulted on the Working Group on Forced Marriages denied that there is a problem, and are hostile to women who refuse these marriages and women's organisations that work with them. Some have argued that issues raised around forced marriage are a form of racism and attack on the community, and on their cultural and religious heritage.

Despite these struggles by women's groups, male community leaders are still influential within certain communities. Ali Jan Haider, a Muslim social worker, relates how male family and community elders personally threatened him and his family when he helped a young 21-year-old woman and her five children escape domestic violence and placed her in a refuge. The young woman had come to the UK aged 16 from the rural Mirpur district of

Pakistan and had been subjected to persistent physical and mental abuse at the hands of her husband and her in-laws for several years. He explains the consequences of his actions:

> The community interference began in earnest. I had a phone call from a local Asian Councillor asking me if I could explain why I had taken mum and children away and broken up this respectable family. I then had phone calls and visits from countless community elders including a local religious leader. He did not waste any time castigating my actions and telling me what I had done was sinful. He told me how I should be personally held responsible for the family's loss of face, and the distress I had caused them.
>
> (Haider 2003: 4)

Haider, in outlining an Islamic perspective to domestic violence, explains the complex interrelationship and confusion between the Muslim religion and Pakistani culture on one hand and the practice of Social Services and his white and non-Muslim colleagues on the other. This confusion often leads to institutional paralysis or community resistance, preventing Muslim women from seeking help when they most need it.

Women's groups such as SBS, KWRO (Kurdish Women's Refugee Organisation) and WLUML (Women Living Under Muslim Laws) argue that the way to tackle the issues of partiarchial community violence is to adopt a global human rights approach when dealing with the issues of honour-based violence. At a round table held to address the issue of honour crimes[20] it was recommended that a true human rights approach would need to take account of a country's civil societal role in addressing honour crimes and should therefore include wider national concerns about sexuality, patriarchy and sexual autonomy in the society more generally. Such an approach calls for a fundamental redefinition of community, citizenship and the individual, and challenges the false dichotomy between community and women, where women are placed outside of the community.

Conclusion

I began this chapter by asking: How do we as socially responsible educators understand and act on the gendered risk faced by many of these young 'ethnicised' women in their own communities in the name of 'honour'? As our discussion reveals, there are many tensions that underpin an analysis of gendered human rights violations in a multicultural context. A key issue is that young women from ethnic minority communities are invisible within the discourse of multiculturalism and are therefore at risk of not being fully protected by the state agencies as equal citizens. They 'fall between the cracks' of the multicultural discourse, as 'race' and ethnicity is prioritised and gender differences and inequalities are rendered invisible. On the other hand, when ethnicised young women become visible they are pathologised as victims in relation to the negative media attention in the current discourse of Islamophobia. Social cohesion which seeks to build on the idea of multi-cultural coexistence with its emphasis on inter-faith dialogue, integration and intercommunity understanding still does not tackle the thorny issue of gender inequality in ethnic communities.

Often, when we are immersed in the cultural context of respecting and accommodating cultural difference we do not see the bigger picture of universal violence against women and the human rights violations of these crimes. The climate that multiculturalism has produced in relation to racism is one of 'walking on eggshells' where cultural differences are respected, often without question, for fear of offending communities and ethnic groups. In these situations young ethnic minority women can suffer from a lack of protection because organisations that deal with their protection are fearful of being seen as racist, or feel they lack the cultural expertise, or do not want to offend the communities' sensibilities. However, domestic violence must never been seen as a cultural matter, but always as a human rights issue (Salim 2003). In 1995 the Beijing Platform for Action at the 1995 UN World Congress on Women declared that culture, tradition and religion could not be used by the state to avoid their obligation to protect women (Kelly 2005). To develop a truly multicultural multi-agency policy framework under *Every Child Matters*, schools need to be absolutely resolute in their approach to cultural forms of domestic violence. When dealing with community groups and state agencies, professionals in schools should be ever vigilant about whose perspectives are being heard and whose voices are being marginalised and by whom. This is not an easy task; it is a front-line position and there are issues of personal safety on all sides which need to be considered, but only by challenging the multicultural status quo can we move towards a more just and equitable response to the global issue of domestic violence that festers within all our communities, whether black, white or Asian.

Part 3

Transcending race and gender expectations

Chapter 7

Black women and real citizenship[1]

This chapter explores the ways in which black women's participation as both mothers and educators sheds new light on traditional conceptualisations of citizenship. First, it is argued that their active engagement in black supplementary schools demonstrates the paradoxical relationship between individual educational achievement and collective community commitment that characterises black female citizenship. Second, in their gendered/racialised version of citizenship the women combine their social capital and emotional capital skills of resourcefulness and networking, enabling them to become collective transformative agents. Finally, the women's radical forms of 'giving back' and quest for educational desire open up a 'third space' of strategic engagement. This 'third space' has hitherto remained invisible as the traditional gaze on the public and private dichotomy in current citizenship theorising has obscured 'other ways of knowing' and thus 'other ways of being' a citizen.

Feminist scholars have argued that a genuine politics of inclusion is impossible to achieve so long as the mechanisms which exclude the demands of minority or marginal groups are not explored (Young 1990). The consistent exclusion of women from the public sphere through restrictions on paid employment, threats of violence, restrictions on speaking in public spaces, and confinement to domestic duties in the feminised private sphere critically affects equal participation and hence the citizenship status of women (Lister 1990; Walby 1994). However, as the starting point of much feminist theorising takes as its terms of reference the gendered exclusion of women from the patriarchal discourse of citizenship, definitions of who counts as a citizen become preoccupied with equality, acceptance and membership into the masculine civic polity. The terrain of feminist academic discourse thus slips into the revalorisation of difference and celebration of the private sphere rather than considering the more challenging position of 'acts of citizenship'.

New forms of engagement have emerged as those deemed to be the socially marginal, such as black women, adjust their strategies to accommodate a changing variety of racially contested public and private spaces (Hill Collins 1998). These 'acts of citizenship' which require 'other ways of knowing' are rarely given legitimacy in the dominant feminist and classical political and social discourse on citizenship. It is argued here that the classical notion of citizenship, in terms of universalist inclusion and participation in a stable political community, requires rethinking in postmodern times. In the context of global economic and political change and increasing social fragmentation, the centrality and stability of traditional forms of belonging and solidarity that bind citizens together in a common public culture have been undermined by the increasing subjectivisation of social actors who are occupied with the politics of self-actualisation and hence the nature of the self (Lash 1996; Mouffe 1993). Inequality now, it is argued, can be explained by how adept some groups are in adjusting to the fluidity of social change. Active participants – the new citizens – are reflexive autonomous 'clever people' capable of changing expert systems and reconstructing new solidarities across time and space (Giddens 1994: 94). Those who are successful advocates of their social and political rights in the public sphere advance the claims of the 'reflexive winners' (Beck 1992). It is suggested that the 'reflexive' losers are those who adapt to their increasing exclusion by ceasing to participate as citizens. In a process of strategic disengagement from the public sphere they defensively withdraw collectively and individually from public participation (Ellison 1997). It is in this latter marginal disengaged category that black women are so often inappropriately positioned as members of the passively constructed 'socially excluded'.

Black supplementary schools: a study of black female agency

Black women's educational strategies and struggles to support their children within increasing social and educational exclusion in Britain call for the necessity to redefine what is meant by 'real' citizenship in late/postmodernity. In this analysis of black women's participation in black supplementary schools the intention is to develop an understanding of citizenship within the context of the dynamics of race and gender. As the data from this study reveal, black women's grassroots activism is not rooted in 'defensive engagement'. On the contrary they have actively evolved gendered/racialised forms of community solidarity and collective voice that refuse to privilege dominant definitions of a decentred, multiply positioned, self-articulating postmodern citizen.

This small-scale study of African–Caribbean supplementary schooling focused on just four black supplementary schools: three London-based schools, Colibri, Community Connections and Ohemaa, and one in a provincial city, Scarlet Ibis.[2] The six black women educators whose in-depth interviews form the main data for this study had been involved in supplementary schooling for periods ranging from four to sixteen years. They had often started out as a member of a small group of black parents, talking in terms of themselves 'and a few other mothers getting together'. Their narratives reveal a 'real' commitment to community through the complex and strategic rationalisation of both their own and their children's educational aspirations. The findings of this study, arising as they do out of a very small-scale investigation based on qualitative interviews and three days of participant observation, are necessarily exploratory and tentative. However, the data show that the participation and commitment reveal a very different vision of citizenship from prevailing orthodoxies which give primacy to the traditional forms of collective social participation.

Black supplementary schools are for the most part self-funding, organic grassroots organisations consciously hidden away from the public 'gaze' of funders and local authorities. Set up by and for the black community, these schools, which are mainly run by women, have a history that reaches back into the 1950s, ever since the first wave of postwar black migrants arrived and settled in Britain (Reay and Mirza 1997). The schools are small concerns run after school on Saturdays or Sundays and are difficult to locate, as they exist deep within in the informal black community and are supported by the black church networks. These small, local, often community-based schools are not regarded in the same light as the voluntary aided separate religious 'ethnic' schools movement. Unlike established Muslim, Jewish or Seventh Day Adventist schools, the supplementary school is based on a philosophy of inclusion rather than exclusiveness. A notable characteristic of these black schools is that no matter if the school's orientation is Methodist, Evangelical, Pentecostal, Rastafarian or Afrocentric (rooted in Garveyism), other children, including white working-class children and children from other dominations or ethnic backgrounds, are welcomed. Their open community membership means that these schools place themselves outside of the contentious discourse for separate religious 'ethnic schools'. Black supplementary schools are in that sense an anomaly within 'ethnic education'.

Ironically the ambiguous status of black supplementary schools has meant that they have been for the most part left alone. The schools are not seen to represent a 'critical mass' in terms of numbers and voice. What is regarded as their fragmented, localised, contingent formation is not perceived as constituting any threat to the mainstream. As funding through the local authority or voluntary sector has always been small, unreliable or resisted, these schools' self-sufficiency and genesis in community activism have placed them outside the local authority gaze. For the most part these schools rely on parental contributions and community donations. As many as 1000 schools have been reported in London (Abdelrazack and Kempadoo 1999). This six-month small-scale study uncovered the presence of 60 supplementary schools in Inner and Greater London. By the time the study ended, through personal and social networks and word of mouth we were hearing of more and more schools every day. Sometimes there would be several on one council estate or in one neighbourhood. They appeared to spring up 'unofficially' in houses, community centres and unused school rooms. The average size of the schools was between 30 and 40 pupils. However, some schools had as few as 15 children and others as many as 90. The age range of pupils catered for was anything between 3 and 18 years old, though the average age of most schools was 5 to 16 years.

Of the 60 schools in this research, over 65 per cent of the teachers were women. Where men ran the school, women's daily work as teachers and carers was clearly the majority input. Mac an Ghaill writes that in the black education movement, 'It is important to emphasise that black women were at the forefront of the implementation of these strategies of resistance' (1991: 134). Similarly, black women writers Bryan, Dadzie and Scafe argue, 'For black women challenging education has been part of a wider struggle to defend the rights and interests of the black community as a whole . . . education struggles have been central to our political development' (1985: 59). In the four supplementary schools in this research black children discovered 'really useful knowledge' (Johnson 1988) which allowed them 'to step outside the white hermeneutic circle and into the black' (Gates in Casey 1993: 110). Each of the four schools in the study were distinct, but they were underpinned by two main pedagogies. Some focused more on black images, black history and black role models. Others focused more on back to basics, the formal teaching of the 3 Rs. Some did both. In the same way as the schools were paradoxically radical and conservative in their aims, so too were the teachers both radical and conservative in their praxis. On the one hand, the women, who were for the most part voluntary unpaid teachers, talked of their 'joy' of what they do, the 'gift of giving back', of their work to 'raise the race'. Many had been giving up their weekends for 20 years. Others had become ill from overwork and dedication. On the other hand, the same teachers saw themselves as complementing mainstream education. They were concerned about 'fitting in', assisting parents with home-school relations and encouraging the children to do better. On the surface these schools appeared conformist and conservative, with their focus on formality and buying into the liberal democratic ideal of meritocracy.

However, black supplementary schools should be seen as more than simply a response to exclusion and evidence of good practice. In their presence and praxis these schools embody an evolving organic critique of mainstream educational 'lacking'. In mapping black supplementary schools' hidden history what emerges is a picture of collective black educational agency that challenges taken-for-granted assumptions embodied within mainstream educational rationale. In the words and actions of the heterogenous black female educators involved in these schools, there is evidence of a radical black agency from which has evolved a unified collective consciousness. It could be argued that such conscious forms of female collective action should be recognised as constituting a new social movement (Mirza 1997c; Reay and Mirza 2000b). An analysis of female collective action offers a new direction in the investigation of black social movements where for too long black female agency has remained invisible. In the masculinist discourse of 'race' and social change, the assumption has always been that the struggle against racist exclusion is contested and fought over in the masculine arena of the streets – riots, rebellion and violent confrontation characterise the struggle of the (male) youth in the city. In privileging such an analysis the subversive and covert transformative action of women is rarely valorised as an act of social change. However, black women struggle for educational inclusion in order to transform their opportunities and so in the process subvert racist expectations and beliefs. In the study the women collectively opened up transformative possibilities for their community through their pragmatic recognition of the power of education to transform and change the hegemonic discourse.

From personal desire to collective radicalism: black women's stories of community and commitment

In *Young, Female and Black* (Mirza 1992) young British African Caribbean women tell stories of their educational commitment and desire to do well. They talk of passing exams, going to college, proving their worth. On the surface their instrumental credentialism appears to be grounded in traditional values of meritocracy. However, an alternative reading in the context of their circumstances reveals that what they do is to strategically redefine success. Following in the footsteps of their mothers and grandmothers they predictably trace the generational line that links back to a seemingly traditional pattern of inclusive educational practice. However, what the young women are actually doing by their inclusive acts of 'doing well' is subverting the individualism of the mainstream educational system. They do so by their pragmatic refusal, using the educational structures and systems that exist to achieve occupational mobility and academic success on their own terms. The young black women work individually on their own at the back of noisy, run-down classrooms. In their actions they are not 'resisting through accommodating', as is so often believed, but they are refusing to fulfil racist expectations by being labelled underachievers. The underlying discourse they identify with is to 'raise the race' – to do well for others in the community through their own achievements. The racialised reality of their world means they recognise that a black person is located very differently than a white person. Thus to be educated is to engage in a radical act, as Kathleen Casey observes:

> In a racist society for a black child to become educated is to contradict the whole system of racist signification . . . to succeed in studying white knowledge is to undo the system itself . . . to refute its reproduction of black inferiority materially and symbolically.
>
> (Casey 1993: 123)

This paradoxical pattern of personal educational desire and collective community commitment is mirrored in other research. Signithia Fordham's research in the USA reveals young black students rejecting formal schooling's achievement-orientated individualism in favour of a collective individualism which valorises the black self's commitment to the imagined or fictive black community. Fordham explains that in hostile contexts controlled by the 'white (an)Other' it was necessary to behave as a collective black self, suppressing the desire to promote the individual self. Presenting an identity that minimises individual distinctions strengthens the possibility of community stability, promoting survival in a system not designed for black survival.

The commitment of African American students to the black fictive kinship system sanctions individual competition only if it compels the individual to give competitively, to use his or her skills to connect or reconnect him or herself to an imagined black community. If individuals possess skills and expertise in an area external to what their peers construct as the black community, people who share or have access to them assume that they will be willing to share this 'gift' or skill unconditionally (Fordham 1996: 91).

What is also marked in the research on black educational orientation is the gendered nature of this educational commitment. The finding that running black supplementary schools was primarily women's work is supported by a growing body of research both here and in the USA which asserts that children's education is predominantly the concern and responsibility of mothers (Reay 1998). Often, as in this study, collective black agency is generated through the efforts of particular women:

> The translation of common experience into collective action requires some additional impetus. That impetus frequently comes from one or more pioneer women. These women have a catalytic impact on the women in a given community or locality and begin the process of awareness raising and mobilisation.
>
> (Sudbury 1998: 87)

The narratives of black women educators in our study mirrored this finding of covert gendered agency, as Charity, a mother and teacher in a black supplementary school, explains:

> It's mainly women who are the ones who are involved in education in this country. Within the Afro-Caribbean community it tends to be mainly women. In my family that was the case and at Colibri it was mainly women who came and that was fine. Obviously, there were a few fathers who were involved and there were a couple of men on the committee but it was mainly women.

Charity's narrative not only highlights the key contribution of women; it also presents a very different version of urban black community to those endemic in popular media and political discourses:

> There was a group of about six parents, who like myself as a black teacher, were dissatisfied with what was happening to black pupils. They felt if they had been in the Caribbean their children would be much further on academically and they decided something had to be done, schools weren't doing anything so it had to be them. I really wish someone had the time to chart the enormous amount of work they put in those first few years. It was immense. The school started off in someone's front room on Saturday mornings. The parents doing all the teaching themselves to start with and it was very much focused on what was their main concern; their children not being able to read and write properly. Then these parents found the group of children grew from 10 to 15 and soon it was 20 and at this point it was unmanageable running a Saturday school in someone's front room so they petitioned the council for accommodation and finally got one of the council's derelict properties. They spent their spare time shovelling rubbish out of the room, tramps had been living there, doing building, repair work, getting groups of parents together to decorate. They pulled together and did all this work themselves, used the expertise they had to get the school on its feet and it was mainly the women organising things, making sure it got done, although in those early days quite a few men were involved as well.

As Charity's words indicate, these four black supplementary schools generate rich opportunities for contesting prevalent discourses about contemporary urban communities.

There is none of the apathy, recalcitrance, fecklessness and aggression which permeate both popular and political discourses on the 'socially excluded'. Dominant discourses of the urban working class, both black and white, paint pictures of apathetic masses, the inactive and uninformed. Once named 'the underclass' by the socially and politically privileged, and now renamed the 'socially excluded' by the New Labour elite, these urban communities have been ritually pathologised as disengaged, disadvantaged and inherent underachievers (SEU 1998).

However, Verna tells a very different story; one of effective agency. The agency she speaks of is not the individualised agency of the white middle classes (Jordan *et al.* 1994; Reay 1998), but rather a collectivised agency grounded in communal responses to a mainstream educational system which is perceived to be failing black children. In her narrative we hear commitment, reciprocity and continuity:

> I really wanted to do Saturday school because so much was given to me
> when I was a child. I had so much positive input I wanted to give some
> of it back. I also wanted to challenge this government's views on
> community – that community isn't important. Not that I'm interested in
> politics. I keep my head down. My work is on the ground with children,
> doing my bit here and it has been rewarding, very rewarding. Children
> have gone through the school that others have given up on and they are
> doing very well. Matthew who was so very, very difficult when he came,
> could not sit down for more than 30 seconds I see him now on his way
> to college. Perhaps it is all right, you know, that this is a stage. The school
> has done a great deal for a number of children. I can see the fruits of my
> labour. (Verna)

Verna is not 'interested in politics', rather her focus is intensive work 'on the
ground with children'. She is engaged in, dare we say, a variant of mother
work (Hill Collins 1994), but one, despite her protestations, that ultimately
has a political edge. Verna's text also speaks of community; a community
grounded in her own labour. Community as a concept may be out of favour
within academic circles (cf. Young 1990), but all the women used the term
extensively in their narratives as something they were not simply a part of
but were also actively engaged in constructing through their work as
educators. As Rose stated emphatically, 'An important part of Saturday
school is about creating community. That's part of what we're here for.'

In order to make sense of the enormous chasm between popular and elite
prejudices in relation to urban communities and the actual practices going
on within them, we need to inject a gendered analysis (Burlet and Reid 1998).
So many successful communities across all fields of society are founded on
women's invisible unpaid labour despite the high profile of *male* leaders. In
her exemplary work on 'reading the community' Valerie Hey differentiates
between male strategies of commandeering social resources and female
strategies of constructing social capital in order to develop effective
community links (Hey 1998). The black women educators had minimal
possibilities of commandeering social resources. Rather, they all worked
incredibly hard to generate a sense of community and develop social capital
out of friends' and neighbours' social relationships. As Hey succinctly puts
it, 'There are at least two versions of community – his and hers' (Hey 1998:
2), and these six Saturday schools were all built on 'her version'.

Similarly, Patricia Hill Collins makes a case for appreciating the specific
nature of black female 'community connectedness'. She suggests we should
rearticulate black women's experiences with Afrocentric feminist thought in
order to challenge prevailing definitions of community. She writes:

> The definition of community implicit in the market model sees com-
> munity as arbitrary and fragile, structured fundamentally by competition

and domination. In contrast, Afrocentric models stress connections, caring, and personal accountability. . . . Denied access to the podium, black women have been unable to spend time theorising about alternative conceptualisations of community. Instead through daily actions African American women have created alternative communities that empower.

(Hill Collins 1990: 223)

Patricia Hill Collins shows that through reconceptualising the work of mothers, other mothers, women educators, church and union leaders, community power is not about domination as in the Eurocentric perspective, but about energy which is fostered by creative acts of resistance. Bourdieu has developed the concept of social capital which illuminates this point of gendered community participation. He defines social capital as 'contacts and group memberships which, through the accumulation of exchanges, obligations and shared identities, provide actual or potential support and access to valued resources' (Bourdieu 1993: 143). Social capital is under-pinned by practices of sociability which require specific skills and dispositions. However, we suggest that there are gender implications which Bourdieu ignores but which would point to a connection between social capital and Helga Nowotny's concept of emotional capital.

Nowotny develops the concept of emotional capital which she defines as 'knowledge, contacts and relations as well as the emotionally valued skills and assets, which hold within any social network characterised at least partly by affective ties' (Nowotny 1981: 148). As Virginia Morrow points out, 'this concept should alert us to the invisibility of women's work in creating and sustaining social networks and hence social capital' (Morrow 1999: 765). The black women through their involvement in supplementary schooling were producing resources to compensate for perceived deficits in state educational provision and thereby enhancing the black community's stock of both social and cultural capital.

All six women were extensively involved in the wider black community, as well as the community they saw themselves as actively constructing through black supplementary schooling. They were all facilitating black parents' groups and working with local black arts and business collectives. Two of the women were involved in national black women's networks. The social capital generated through such contacts was fed back into the schools, benefiting the pupils in a variety of ways: through additional funding, sponsorship and curriculum enhancement. For example, in Scarlet Ibis a local black business had paid for computing equipment, while members of the black arts collective had volunteered their services and provided sessions on pottery making, set design and printing.

There are a variety of competing tensions within representations of black supplementary schools as forms of private sector schooling and evidence of black enterprise. They may be depicted as autonomous self-sufficient organisations; part of a vibrant, growing, largely unacknowledged black enterprise culture which spans commerce, the voluntary sector, and arts and education fields. Aligned with such understandings of black supplementary schools are views of them as predominantly community self-help projects. Such representations coalesce around New Right, and increasingly, New Labour emphases on enterprise and local initiatives. Yet at the same time, there are other images which cut across and powerfully contradict such representations, in particular, black supplementary schooling's association with the political Left's project of anti-racism and the rediscovery of marginalised groups' histories.

In addition to extensive links within and beyond the immediate community, the women were firmly rooted in the localities which their supplementary schools served. Both Rose and Verna lived on the large, sprawling council estate that Scarlet Ibis was situated on, while Charity, Nadine and Maxine all lived within walking distance of the schools they helped to run. The women's narratives, with their emphases on material notions of community grounded in a specific geographical locale, render problematic new notions of 'community' in which the developing agenda of communitarianism has detached understandings of community from its grassroots connotations. In this new notion of community the association of community with groups of working-class workers has been prised apart and into the gap has been inserted a 1990s view of communities as diasporic collectivities of individuals who share one or perhaps two or three characteristics in common (Etzioni 1993). It is important not to overlook the work of regulation and governance which such changes achieve:

> One of the ways the discourse of the new works to maintain the symbolic order is through a strategy of transference. Under pressure from overdetermined shifts in the social formation, modes of thinking and desiring which had been thoroughly sanctioned in one ideological formation become inadequate to the reproduction of social subjects in another.
>
> (Hennessy 1993: 104)

As a result, the circulation of new modes of thinking and desiring in the social imaginary must be publicly inhibited and repressed. Community in the sense of any 'true' sense of collectivity has been discursively reworked to fit the competitive individualism of the 1990s.

Through the 'third-way' rhetoric of self-help, choice, and individual and family responsibility, community has been remodelled and appropriated by the intellectual elite and white middle classes (SEU 1998). It is in an ironic reversal of 'community' which obscures the unspoken self-interested individualism that has always accompanied middle-class activities (Jordan *et al.* 1994) and renders any understandings of middle-class community paradoxical. The classic ethnography of a working-class English community described Bethnal Green in the 1950s as:

> a community which has some sense of being one. There is a sense of community that is a feeling of solidarity between people who occupy the common territory which springs from the fact that people and their families have lived there a long time.
>
> (Young and Willmott 1957: 113)

The associations implicit in Young and Willmott's work (of family, kinship, rootedness, localism and collectivity) are no longer apparent in contemporary understandings of community. Community in the Young and Willmott sense is perceived to have disappeared. Yet, paradoxically, it is in 1990s Bethnal Green that we actually do have a community in the Young and Willmott mould. The difference is that this community is no longer only white working class but is also made up of a new urban Bengali working class.

Similar notions of working-class community are to be found in the discourses of both black women educators and of parents whose children attend supplementary schools. The use of community in the discourses of these black women educators operates as a challenge to the consumerist individualism of the late 1990s communitarianism. Ferree has argued that women, working-class people and black groups in society are especially likely to reject competitive individualism as a feasible value, instead emphasizing the construction and maintenance of viable networks of relationships (Ferree 1992: 37).

The sense of community engendered through these black women's activities, embracing as it does an interdependency of the individual and the necessity of the communal, is very different to the sterility of academic injunctions of communitarianism. It is also a gendered form of black activism quietly taken up by women that sharply contrasts with the far more high-profile agitations valorised by black male activism. However, black female activism shares neither the inherent ephemerality usually attributed to the former nor the self-defeating qualities often assumed of the latter. Iris Marion Young warns against the tendency to ascribe essentialist male and female ways of working to notions of community and individualism respectively. She argues that modern political theory and bourgeois culture:

> identifies masculinity with values associated with individualism – self-sufficiency, competition, separation of the formal equality of rights. The culture identifies femininity, on the other hand, with the values associated with community-affective relations of care, mutual aid, and cooperation. Asserting the value of community over individualism, the feminine over the masculine does have some critical force with respect to dominant ideology and social relations. [But] merely revising

their valuation does not constitute a genuine alternative to capitalist patriarchal society.

(Young 1990: 306–307)

Black supplementary schools paradoxically embody elements of both masculine individualism and feminine cooperation. Within a wider social context in which British consciousness, whether black or white, is currently preoccupied with individualism, black supplementary schools are simultaneously places of collectivity at the same time as they focus on individual achievement. hooks discusses the trend in the USA for black people to buy into liberal individualism and cease to see their fate as in any way linked to a collective fate (hooks 1995). Similar discursive shifts are happening in Britain across racial divisions and within all sectors of society. According to Shotter (1993), processes of postmaterialism are breaking down traditionally homogeneous notions of culture and identity allowing individuals to free themselves from the constraints of religion, class and traditional community bonds.

However, the ability to surrender the familiarity of the (national, ethnic, religious) community in favour of the unknown, individualistic autonomy appears to be the preserve of the few. It is these few (for example, web surfers and nomadic academics) who are used to justify postmodern explanations of the obsolescence of traditional means of social organisation. Yet contrary to the fragmenting forces of postmodernity, black supplementary schooling's traditional means of community organising can be seen to be flourishing. It would seem that:

Inspite of postmodernism, little has changed for the majority of black women, globally and nationally. For them power is not diffuse, localised and particular. Power is as centralised and secure as it has always been, excluding, defining and self-legitimating.

(Mirza 1997a: 20)

Conclusion: Grassroots citizenship and the 'third space'

Black women educators in black supplementary schools work for the reinscription and revitalisation of traditional notions of community. The idea of 'community' as practised among the women was less about creating symbolic markers and more about the conscious, pragmatic construction of a 'black home'. While the schools themselves were set up as physically bounded 'spaces of safety', these 'sacred spaces of blackness' were not just symbolic – they were a lived reality in which the women's energy and creativity generated 'social capital' (Bourdieu 1993). Notions of community were thus grounded in the women's own labour. They were not simply a part of the community, they were also actively engaged in constructing it through their work as radical black educators. Hidden from view, in covert, quiet ways, black women work to keep alive the black communities' collective desire for self-knowledge and 'belief in the power of schooling to mitigate racial barriers . . . and make dreams come true' (Fordham 1996: 63).

Feldman *et al.* (1998) argue that the realm of community which women create through their everyday activities becomes the 'third element' that mediates between the public and private spheres and provides the base for a new politics. However, it is argued here that black women's agency and strategic self-determination does not simply mediate between the public and private spheres but instead disrupts the static modernist distinction between the public and the private which dominates feminist theorising on citizenship. As Patricia Hill Collins demonstrates, the racialised context of public and private means the black female experience is different than for white women. Although they enjoy formal legal citizenship, for blacks in America the public has become a place of danger characterised by the containment and surveillance of the 'private' lives of the so-called black 'underclass' through welfare regulation and racist institutionalised market inequalities (Hill Collins 1998: 35).

In this context of public danger black female participatory politics has to be strategic and contingent, using formal institutional structures that are advantageous and finding ways around those that are not. However, black female agency has remained invisible in the emerging masculine discourse on postmodern citizenship. Gilroy suggests that spontaneous black grassroots schools, which as this study shows are mostly female led, are 'defensive organisations with their roots in a radical sense of powerlessness' (1987: 230). Similarly Ellison argues that marginal groups, unable to deal in the public realm with the fragmenting effects of social change, take up positions of defensive engagement resorting to fundamentalist solidarities and recidivist social forms in an attempt to mitigate the effects of exclusion:

> the limitation of effective citizenship to those with the personal or collective resources – material cultural and intellectual – to construct solidarities and imagine new identities and modes of belonging carries the danger that those excluded from the sphere of reflexive engagement could be forced in to a 'non-reflexive' defence of interests.
>
> (Ellison 1997: 715)

What both Gilroy and Ellison fail to understand is the creative contingent engagement of black women who effectively subvert the subjectivisation and individualisation inherent within the processes of postmodern fragmentation. Operating in the interstices of a range of constituting identifications and subject positions, the women decentre fixed notions of citizenship that still prevail by simultaneously employing the contradictory discourse of individual self-achievement and educational self-improvement in an ingenious patch-work quilt of collective community reciprocity.

In this study what the black women appeared to have learnt is an awareness of the need for social support and collaborative action through their experience of marginality in a white racist society. From this awakening of consciousness and socioanalysis (Bourdieu 1990: 116) the women created their own cultural capital. Their habitus embodied 'real intelligence' in their ways of knowing and understanding (Johnson 1988; Luttrell 1992). As their words show, this ultimately led to collective action and social change through self-determination and educational urgency to succeed within the main-stream.

Black women's community action creates, in effect, a 'third space' of radical opposition. In the context of white hegemony this third space constitutes a subaltern counter-public. Nancy Fraser writes about hidden counter-public spheres which have always existed, including women's voluntary associations and working-class organisations. She describes such subaltern counter-hegemonic spaces as:

> parallel discursive arenas where members of subordinated social groups invent and circulate counter discourses, which in turn permit them to formulate oppositional interpretations of their identities, interests and needs.
>
> (Fraser 1994: 84)

It is in the 'third space', a de-essentialised but invisible counter-hegemonic space, where the marginal and the excluded – those situated as such through their gender and radicalised construction – find a voice. That voice, as the black women's narratives show, is subversive and radical. In the third space black women educators' acts of belonging and sustenance of community demonstrate new and inclusive forms of 'real' citizenship that deserve to be recognised.

Chapter 8

(In)visible black women in higher education[1]

> Young black women set off into the white world carrying expectations of mythic proportions . . . their odysseys, they believe will transform their lives . . . but separated from their cultural communities these young women's passages turn out to be isolated individual journeys . . . 'into the heart of whiteness'.
>
> (Casey 1993: 132)

Higher education in Britain remains a 'hideously white'[2] place, rarely open to critical gaze (Back 2004). It is not a place where you expect to find many 'black bodies'. Being a body 'out of place' (Puwar 2001) in white institutions has emotional and psychological costs to the bearer of that difference. Simmonds, a black woman academic, writes, 'The world I inhabit as an academic is a white world . . . in this white world I am a fresh water fish that swims in sea water. I feel the weight of the water on my body' (1997: 227).

In this chapter I wish to explore the personal costs of the position of marginality for black women in higher education. Lifelong learning is about the profound experiences you have when moving between 'worlds' of difference. We need to ask questions about what shapes these worlds and how we are implicated through our inclusion, exclusion, choice and participation in reproducing it, for, as Casey describes in her poignant passage above, black women's innocent expectations and eager quest for knowledge can take them on an unexpected journey 'to another place' where they are transformed, but are also transforming.

There is a paradox concerning black women in higher education. On the one hand they are almost invisible in the higher and senior levels of the academe – a state that has persisted in the 25 years since I have been teaching and researching in higher education. Recent figures suggest there are only 10 black women professors in the UK (THES 2004). Black and minority ethnic staff, 92 per cent of whom are on low-grade, less senior posts, make up 2.5 per cent of those working in higher education, and of these only 1.6 per cent are female (Carter *et al.* 1999). On the other hand black women are present in new universities as students in significant numbers, a phenomenon that I have seen grow over the same time (Connor *et al.* 2004; Modood and Acland 1998).

Although ethnic minorities make up 6 per cent of the working population in the UK, they make up 15 per cent of all students. Young black people of African and Asian origin are nearly three times more likely to be in university than their white counterparts. If we look at the percentages of young people under age 21 on full-time undergraduate courses, black and minority ethnic women are the highest participants of all. As a proportion of the average 18 to 19-year-old population we find 59 per cent of young black women going to university to study for a degree, as are 48 per cent of young black men.[3] I am intrigued by this invisibility/visibility split between staff and students, and the significance it has in terms of understanding the experience of black women in higher education.

The duality of invisibility/visibility characterises black women's appearance and disappearance more generally in our telling of our social (his)story.[4] However, I am not concerned with a simple disappearance and appearance of the physical – 'now you see black women, now you don't'; I am concerned more with the shifting constructions of their messy, complicated 'otherness' in our changing troubled higher educational institutions.

Outsiders within

I first began to think about the invisibility/visibility couplet when I was asked to give a keynote address at the centenary celebration of women's first admission to Trinity College Dublin in 1904.[5] Trinity College was a grand place, and as I walked through the cobbled courtyards, dined in the Commons and gazed at the grand, vaulted Old Library I saw that young women now moved with seeming ease and authority in these ancient and 'hallowed' spaces. I wondered what it was like 100 years ago to be Alice Oldham, the first female in an all-male college. Women were seen as being a 'danger to the men', and as the College Board cautioned, they had to be watched: 'If a female had once passed the gate it would be practically impossible to watch what buildings or chambers she might enter, or how long she might remain there' (Parkes 2004: 2).

But what must it have been like for the first woman of colour in an elite white male university in Britain? Preparing for my paper at Dublin I did some research and to my surprise I found a hidden genealogy of black women's presence in higher education in England that began before the admission of white women in Ireland.

Cornelia Sorabji, who was Indian, went to Somerville Hall Oxford in 1889. She was the first woman ever to study law in a British university (Burton 1998; Visram 2002).[6] Continuing my search I stumbled upon a small, crumpled photograph tucked away in the corner of a dark display cabinet on the suffragettes at the back of the 'World City Gallery' at the Museum of

London. The photograph was of the Indian suffragettes at the 1911 Women's Coronation Procession. The procession was a huge rally organised by the suffragettes to highlight their struggle during the coronation celebrations of George V. There were 60,000 women, 1000 banners and the column of marchers snaked for seven miles. Under a banner with their emblem of an elephant were assembled several Indian women suffragettes (Visram 2002). I learnt that one of the most active Indian suffragettes was Sophia Duleep Singh, whose sisters Bamba and Catherine (daughters of the Maharaja of the Punjab) also went to Somerville College in 1890.

I never knew Indian suffragettes existed. Indian women remain largely outside the historiography of British Suffragettes (Visram 2002). Excavating such an erasure of black women's genealogy in British academia exposes a 'counter-memory' which tells a different 'truth'. Similarly, our collective amnesia about black women's presence in higher education exemplifies the continuous battle for the reappropriation of cultural difference in the constantly shifting and changing hegemonic war against racism. Spivak calls such conscious negation of black women from discourse a form of 'epistemic violence' (Spivak 1988). I had always thought the struggle for a space in higher education was a 'white woman's history' – as indeed I thought that the suffragette movement was a white woman's movement. But I have been

Figure 8.1 Indian Suffragettes on the Women's Coronation procession, London, 17 June 1911

Source: Reproduced by kind permission of the Museum of London Picture Library.

learning[7] that history is about what gets chosen to be revealed by whom and when. Mohanty writes against a hastily derived notion of 'universal sisterhood' that assumes a commonality of gender experience across race and national lines; she writes:

> I have tried to demonstrate that this (feminist) scholarship inadvertently produces Western women as the only legitimate subjects of struggle, while Third world women are heard as fragmented, inarticulate voices in (and from) the dark.
>
> (Mohanty 1993: 42)

Embodying difference

I was however excited by the excavation of Indian women as activists, scholars and writers. Women like me, in demonstrations back then, in a time when we were not even supposed to have an existence (Spivak 1988)! However, for me the question in this instance of revelation is as Mohanty suggests not just acknowledging their 'difference', but rather the more difficult question of the *kind of difference that is acknowledged* and engaged (Mohanty 1993). But the kind of difference I found should not have surprised me. The Indian women at the procession were described by a governor of an Indian province in terms of their 'oriental' appearance as:

> Particularly striking and picturesque . . . in beautiful dress . . . the most significant feature of the whole procession, as they demonstrated the 'women's' question was without race, or creed, or boundary.
>
> (Visram 2002: 164)

In contrast to the staunch, serious, defeminised white middle-class suffragettes these 'strange and exotic creatures' were described as non-threatening in their ability to bring about change through their harmonious multicultural 'otherness'. A spectacle to be gazed upon, it was as if these Indian women were 'known better than they know themselves' (Mirza 1997a: 20). Simmonds discusses how racial knowledge is constructed about the other and the experience of being a 'curiosity'. She writes,

> Adorned and unadorned I cannot escape the fantasies of the western imagination . . . this desire for colonized bodies as spectacle . . . is essentially an extension of the 'desiring machine' of capital.
>
> (Simmonds 1997: 232)

Similarly, Cornelia Sorabji who was by no means a feminist or a radical (she was pro-British rule and against Gandhi's independence movement for India) talks of her special treatment at Somerville. She was introduced into

Figure 8.2 Cornelia Sorabji at Somerville Hall Oxford, 1891 (top left); princesses Catherine and Bamba Duleep Singh (bottom left and centre)

Source: Reproduced by kind permission of the Principals and Fellows of Somerville College, Oxford.

influential literary and political circles and always wore a sari. She was given special privileges (a fire to dress before in the mornings) and was chaperoned to lectures. Although she was never later allowed to practise as a solicitor in Britain she demanded and got special dispensation to sit her law exams as a woman in college. She writes that the men students were so kind, giving up a book if the librarian said she wanted it. This special treatment exasperated her and she said of her tutor, 'I wish he would treat me like a man and not make gallant speeches about my intellect and quickness of perception' (Visram 2002: 95). For black women it is impossible to escape the body and its reconstructions as we daily negotiate our embodied social situations. Cornelia returned to India and championed the property rights of the Purdahnashin (veiled women confined to the private domain by religious practice), but lived her final years in England in an asylum where she died in 1954 (Vadgama 2004). Such sad revelation makes me wonder about the 'weight' of living a non-white existence in a consuming white world.

Being a curiosity, a special case, 'one in a million', can be an emotional and professional burden to black women in the academy. To be an exotic token, an institutional symbol, a mentor and confidant, and a 'natural expert of all things to do with 'race', is something that many black women academics recount in their careers in academe (Essed 2000; hooks 1994; Mirza 1995; Razack 1998; Simmonds 1997; Spivak 1993; Williams 1991). However, we need to be careful in how we situate these 'tales of women with dark skin', for as Bhattacharyya eloquently argues such heroic 'new' stories in themselves do not counter invisibility and negative stereotypes deeply embedded in our thinking (Bhattacharyya 1998).

By telling the stories of Sophia and Cornelia I am not advocating the 'black women were there too' as some sort of a triumph, that numbers and presence are all. This would be to invoke a benign multiculturalism which suggests that diversity in and of itself – that is, the mere presence of black women – signals the attainment of equality. I tell the stories of these lost and invisible pioneers because as Mohanty explains,

> The challenge of race resides in a fundamental reconceptualization of our categories of analysis so that differences can be historically specified and understood as part of larger political processes and systems . . . difference seen as benign variation (diversity), for instance rather than as conflict, struggle or threat of disruption, bypasses power as well as history to suggest a harmonious, empty pluralism.
>
> (Mohanty 1993: 42)

For black women existence is not just about physical space, it is also about the power to occupy a historical space.

Is diversity desirable?

The visibility/invisibility distinction that characterises black women's presence in higher education must be contextualised within the pervasive, all-consuming discourse of 'diversity in higher education' (Law et al. 2004). The question here is: 'What has diversity done to open up (or close down) possibilities for black women as students and teachers in higher education?' In the context of policies on widening participation in higher education, and the media exposition of the continued lack of equity in access, particularly for working-class black and white young people, 'diversity' has become an all-consuming discourse that no right-minded university, old or new,[8] would dare be without as an intrinsic part of its identity and image. However, as the Higher Education Funding Council for England (HEFCE) declares in its policy statement, *diversity* is less about equity and more about diversity of HE provision so as to secure the 'best fit' to meet the diverse needs of students, the economy and society:

> Diversity is widely agreed to be a desirable feature in higher education . . . the goal must be to secure the pattern of diversity that most cost-effectively meets the needs and aspirations of the greatest number of stakeholders.
>
> (HEFCE 2000: 3–4)

Diversity as a discourse of social inclusion is based on the philosophy of 'getting the right people for the job on merit' and the 'business benefits of a more diverse workforce to reach a wider market' (Cabinet Office 2001: 18). Government strategy overtly claims that diversity is about good public relations, and 'inclusivity' as good for business. The Ministerial Foreword to the official guidance for the higher education sector embraces the business principle, stating:

> It is vital for the continuing health of the higher education sector that it should recruit from a wide and diverse human resource pool. This is not only on the grounds of equity, but equally sound for business reasons.
>
> (ECU and JNCHES 2003: 2)

The driver for change comes from a pragmatic recognition of demographic changes with a projected ageing population and reduced fertility in Britain. This has led to a concern about underused labour and need for black and 'ethnic minority' groups to be included in an expanding service sector in a global economy (Metcalf and Forth 2000). The employment of these groups it is argued will bring added benefits since they will increase access to certain customer groups. Public changes on ethical and social responsibility have persuaded companies that a 'rights'-based approach may also be good for business (Fredman 2002).

Unmasking diversity and difference

The discourse on 'diversity and difference' which emerged in the 1980s evolved in response to the recognition that equality is not simply about sameness, but about inclusive difference. Calls for the recognition of the difference which age, gender, sexuality, disability, ethnicity, culture and religion make signalled an important and liberating time for many silenced minorities. The black feminist critique was a destabilising force for the modernist epistemological standpoint of white feminism which had failed to embrace the diversity of women's experiences across class and race lines (Collins 1991; Mirza 1997a). The assumption, as Chandra Talpade Mohanty explains, is that:

> feminist studies discursively present Third world women as a homo-genous, undifferentiated group leading truncated lives, victimized by the combined weight of 'their' traditions, cultures and beliefs, and 'our' (Eurocentric) history.
>
> (Mohanty 1993: 42)

However, while postmodern notions of 'difference and diversity' were important for hearing marginalised voices it also led to fragmentation which not only dissolved the notion of a universal subject, but in so doing undermined the basis for collective political projects along the old modernist lines such as in the Civil Rights and Feminist movements of the 1960s.

Kenan Malik has delivered a sharp critique of the shift from equality to diversity. Diversity, he suggests, evolved from the identity politics of the 1980s where the politics of recognition gave voice to hitherto silenced minorities such as those who were black, gay or female. He writes: 'where once I wanted to be treated the same as everybody else despite my skin colour now activists want to be treated differently because of it' (Malik 2003). Malik has a point. This new-found focus on 'difference' is not innocent – it obscures the nature of racism, as Stuart Hall explains:

> The Black subject and Black experience are constructed historically, culturally; politically . . . the grounding of ethnicity in difference is deployed, in the discourse on racism, as a means of disavowing the realities of racism and repression.
>
> (Hall 1992: 257)

Why does diversity get 'stuck'?

In higher education many diversity action plans and equality statements have been produced by universities to meet the requirements of positively promoting racial equality required by the Race Relations (Amendment) Act (2000). Armies of consultants and professionals have been recruited to produce complex bureaucratic, target-led, glossy action plans and strategies which are underpinned by the notion of 'respecting diversity in order to achieve equality' (Bhavnani *et al.* 2005). However, despite these action plans endemic racialised class and gender divisions show little sign of abating (Blanden *et al.* 2005; Connor *et al.* 2004; Reay *et al.* 2005). The question then becomes: Why is there such little real diversity on the ground when we talk so much about achieving the goal of diversity as a moral and social good at the top? How can so much 'diversity talk' engender so much 'diversity paralysis?'

Sara Ahmed (2005) argues that diversity does not simply bring about institutional change. The question we must ask is: 'What work does "diversity" do in education?' Ahmed suggests that institutional 'speech acts', such as a university making a commitment to diversity, or admission that they are non-racist and 'for equality', are 'non-perfomatives' (that is, such speech acts 'work precisely by *not* bringing about the effects they name'). Thus she explains that having a good race equality policy gets translated into *being good at race equality* – 'as if saying is doing'.

> Declaring a commitment to opposing racism might function as a form of organization pride . . . the university now says: if we are committed to antiracism (and we have said we are), then how can we be racists? . . . The work of such speech acts seems precisely how they function to block rather than enable action.
>
> (Ahmed 2005: 8)

Thus, as Ahmed argues, newer universities which are seen as 'diversity-led' (as they have many students from ethnic minorities and lower socio-economic backgrounds) present themselves as 'being diverse' without having to do anything. Simply 'being diverse' means such new universities need not commit to 'doing diversity'. On the other hand the 'ideal' research-led 'sandstone' universities are elite precisely because they have an image that is not diversity-led. They use the language of globalisation and internationalism where diversity for them means appealing to a wide variety of diverse people across cultures. Ahmed explains that diversity here is not associated with challenging disadvantage, but becomes another way of 'doing advantage'.

To explain why diversity remains 'undone' in higher education, Ahmed explains that while the term 'diversity' may 'circulate', its documents and statements get 'stuck', 'cut off from histories of struggle which expose inequalities' (Ahmed 2005: 19).

Counting the costs of 'just being' in higher education

But what happens to those who come to represent 'diversity' in higher education – the black and minority ethnic groups targeted to increase the institutions' thirst for global markets? Higher education research shows black and female staff are likely to be concentrated in lower status universities, be on lower pay and more likely to be in short-term contracts (Carter *et al.* 1999; NAO 2002). Similarly, students are to be found in lower status new universities and concentrated in particular subject areas. In particular, those of African origin are more likely to be performing on the 'lower tail-end' of attainment (Connor *et al.* 2004; Modood and Acland 1998). However, despite these endemic inequalities black women persist in their desire for education as social transformation (Mirza 2005). Levels of participation in further and higher education are as high for women of black African, Caribbean and Indian origin as among white women, both 23 per cent (WEU 2002).[9] The question here is: 'Why does this persistence prevail in such hostile places' and 'What is the cost of just being there?'

Black women and the politics of containment

Black women are increasingly visible in public spaces as professionals in previously race/gendered homogeneous places such as universities, the judiciary and the media. The black feminist writer Patricia Hill Collins suggests that this shift in the positioning of race and gender and class through changing power relations and privatisation has led to reconfigured patterns of institutionalised racism. In what Collins calls the 'new politics of containment' surveillance strategies become increasingly important when middle-class black women enter institutional spaces of whiteness in the increasingly devalued public sphere from which they were hitherto barred. She explains:

> Whereas racial segregation was designed to keep blacks as a group or class outside centers of power, surveillance now aims to control black individuals inside centers of power when they enter the white spaces of the public and private spheres.
>
> (Collins 1998: 20)

Collins argues that black women are watched in desegregated work environments to ensure they remain 'unraced' and assimilated (Collins 1998: 39). Being seen to be assimilated is important, as standing out can invoke deep feelings of need, rejection and anxiety within the 'white other' (Ahmed 2004). To be unassimilated or to 'stand out' invites a certain type of surveillance that appears benign but can be deeply distressing for black women.

For example, surveillance means being accountable and having more attention than others heaped upon you. A black female professor related when she was first appointed with fanfare and excitement. She was a 'special case'; one in 'a million'; a black female trophy. She was in the university news (front page and the Web) and she was invited to many high-profile functions and events. Although it was not her job, in the first week she had to publicly present a detailed plan for delivering equal opportunities and race equality for the next five years to the senior managers and executives of the university. By three months she had been required to write five reports on her targets, attainments and strategies, and also found herself accountable to three different line managers (as it could not be decided to whom she should report: the executive, academic area, or the faculty). Their 'kind and supportive' attention was all-consuming but she received no real support for her academic research and teaching. Finally she became ill. No other professor had received this exhausting and intense level of scrutiny or expectation over such a short space of time.

There is an irony to heightened visibility for the 'invisible' in our polite and gentile corridors of higher education. A national survey of ethnic minorities in higher education found that black women were more likely than any other group to report being the victim of sexual harassment and discrimination at work (Carter et al. 1999). This raises many questions about the safety of black women in public spaces. The example of Anita Hill, the African American woman who brought a high-profile case against the African American Supreme Court Justice Clarence Thomas, demonstrates how sexual harassment can be racialised within an institutional context. Anita Hill lost her case, and it is argued that this happened because of the way the 'black woman' is constructed and given meaning in the public discourse on 'race' (Collins 1998; Morrison 1993b). Anita Hill did not fit any of the stereotypes of 'the black woman' (i.e. she was not an 'overachiever' or a 'welfare mother'); thus she could not be easily understood and received no sympathy in the public mind. She was not seen as a credible defendant and was labelled as a 'traitor-to-the-race' because of her public denouncement of a senior black male colleague. As Collins points out, the 'black woman' is predetermined by an already written script:

> surveillance seems designed to produce particular effects – black women remain visible yet silenced; their bodies become written by other texts, yet they remain powerless to speak for themselves.
>
> (Collins 1998: 38)

Black women's journeys into higher education, as Kathleen Casey writes in the opening quote of this chapter, are journeys into the 'heart of whiteness' where a homogeneous identity of 'the black woman' is created by 'a white gaze which perceives her as a mute visible object' (Casey 1993: 111). Being a 'mute visible object' is something that consumes one's very being and, as bell hooks argues, black women need healing strategies and healing words to enable them to deal with the anguish that sexism and sexist oppression creates in daily life. She suggests that black women need to theorise from a 'place of pain . . . which enables us to remember and recover ourselves' (hooks 1994: 74). She explains that such a location is experienced and shared by those who are 'aware' of the personal and collective struggle that all forms of domination, such as homophobia, class exploitation, racism, sexism and imperialism, engender. She suggests courageously exposing the 'wounds' of struggle which will teach and guide us on new theoretical journeys which challenge and renew inclusive feminist struggle.

Such a 'place of pain' manifests itself in many ways. Recently I attended an equal opportunities workshop where we were asked to identify experiences of institutional racism. A young Iranian woman, a graduate student, recounted how her husband, a qualified medical doctor, was experiencing racial discrimination when trying to get a placement in the National Health Service. A white male member of the group, an established academic, piped up and said, 'Don't worry love . . . it wouldn't happen to you as you are so attractive.' In that one moment all the black women in the group were reduced to no more than their embodied 'otherness' – mute, visible objects. His unthinking comment was made possible by the unspoken power of his authoritative gaze.

Patricia Williams, an eminent African American professor, talks of the collective trauma such everyday incursions into one's self-hood engenders:

> There are moments in my life when I feel as though part of me is missing. There are days when I feel so invisible that I can't remember the day of the week it is, when I feel so manipulated that I can't remember my own name, when I feel so lost and angry that I can't speak a civil word to the

people who love me best. These are times I catch sight of my reflection in store windows and I am surprised to see the whole person looking back . . . I have to close my eyes at such times and remember myself, draw an internal pattern that is smooth and whole.

(Williams 1991 quoted in hooks 1994: 74)

Excluding practices

There are costs to 'just being there' in higher education. Many black and minority students are more likely to leave university before completing the course. As Connor *et al.* (2004) argue, the most influential reasons are unmet expectations about higher education. While financial and family difficulties, institutional factors, such as poor teaching and wrong subject choice also feature, ethnic minority people also reported 'the feeling of isolation or hostility in academic culture' (Connor *et al.* 2004: 60). These are worrying findings, since they signal the fact that many black students do not feel they 'belong'. The findings of Diane Reay, Miriam David and Stephan Ball (2004) have shed some light on the process of exclusion 'felt' by young working-class and ethnic minority people seeking to enter higher education. Reay *et al.* suggest young people can engage in a process of self-exclusion when making university choices. Drawing on Bourdieu, they write that processes of exclusion work through having 'a sense of one's place which leads one to exclude oneself from places from which one is excluded' (Reay *et al.* 2005: 91). As one working-class student in their study says about going to an elite university, 'what's a person like me doing in a place like that?'

> Choosing to go to university . . . for the working classes is about being different people in different places, about who they might be but also what they must give up.
>
> (Reay *et al.* 2005: 161)

Processes of exclusion in higher education are difficult to unpack as they are underscored by the complex dynamics of class, gender and race. Experiences are complex and relational, and are located at the intersection of structure, culture and agency (Brah 1996). For some students university can be a positive experience. As Shirin Housee demonstrates, South Asian young women can find a space at university to express assertive, independent personas which enable them to freely express their religious identity. In opposition to the stereotype of Asian women as victims and recipients of patriarchal culture they were 'fighting back . . . and were not going to accept racism, sexism or any other -ism' (Housee 2004: 69).

However, while spaces of opposition can and do open up, Back (2004) suggests that there are two antagonistic forces at play in higher education: one moves unconsciously and haphazardly towards what Hall has called 'multicultural drift' (Hall 2000), and the other remains the 'sheer weight of whiteness' (Back 2004: 1). With regard to the latter, in some institutions the 'sheer weight of whiteness' is overt and almost impenetrable. Research looking at the University of Cambridge shows how elite culture is self-reinforcing. It was seen by others as a white, male, 'tough and macho' culture that was 'secretive, intimidating and insular'. It was assumed by those at Cambridge that those in privileged positions were there because of their ability and merit. However, over 70 per cent of readers and professors had a degree from Cambridge and one-third of academics had no experience of any other university, the majority being there for over 20 years (Schneider-Ross 2001).

Puwar (2004) draws on the social theorists Bourdieu and Foucault to explain how cultures of exclusion operate within contested social spaces such as universities:

> Social spaces are not blank and open for any body to occupy. Over time, through processes of historical sedimentation, certain types of bodies are designated as being the 'natural' occupants of specific spaces. . . . Some bodies have the right to belong in certain locations, while others are marked out as trespassers who are in accordance with how both spaces and bodies are imagined, politically, historically and conceptually circumscribed as being 'out of place'.
>
> (Puwar 2004: 51)

Puwar suggests that black bodies out of place are 'space invaders'. She argues that there are several ways in which black bodies are constructed when they do not represent the 'racial somatic norm' within white institutions (Puwar 2001, 2004). First, there is 'disorientation', a double-take as you enter a room, since you are not supposed to be there. You are noticed and it is uncomfortable. Like walking into a pub in a town where you don't live. There is confusion, as you are the not the 'natural expected occupant of that position'. I know this well; in many meetings, even though I am a professor, I have been mistaken for the coffee lady! Even students do a double-take when they see you are the social theory lecturer.

Second, there is 'infantalisation': here you are not only pigeon-holed into being 'just a race expert', but black lecturers are seen as less capable of being in authority. This can mean that black staff are assumed to be more junior than they are (I have been told to get off the photocopier as it is not for administrators). There is constant doubt about your skills, which can affect career progression. Third, there is the 'burden of invisibility', or hyper-surveillance. Here you are viewed suspiciously and any mistakes are picked up and seen as a sign of misplaced authority. You have to work harder for recognition outside of the confines of stereotypical expectations, and may suffer disciplinary measures and disappointment if you do not meet expectations in your work performance.

Sometimes I am shocked by the deeply racist comments I hear in everyday life in the higher echelons of our 'civilised' universities. Recently I was on a search committee for the appointment of a chair in a prestigious university. I was sent an email by a senior white male academic about the applications. He stated that there had been several who were described in terms of their research (they were not racialised), and one application from a 'not very credible Indian'. Why was 'the Indian' racialised and none of the others? What difference did it make that he was Indian? What was I being 'told' in this coded message? Was it that 'all Indians want to come to England and will try anything'? Or that other trope that 'Indian qualifications are not very good, and anyway an Indian can never be as good as a white (British) academic'. Why did the white *male* academic who sent the email not think about what he was saying to me – a woman of Indo-Caribbean heritage? Was it because even though I am one of them (an Indian) I am now 'one of us' (i.e. an honorary 'white' who can speak their language)? Why did he say it at all? Perhaps because he could.

Franz Fanon's timeless prose can help us understand the personal costs of the racialised phenomena of 'a not very credible Indian':

> We have a Senegalese teacher. He is quite bright. . . . Our doctor is coloured. He is very gentle. It was always the Negro teacher, the Negro doctor . . . I knew, for instance that if the physician made a mistake it would be the end of him and all those who came after him. What could one expect after all, from a Negro physician? As long as everything went well he was praised to the skies. But look out, no nonsense under any conditions . . . I tell you I was walled in; no exception was made for my fine manners, or my knowledge of literature, or my understanding of quantum theory.
>
> (Fanon 1986: 117)

Relocating the self

From the diaries of Cornelia Sorabji (Burton 1998; Visram 2002) and the eloquent lectures of Patricia Williams (Williams 1997) we can begin to open up and understand the complex multidimensional world black women inhabit on the margins of white institutions. Moreover, we need to understand black women's agency and subjectivity in relation to their space on the margins. Marginality, as bell hooks argues, can be a radical location in which black women can situate themselves in relation to the dominant group through 'other ways of knowing'. hooks recounts her own story of leaving home and going to university and becoming a successful academic:

> When I left that concrete space on the margins, I kept alive in my heart ways of knowing reality . . . . (I was) sustained by remembrance of the

past, which includes recollections of broken tongues that decolonise our minds, our very beings.

(hooks 1992: 150)

She argues that we should reclaim the word 'margin' from its traditional use as a marker of exclusion and see it as an act of positive appropriation for black women:

> Marginality is a central location for the production of a counter hegemonic discourse – it is found in the words, habits and the way one lives. . . . It is a site one clings to even when moving to the centre . . . it nourishes our capacity to resist. . . . It is an inclusive space where we recover ourselves, where we move in solidarity to erase the category coloniser/colonised.
>
> (hooks 1992: 149–150)

Black women appear to occupy parallel discursive spheres in what Diane Reay and I have called a 'third space' (Mirza and Reay 2000a). Nancy Fraser calls this third space 'hidden counter public' spheres which are arenas where 'members of subordinated social groups invent and circulate counter discourses, which in turn permit them to formulate oppositional interpretations of their identities, interests and needs' (Fraser 1994: 84).

In our research on African Caribbean women educators working in black community schools (sometimes called supplementary or Saturday schools), Diane Reay and I found black women working alongside the dominant educational discourse. In their space on the margins, with their quiet and subversive acts of care and 'other ways of knowing', these women:

> operate within, between, under and alongside the mainstream educational and labour market structures, subverting, renaming and reclaiming opportunities for their children through the transformative pedagogy of 'raising the race' – a radical pedagogy, that ironically appears conservative on the surface with its focus on inclusion and dialogue with the mainstream.
>
> (Mirza 1997c: 274)

Black women appear to seek social transformation through educational change. The African Caribbean women teachers in black supplementary schools (as indeed do those working and studying in universities and schools) struggle for educational inclusion in order to transform opportunities for themselves and for their children. In covert and quiet ways (unlike street riots which signal masculine social change) these women work to keep alive the black communities' collective desire for self-knowledge and a belief in the power of schooling to militate against racial barriers (Fordham 1996: 63).

As Casey writes education acquires a different meaning in the context of racist oppression:

> In a racist society . . . to become educated is to contradict the whole system of racist signification . . . to succeed in studying white knowledge is to undo the system itself . . . to refute its reproduction of black inferiority materially and symbolically.
>
> (Casey 1993: 123)

For African Caribbean women educational institutions were not just mechanisms through which individuals are unconsciously subjected to the dominant ideological system but rather, as Freire argues, education is the terrain on which they acquire consciousness of their position and struggle (Freire 2004). Just as the black women educators had developed through their experience a strategic rationalisation of their situation and opportunities, so too have black women in higher education developed a sense of their space on the margins through self-actualisation and self-definition.

Conclusion

> The black woman's critique of history has not only involved us coming to terms with absences: we have also been outraged by the ways in which it has made us visible, when it has chosen to see us . . . we cannot hope to constitute ourselves in all our ill conceived presences that invade herstory from history, but we do wish to bear witness to our own herstories.
>
> (Carby 1997: 45)

Black women have been virtually invisible from higher education as professional lecturers, researchers and teachers. In tiny numbers they are often the only member of staff in a department, and often in part-time work and in lower, less stable contracts (Carter *et al.* 1999). On the other hand they are visible in large numbers in certain new universities as students. For example, at Middlesex university where I teach, black women can make up as much as 65 per cent of the students on health and social science courses. But by flagging up this paradox of invisibility/visibility it is not just the numbers I am concerned with here. It is the construction of the invisibility/ visibility split in terms of black women's embodied experience as black bodies 'out of place' in higher education.

Diversity documents in our higher education institutions highlight gender, race (or sometimes socioeconomic class) numbers to show how successful (or not) they are at achieving equality. Black women are highly visible when our bodies help higher education institutions achieve their wider moral and ethical goals, and to appeal to a wider global market. But this is not a true representation or equality. In our universities 'diversity' is 'skin-deep'. Black people are celebrated in colourful brochures with smiling 'brown' faces – like a box of chocolates there is one from every continent and one of every colour: Chinese, African, Indian. Objectified and commercialised, no one asks 'How do they feel about that?' They find themselves appropriated, their bodies comodified, 'for the desiring machine of capital' (Young 1995 in Simmonds 1997: 232).

However, black women slip into invisibility in the site that matters the most: how they are valued and embraced in everyday practice and the transforming difference they bring to their institutions. Such absences are not simply a silence, a forgotten oversight, but an erasure of their very being. With the new-found 'fetish for difference' that diversity brings, black women have become 'hot' property in the academy in terms of research projects and teaching, once they stay in their place as 'natives in the academy' (Puwar 2004). In universities black women struggle daily against the

> presumption that scholars of colour are narrowly focused or lacking in intellectual depth . . . whatever our history what ever our record, whatever our validations, whatever our accomplishments, by and large we are perceived as one-dimensional and treated accordingly . . . fit for addressing the marginal subjects of race, but not subjects in the core curriculum.
>
> (Madrid in Lopez 1993: 127)

Paulo Friere, the visionary Brazilian educationalist, argued that education is the struggle over meaning as well as power relations (Friere 2004). For black women universities are not simply a place to achieve qualifications and pass exams in an increasingly instrumentalist market-driven educational culture (Giroux and Giroux 2004). As Mohanty argues, for black women,

> Educational sites represent accommodations and contestations over knowledge by differently empowered social constituencies . . . thus education is a central terrain where power and politics operate out of the lived culture of individuals and groups situated in asymmetrical social and political positions.
>
> (Mohanty 1993: 43–44)

Manuel Castells (2004) argues that universities are global elite information networks that are important to sustain because, with encroaching neoliberal market forces, the university is the last remaining space of freedom. However, as we have seen, here within these precious places of freedom, academic institutions still create paradigms and knowledges that transcribe race and gender power relations. If we are to transform our academic institutions into truly democratic inclusive spaces we need to be ever vigilant of excluding practices as we journey through higher education.

Part 4

Reflections on race
and gender

Chapter 9

Race, gender and educational desire[1]

The text for this chapter is taken from a spoken lecture.[2] As such it is a personal retrospective that seeks to move our understanding of educational inequality forward by examining what appears to be disparate, but intimately linked issues and discourses. Through the lens of gendered autobiography this chapter brings together the dynamics of racist educational policy and practice in Britain in the context of the shadow of colonial history and migration. Finally it reflects on subsequent black strategies of transcendence and overcoming and their struggle for equality through education. It is written in a reflexive and rhetorical style addressing the reader directly, which is characteristic of traditional storytelling.

This chapter centres around three consuming issues which I address in my academic work: the intersection of 'race', gender and the relationship this has with educational aspirations, what I call 'educational desire'. Reflecting on my scholarship over the past 25 years I realise it has been underpinned by a need to ask a fundamental question, 'Why is it that those who are the most committed to education often struggle the most to succeed?' To answer this question, I bring together seven stories of educational desire.

Telling stories is traditional in many cultures. The African Griot or storyteller uses the oral tradition to pass on tales from generation to generation. In India the Hindu Ramayana, with its miracle plays and parables, tells epic stories of the battle between the Gods for good and evil. In the academic world we use critical race theory which is based on situational and reflexive knowledge to illuminate hidden or marginal social realities. Stories are a powerful way to talk.

Story 1: 'The Quilt'

Recently I went to India, a pilgrimage of sorts, to find my health and my roots. I visited Tamil Nadu at the southernmost tip of India. This is the place of my ancestors. One hundred and sixty years ago they were brought by the British as indentured labourers to work on the sugar plantations in Trinidad. This was the 'new slavery'. Hidden in the history of Empire, the trail took impoverished Indians on the so-called 'curry trail' to Malaysia, Mauritius, Fiji, Kenya, South Africa and Central America (*Caribbean Quarterly* 1986: Ramdin 1999).

In Tamil Nadu I met women who wove and stitched. In the shameful face of vast capitalist profits of high street shops this woman made cloth for less than a dollar a day. She was so proud of her craft and showed me her loom where she sat for 12 hours a day (Figure 9.1). She asked for a pen for her children's schooling. She touched my soul. Why is education so important?

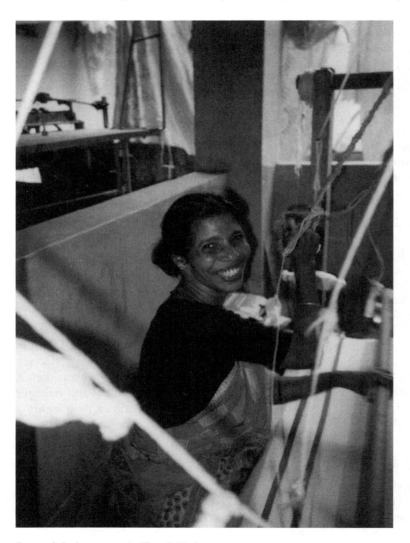

Figure 9.1 A weaver in Tamil Nadu

A way up, a way out, a way to transform one's life? What is the relationship between the marginal and dispossessed and the desire for education as transformation? I needed to know. I needed to find the answer.

On that trip I bought a beautiful quilt, a tapestry made of fragments of bridal dresses worn by the women who made it (Figure 9.2). Who are they and what is their story? Quilting is the art of stitching together pieces of cloth, fragments of memory, linking the past to the present and making it whole (Flannery 2001). This has a powerful meaning for women across cultures and time. The women are marginal on the peripheries of their societies, yet in slow, painstaking, silent rhythm they take scraps of cloth making patterns for us to see. With care, warmth and love they rework the quilt over and over again, remaking their story. The batting and back layers are unseen, but without them the patches have no foundation. When we stand back and look at their finished quilt the whole experience becomes coherent.

Black British Feminism (Mirza 1997), the framework that has inspired me, is like the quilt. It is about situated knowledges, building a framework for understanding whose stories we hear or choose to hear in the construction of our reality. The hidden voice of the women or the dominant paradigm of the powerful? We hear of policies, plans and Acts of Parliament but what can we see if we look at things differently? In so doing how can we build a

Figure 9.2 Indian bridal tapestry quilt – Tamil Nadu

new science of critical understanding that centres gender and 'race' as a critical space? *Black British Feminism* asks critical questions about processes, relationships and power from the standpoint of women who are rarely seen and heard. We map hidden patterns in subjugated and suppressed knowledge, and illuminate 'other ways of knowing'.

In this chapter, I want to unpick the stitches and look beneath the patches, to see the backing and hear the voices which tell stories of educational desire among tails of educational despair in the women's struggle for themselves and for their children.

Story 2: 'The Caribbean Awakening'

I never met my Trinidadian grandmother (Figure 9.3). I was born in Britain and by the time I went as a child to Trinidad aged 4 she had already passed away. I only heard folktales of her indomitable spirit, excellent cooking and powerful singing voice. Everyone loved her. She was mother earth. I thought this is a good place to start excavating my feminist roots for this chapter. In Trinidad last Christmas I visited a contemporary of my grandmother, Mrs Nobbee, now aged 92. She told me my grandmother had been the force behind the founding of one the most prestigious girls' schools on the north of the Island, St Augustine Girls. I went to the sister school in the south of the Island, Naparima Girls. This picture is how I remember it (Figure 9.4). These were Presbyterian schools initiated by the Canadian missionaries who began their work, educating, training and converting when the first indentured Hindus and Muslims arrived in the Caribbean in the 1860s.

Yet it was my grandfather, one of the first local men to become a Christian minister on the island, who is remembered as a social reformer in our history. Not my grandmother, not his wife Theresa, one of the first 'bible women' who travelled the island to teach the catechism to daughters of impoverished labourers like herself. I was both indignant and excited by this revelation. My grandmother must have been a feminist like me! A kindred spirit!

But the things Mrs Nobbee told me did not fit my neat paradigm. She told a proud and different story of women's campaigning, not a story of radical women fighting for radical change but a story about women working within the system. Conservative, traditional, tropical 'genteel' women, schooled in Victorian colonial manners. They were trained to be good, accomplished wives and mothers who cooked, sewed and sang hymns while doing algebra and Latin. They worked with the men to do the negotiating, and never asked for, or got, recognition. Women like my grandmother were transformative agents and educators. They worked not against the grain but within and alongside the mainstream in order to challenge and change from within the structures and institutions in which they found themselves. As women they are too often forgotten souls in the history of time.

Figure 9.3 The author's grandmother Theresa Hosein *c.* 1940

This theme of radicalism and conservativism is one that courses through Caribbean and Asian educational experiences in the UK. It is the tension that determines the juxtaposition of the patches in the quilt, where we put them, how we construct social reality on our educational journey. Notions of resistance are nearly always masculine. Our ideas of social change are often

Figure 9.4 Naparima Girls' High School, Trinidad, c. 1960

about confrontation and clamour, gladiators and heroes, the men that led the movements like my grandfather, not about quiet women's work like my grandmother's. In the USA when we think of Civil Rights we think of the charismatic Martin Luther King. But it was Ella Baker's 'Learning by Doing' literacy programme that stretched across the nation, powering the drive for voter registration.[3] In South Africa we hail Nelson Mandela is but it is the women who are the backbone of the everyday struggle in the townships, the amazing unsung women who work the healthcare trains that criss-cross the country in the battle against AIDS, educating as they go.[4]

In the UK there are thousands of women and mothers who give up every weekend to teach their children in the black community. Often becoming ill through overwork, they are the vanguards of change in their important work to 'raise the race'. This is what Diane Reay and I found when we did our research on black supplementary schools (Reay and Mirza 1997). These schools are amazing places; set up by and for the black community to 'supplement' the failing education system, they are hidden from the mainstream. They are autonomous, getting little or no state funding yet working alongside the mainstream. These schools have been core grassroots black organisations since the 1970s. Here is a rare picture from this time (Figure 9.5).

Set up against the odds in cold church halls, damp basements and dilapidated houses they thrived with the support of the black church and the overwhelming commitment of the parents. Armies of black women have worked alongside men to fuel this radical movement, which was often seen

Figure 9.5
Black Saturday School,
c. 1970

Source: Runnymede Collection:
Times Educational Supplement,
6 January 1984.

by the authorities as a separate, dangerous 'black power' place. But what is clear is that these schools are much more than a response to mainstream failure. They are spaces of hope and transcendence underpinned by invisible women's work. They present the paradox of what appears to be radical separate black provision operating as a mechanism for mainstream educational inclusion. On the one hand we found the schools work to 'fit in' and build a dialogue with the mainstream schools and the curriculum. With a traditional and often disciplinarian focus on the 3 'R's ('reading, writing and arithmetic'), they have been seen to be buying into the conservative ideas of 'back to basics',[5] 'formal is best', and the instrumental meritocratic ideal of gaining educational credentials.

On the other hand the women are also radical. They provide an alternative world with different meaning and what we have called 'other ways of knowing'. The women in our study talk of the *'joy'* of what they do, their work *'to raise the race'* and the *'gift of giving back'*. In their stance against racism, these teachers have developed a radical pedagogy that centres on black history and knowledge. These schools are places where whiteness is displaced and blackness becomes the norm, creating a sanctuary for the black child in which he or she is celebrated and recentred. In the same way as my grandmother was both racial and conservative in her approach to education so too are these black women. It is a strategy borne from their understanding of the value of education in the struggle for group survival. In their space on the margins they operate between under and alongside the mainstream educational and labour market structures, renaming and reclaiming opportunities for their children, and in the process subverting racist expectations and beliefs. In this sense education is a transformative mantel – a Golden Fleece.

Story 3: 'The Golden Fleece'

In the Greek myth *Jason and the Argonauts*, Jason goes in search of the Golden Fleece. It is a journey of courage, love and endurance, which, at the end, transforms him and makes him King. I heard a touching story about a Nigerian father who told his son to go to England and get educated. *'Leave'*, he said, *'go in search of the Golden Fleece'*. I think the idea of a Golden Fleece, a journey that transforms your life, is a useful way for us to think about the postcolonial educational experience.

My father and mother were part of the postwar migration to Britain (Figure 9.6). My mother came from Austria, my father from Trinidad. He was part of what the black activist and author John la Rose calls the 'heroic generation' (La Rose 1999). We have heard of the *Empire Windrush*,[6] but there were many other ships and my father came on the less romantically named *Colombie* – which he told me was a real banana boat. He arrived in December 1950 and to keep warm he took hot showers in his bed-sit. His theory was that the hot and cold temperatures caused him to lose his hair! He struggled to get into college, find a job and raise his family. It was a difficult time of overt racism. 'No blacks, no dogs, no Irish' was the landlord's slogan of the day. He had a Muslim name and even in the 1950s, 50 years before the wave of Islamophobia after 11 September, he had to change his surname to protect us, get a job and get a house. In 2005 my daughter too had to do the same, i.e. change her Muslim name just to get a job interview.

White women, like my mother, who married black men, those 'dark strangers' (Patterson 1965), are the silent heroes of this generation. They

Figure 9.6
The author's parents,
Ralph and Hilda Hosier
(wedding picture,
London 1956)

were true pioneers, those who crossed over in another way. They too have a story to tell of racism and transcendence, of love and care for their children. My mother protected her children's identity and made me understand both sides to my heritage. She gave me what the African American writer Ralph Ellison describes in his book *The Invisible Man* (1965: 15) 'the gift to see around corners'. The ability to see things differently. Their story of mothering work to shape a new generation of 'dual heritage' children is one that is largely forgotten in the postcolonial story on diaspora and displacement. It is she who gave me the desire for education – the quest of the Golden Fleece.

Sometimes you read a book that transforms your life. My book was not an inspirational novel or a grand Shakespearian tome. It was an ordinary text book we used on my undergraduate degree course in development studies at the University of East Anglia in 1978.[7] It was called *The Diploma Disease* by Ronald Dore (1976). The irony was that a book about the narrow goal of education and the instrumentalism of qualification-getting in countries like Trinidad opened up my thinking about the possibilities of education as transformative. What was my father chasing when he came to Britain? Was it education for bureaucratic self-advancement or knowledge to transform his newly independent country? Were his motives radical or conservative? Can education be revolutionary or is it always about containment? I went back to my school in South London, near Brixton, to do a Ph.D. and to find some answers.

In *Young, Female and Black* (Mirza 1992), the book from that study, I found that second-generation young Caribbean working-class women appeared to deeply identify with the ideology of meritocracy. On the surface they wanted to climb the career ladder and were seeking academic success through obtaining more and more qualifications. But as I dug deeper I found their motivation was not simply driven by a desire for educational credentials; they were engaged in a strategic rationalisation of their schooling. The schools they were in were poorly resourced and teaching was stretched. The young women sat in the back of the classroom and got on with their work. They often pretended to not be working, but did their homework. Most of all they had to stay on longer and go to college to achieve academic success.

They are driven by what I have called 'educational urgency', a desire to succeed against the odds. Ironically, because the young women's aspirations were linked to the growing gendered labour market, they could do access courses in social work or nursing, which opened a path to a degree. In this way they could climb the ladder into further and higher education, a kind of 'backdoor entry' which was not often available to young men in the same way. For them, as in the postcolonial experience, education was linked to job opportunities. But herein lies the difference. They were no longer in the Caribbean; they were in the UK, and their experience was deeply racialised in a particular way. I found they were forging new identities, identities that were grounded in a refusal to be quantified as failures, what *The Sunday Times* has called the 'Ms Dynamite' phenomenon.[8]

They were not, as is assumed in theorising about black female success, building on strong role models of their mothers and grandmothers. Neither were they resisting through accommodating the system, as many have also argued.[9] Their educational stance was much more related to the context in which they were in, what was actually happening to them in Britain. Indeed it had happened to me. When I came to England at age 16 I was deemed a failure. They said I couldn't speak English and put me down a year. They even thought I cheated when I passed my entrance exams with flying colours. I had to remake my identity to succeed. I learnt to speak like them. But like bell hooks, the black feminist writer, I too kept alive in my heart and mind 'other ways of knowing' when I moved from the margins to the centre (hooks 1991: 150).

You may ask: How can I claim educational urgency when so many young people are being failed at school? But young black and Asian people are nearly three times more likely to be in university then their white counter-parts. Although they comprise only 6% of the working population they make up 15% of students (NAO 2002).[10] Black and minority ethnic women are the highest participants of all – 60% are in higher education, as are 48% of ethnic minority men.[11] I am privileged to teach many of these students here at Middlesex University. Young black woman appear to transcend many obstacles and work their way through the cracks of educational opportunity in Britain. But what if these cracks are closing? A recent study by The Sutton Trust shows there has been little social mobility through educational routes since the 1970s (Blandon et al. 2005). The expansion of higher education has benefited the middle classes, those who can afford to make choices. With the scrapping of grants, increasing tuition fees, and the realities of long-term debt – educational desire – the sheer motivation to succeed is not enough if the structures and systems mitigate against you.

Many 'top-down' schemes such as 'Widening Participation'[12] have been put in place to remedy the class bias in higher education – as Diane Reay, Miriam David and Stephan Ball (2004) show in their new book on the subject. These schemes focus on motivating black and working-class students to come in with the promises of access and support as the mechanism for change. But what about the cultural context of learning in ethnic communities? What about the complex interrelationship of educational desire linked to increasing debt? The issues are structural not cultural. Inequalities are now built into the monolithic educational market system. You may want the Golden Fleece, but now it is more illusive than ever.

Story 4: 'The Motherland'

This is a hard story to tell; it is the story of racism and xenophobia in Britain. It is the backing on the quilt, the part we don't like to see but is always there giving shape to everything else. In this story we begin by asking: How do mothers and fathers protect their children in a place where you are told you don't belong? How do young black and Asian people, from Malaysia, Sri Lanka, Somalia, Nigeria, Iran, Caribbean, India, Pakistan, Bangladesh, Vietnam, live and go to school in a place where the subliminal messages are that we scrounge, take what is not ours, steal the housing, health and education? How do you protect your children and feel safe in a country where young people are still killed for simply being black like Stephen Lawrence,[13] among many others? How do you keep your dignity in a country where they spit at you in the street, where they whisper Paki under their breath (something I know about)?

In this story of the Motherland, the Britain to which we came, Denise Lewis and Kelly Holmes, our black female Olympians, may wrap themselves in the British flag, and we may celebrate 'our multiculturalism' with Chicken Tikka Masala, but as Gary Younge writes in the *Guardian* on the elections and immigration, there is still no sense of a truly inclusive Britishness.[14] In *The Commission for the Future of Multi-ethnic Britain*, Bhikhu Parekh calls for a 'Community of Communities' in which we have shared values, but also have group concessions to wear the hijab or eat halal meat (Runnymede Trust 2000). But as the black cultural theorist Stuart Hall (2000) observes, in reality we are in a state of 'multicultural drift'. A haphazard and piecemeal resentful acceptance of the ethnic postcolonial presence. Now on the Census you can tick the box to be 'Black British' and 'Asian British' (whatever that means), but after four generations here we are still not plain old English, Scottish or Welsh. This is the tightrope of multiculturalism, a balancing act. As the black feminist Sara Ahmed (2004) has eloquently argued, multiculturalism is a 'love/hate' relationship. If you show 'love' for the nation by not rejecting its 'hospitality', if you are not too different, not too outstanding, don't make too many claims – like insisting on wearing your hijab – you can be embraced and tolerated. All can belong in a state of 'mutual tolerance' as Roy Jenkins once famously said;[15] if you accept the common norms, sign up for the citizenship test[16] and support the English cricket team.[17]

In the British Council Lecture on Britishness, Gordon Brown, then Chancellor of the Exchequer, talked of the golden thread that runs through Britishness.[18] The thread of liberty, tolerance, fair play, social justice and the rule of law. But, he argues, the shame of post-imperial national economic decline hangs like a shadow over any proud sense of celebrating these threads. This is what Paul Gilroy calls the British condition of melancholia (Gilroy 2004). This is the backward-looking nostalgia for Britain of old. The harking back to Empire and return to greatness is a place where Britishness is stuck, unable to see the true 'multiculture' that has always been at its heart. But what of the lives, bodies and souls upon which this so-called greatness was built? In the context of colonial oppression, slavery, indenture, racism and discrimination what is the meaning of fair play, tolerance and the rule of law? How can we conceive of fair play when for 40 years there has been a press and media barrage against you and your kind?

In the 1970s *The Financial Times* headline read, 'Drowned by Coloured Flood' in response to the Ugandan and Kenyan migrants. In 1978, the headline 'Stem the Tide of Migrants' graced the Evening News in response to new rules to curb the numbers of so-called 'bogus' and illegal immigrants. The new rules led unbelievably to the virginity testing of Asian women. Violated as subhuman they were subjected to forced checks to see if they were really 'pure' brides claiming to be dependants on future Indian migrant husbands. More recently David Blunkett (then Labour Home Secretary) has invoked Margaret Thatcher's 1980s image of being 'Swamped' in the *Mail on Sunday*. Now 'waves of immigrants descend' on us (*Sunday Telegraph*).[19] The media tell us of ceaseless tides of economic migrants and bogus asylum seekers who bring with them diseases such as TB and HIV to infect us in our 'pure' nation. This hysteria is not unlike 100 years ago when the Jewish migrants were also seen as infectious 'alien' invaders. It is ironic that Britain, a maritime nation, a small island, unconsciously invokes these embattled headlines of human waves beating down their doors, 'flooding in' and 'swallowing up' what is left of Britishness.

In the 1960s politicians such as Enoch Powell mined this political gold of race hate, just as then Labour Home Secretary David Blunkett and Michael Howard, leader of the Conservative Party, have also done. As Phillip Gourevitch (2000) shows in his disturbing book on the genocide in Rwanda, political ideology combined with a strong state media can effectively be used to exploit the mythologies of tribal and ethnic divisions and create unspeakable acts of human hate. Of course we say to ourselves, 'we are not like that, it could never happen here', until the first asylum seekers are hunted down and killed in Glasgow or chased out of town in Dover with baseball bats.[20] Reena Bhavnani, Veena Meetoo and I argue in our new book *Tackling the Roots of Racism* (2005) that these racist responses to 'the other' in our midst are sanctioned by the elite, the politicians and the media and the powerful. Racism becomes everyday speak, it becomes normalised. Now 'asylum seeker' is the new swear-word in the playground.

Story 5: 'Assimilating Hope 1960–1970'

Forty years ago there were many theories as to why black children may not do well at school. In 1960s Britain black children were bussed out to cool and water down white fears whipped up by the conservative politician Enoch Powell during the racist Smethwick by-election and the Notting Hill riots. It was believed that the children of migrants needed to assimilate, lose their cultural markers and blend in. It was believed that they were not only culturally and socially deficit, coming from less civilised societies, but also that they were inherently intellectually lacking. The now discredited pseudoscientific IQ tests of Jensen and Eysenck claimed to show that black children were racially different and as such had lower intelligence (Mirza 1998).

But 'natural ability' is still an issue. In what Gillborn and Youdell call the 'new IQism' (2000), the pressures of educational policy, such as league tables, cause the sifting and sorting of pupils into tiers and streams by perceived ability. The patterns are often racialised with black children locked into the lower streams.

I was a little girl in the 1960s, but I remember being given a doll and asked which one I liked (Figure 9.7). Later refined into the Milner's scientific doll studies in the 1970s, the study suggested that if you chose a white doll rather than a dark one like yourself you were exhibiting negative self-esteem and low self-concept (Milner 1975). This in turn affected your feelings of alienation and disaffection to be integrated and thus learn. Does this seem improbable now? Work on raising achievements of young black people

Figure 9.7 The author and her brother Gerard Hosier at their London primary school in Balham, 1962

through raising self-esteem is still with us today, though in its more sophisticated form of positive role models and mentoring. While it has been a lifeline to many young black and Asian people who have been damaged by the effects of racism, we still need to acknowledge its roots in the cultural deficit model and to understand its limitations.

English as a second language was also seen as a problem. Not just Pakistani and Bengali but also Patois and Creole. Over 30 years ago Bernard Coard (1971)[21] brought to light, in his seminal pamphlet, the scandal of disproportionate numbers of Caribbean children being labelled as educationally subnormal (ESN). They were being put in special units, what were then called 'sin bins'. The Black Parents Movement[22] was an important grassroots political response by the black community to the criminalisation and the wanton discarding of their children.

Yet this seems so long ago; surely it is not happening now? But now we have PRUs (pupil referral units). The issue that drives it now is the discourse on discipline and antisocial behaviour. As Tony Sewell (1997) has shown in his research there is no doubt that black masculine peer pressure to be 'cool', urban youth culture and interracial gangs are issues for schools. This clearly relates to underachievement. However, there has been no attempt to decouple these issues of social control from the issues of 'race' and racism. David Gillborn's (1990) research shows that we have effectively criminalised generations of black children, particularly boys, by not recognising the subtle consequences of stereotyping, particularly what he calls the 'Myth of the Afro Caribbean Macho' which has seeped into the classroom and the consciousness of teachers. We now find that black boys are three times more likely to be excluded from school.[23] It's an epidemic, a *real* crisis for the children and their parents.

Story 6: 'The Multicultural Dream? 1980–1990'

Barry Troyna, one of our important educational theorists, called this period the three 'Ss – somas, saris and steelbands (Troyna 1992). It was an apt description of the day-to-day interpretation of Roy Jenkins' famous call for multiculturalism as 'not a flattening out process but one of equal opportunity and cultural diversity in an atmosphere of mutual tolerance'.[24] My daughter Aliya was at primary school then and we did a lot of sari wearing and bringing of food. Here she is with her class being an African bird (Figure 9.8).

In the 1980s, there were the Brixton uprisings. Aliya had just been born and as we lived near Brixton I remember being caught up in the riots. The hate was consuming, but this explosion of anger and frustration was also a

Figure 9.8 The author's daughter Aliya Mirza (centre front) at her South London primary school, 1985

watershed. The Scarman Report (1981) that followed uncovered the racism of the criminal justice system. The Rampton (1981) and Swann Reports (1985) on multiracial education showed that educational underachievement had taken root, and for the first time linked it to socioeconomic concerns of race and class. During this time dedicated scholars saw the visionary potential of multicultural education and engaged in radical, expansive and inclusive scholarship. I have had the privilege of working with many of them, such as Sally Tomlinson (1983; 2008) and Peter Figueroa (1991). In a critique of existing theories and the limitations of the 1988 Educational Reform Act they called for a more coherent approach to multicultural education. They showed that many complex factors make a difference. Schools make a difference, as does the curriculum, poverty and class inequality, and regressive colour-blind government policy.

The anti-racist teachers' movement also identified institutional and structural racism in the school system. Teacher expectations had always been at the core of theories on the self-fulfilling prophecy of how educational underachievement operates in a cycle of low expectations followed by low pupil outcomes, but 20 years on there is still no integral anti-racist training for teachers. Seventy percent of newly qualified teachers say they do not feel equipped to teach pupils from different ethnicities (Multiverse 2004). They may get a one-hour class on diversity in their whole training, and I am often the invited guest speaker.

In the 1980s the right-wing backlash against multicultural education was all-consuming. From the USA to the UK they ridiculed any attempts at cultural inclusion as 'political correctness' and 'dumbing down'. Now, after the 2001 summer disturbances in the northern towns of Bradford and Oldham, Trevor Phillips, Head of the Commission for Racial Equality, has declared that 'multiculturalism is dead'.[25] It is argued that this has led to segregation and caused ethnic enclaves, particularly in schools which have held young people back. But now in the government's sophisticated language of social cohesion and social inclusion – which embodies the notion of inter-faith and inter-cultural understanding, citizenship and community engagement – we see again that communities must integrate, and lose their cultural markers to become viable (Home Office 2005). Is this a return to assimilationism? Has the wheel turned full circle? Are we back where we were 40 years ago? Is this just a new take on the same old problems? What is our vision for a *real* multicultural Britain?

Story 7: 'The Difference of Diversity: 2000–2005'

We have entered a new era in 'race talk'. Now we talk of 'diversity and difference'. This has fundamentally changed the patterns on the quilt. As Kenan Malik[26] powerfully argues, we no longer focus on old-fashioned ideas of equality and the universal qualities that make us, humanity, the same.

Now, in the wake of the identity politics of the 1980s we celebrate our differences; being a woman, being black, being Muslim, being gay. Discrimination based on gender, sexuality, race, disability and age and religion are now high on the legislative agenda.[27]

This politics of recognition enabled those who had been marginalised to find a voice. It was a liberating time but not without its problems. It has been translated into a bureaucratic approach to diversity which monitors our progress and tracks our differences. We now have glossy brochures with our multi-coloured faces and wonderful policies and institutional statements that promise inclusion and change. However, in reality, as a recent LDA report (2004) shows, there has been little progress towards equality. Good intentions remain locked in an institutional paper trail, unable to translate to our in hearts and minds. Now we hear of diversity as 'good business sense'. We can expand the market more effectively by embracing difference. Diversity, we are told, opens up human potential and enables the best to excel. Ironically in the marketplace difference and diversity have led to the 'declining significance of race'. Now in a colour-blind approach we are told we are all the same. Fair treatment is based on merit. But what if we don't all have the same equal opportunities to achieve that merit?

In the story of education how does this notion of merit translate? Under-pinning the *Aiming High* programme (DfES 2003b) to raise achievement for black and minority ethnic young people we see tables that chart hierarchies of difference between ethnicities (DfES 2005; and see Figure 9.9).[28]

Here we use the measure of achieving five examination subjects at GCSE to rank ethnic groups in order of ability.[29] It is seen as a good thing, with Indian and Chinese (the so-called 'model minorities') at the top, and Africans

Percentage of Ethnic Minority Pupils with 5 Grade A*-C GCSEs

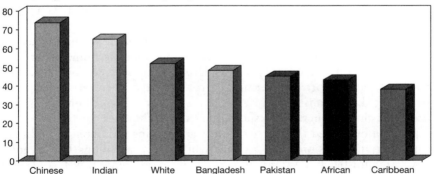

Figure 9.9 Percentage of ethnic minority pupils with five Grade A* to –C GCSEs

Source: DfES (2005).

and Caribbeans (the so-called 'failing' minorities) at the bottom. But what does this tell us? That some are gifted, others are not? Are Asians docile and hardworking (like the coolies of the past)? Do blacks have a chip on their shoulder and rebel (like the uppity slaves of the past)? What do you think? What do we think? What do teachers think? We can ask, 'What about class, gender and regional difference in attainment?' We know these make a difference, but this complexity is rarely highlighted in the 'race' and achievement debate (Gillborn and Mirza 2000).

Now, as shown in Figure 9.9, ethnicity and cultural difference have become signifiers for 'race'. This is the new racism. We have moved from biological notions of innate differences in the nineteenth century to religious, national and cultural notions of innate differences in the twenty-first century. It is as if cultural and religious differences are embodied in nature. In the new cultural construction of 'race', cultural and religious difference is played out when we say, 'blacks are good at sport, not so good at school. Chinese are good at maths, and make good food. Asians are good at business and love family life. Muslims cannot be trusted, they are aggressive, sexist and under all those clothes, usually a bit wild-eyed.' Racism in this cultural and religious guise seems less overt. We understand these differences. Recently a student asked me, 'What do you mean by We?' What I mean is the pervasive way We all talk about race, as if cultural and religious differences are fixed and immutable. It is a racialised way of being that infiltrates our daily language, personal interactions, professional practice, and what's more our social and education policies.

There has been some excellent policy research on diversity. Maud Blair at the DfES has shown that what makes a difference is strong leadership, clear management and a positive school ethos which facilitates open discussion about difficult issues, such as racism, sexism and bullying (Blair et al. 1998). But when we look at the evidence of raising achievement projects under the government initiatives of EIC (excellence in cities) and EMAG (ethnic minority achievement grant), what we find is not a focus on the 'hard' structural issues identified by Maud Blair and her team. We find instead a 'soft' approach focusing on culture, behaviour and the home. There are schemes for motivational and personal development, schemes for counselling and pastoral support, mentoring and role models. There are projects on parenting skills, translation services and summer schools; homework and breakfast clubs, writers' workshops and exam techniques.

It could be argued that these schemes are making a difference, and I am sure special provision, such as that which Trevor Phillips has recently advocated for black boys, can and does make a difference if well conceived and delivered.[30] The most recent figures show Bangladeshi, African, Caribbean and Pakistani pupils' GCSE results are up by nearly three points.[31] But the approach to raising achievement is still located in the old multi-cultural palliatives of the three 'Ss', with concepts of negative self-esteem and cultural deficit. The new cultural racism has slipped in by the back door. In this story it does seem that 'the more things change the more they stay the same'.

Conclusion: Where is the love? Towards a sociology of gendered aspirations

Where do these seven stories take us? There are always two sides to every story and the story of race, gender and education is no different. On one side is the harsh story of failure and being failed by the educational system. It is the story of racism and hate. On the other hand, educational desire remains hopeful and enduring. It is the story of love. In my research women weave together stories of love, transcendence and hope. Hope, as Paulo Freire, the Brazilian educational visionary, says, is at the centre of the matrix between hope, indignation, anger and love – this matrix is the dialectic of change (Freire 2004: xxx). Like him I too argue for an understanding of the energy and commitment and love of education through teaching and learning as the mechanism for social change.

Plato argued that education is fundamentally about love. The philosopher Raimond Gaita draws on this and tells us that nothing goes deep in education unless it is under the inspiration and discipline of a certain kind of love. A teacher's privileged obligation is to initiate students into a 'real and worthy love' for their subject: 'there is nothing finer that one human being can do for another' (Gaita 2000: 231). The struggle for humanity, as the Black and Asian community know, is fundamentally linked to the struggle for education. For a black person to become educated is to become human.[32] The black philosopher Franz Fanon writes in his seminal text *Black Skin White Masks*: 'Nothing is more astonishing than to hear a black (woman or) man express him (or herself) properly, for then they are putting on the white world' (1986: 36). Education in this sense is not about the process of learning or teaching; it is about refutation.

From this evidence how do we build a sociology of gendered aspirations? We have to look for patterns in the quilt, patterns which go against the grain of formal social expectations. We have to 'see round corners' and look at things differently, chart the hidden histories. If we look at what appears to be on the surface the conservative act of self-improvement through women's individual expressions of educational desire for themselves and for their children in time and space, we can see patterns of what I have called a new social movement (Mirza and Reay 2000b). Women educators like my grandmother, the supplementary schoolteachers, and the young black women in schools and universities should be seen as more than fragmented players. They seek social transformation through educational change. They struggle for educational inclusion in order to transform their opportunities and in so doing subvert racist expectations and beliefs.

If we look at the story of the racialisation of education, where young black men are three times more likely to be excluded and failed at school, where theories and approaches to black and Asian educational underachievement have been based on low intelligence, cultural confusion, negative self-esteem, alienation and bad behaviour, then the struggle for education becomes a battlefield. And if it is a battlefield, then the women are postmodern warriors. They are, as the *Guardian* said recently, a 'Quiet Riot'[33] strategically using their social and cultural knowledge drawn from their experience to educate themselves and their children. These women occupy a 'third space', a space of radical opposition in which they struggle for new forms of citizenship, what I call 'real citizenship' that deserves to be recognised (Mirza and Reay 2000a).

But is all this talk of love and new social movements naive, a black feminist Utopia?

In the ideological and actual war against racism nothing stays the same, nothing is what it seems. You have to be contingent, strategic, strong and vigilant. When I was appointed to the Labour government's Task Force on Standards in Education in 1997, David Blunkett, the then Secretary of State for Education and Employment, was interested in capturing the energy and commitment of the black community to drive forward the schools standards agenda. Since then I have seen supplementary schools prevalent in the 1970s and 1980s decline as the government swallows them up and uses them to build its out-of-school programmes. This is the new outsourcing. Just as the socialist Sunday Schools set up by the working-class communities at the turn of the twentieth century were absorbed by the expansion following the 1944 Education Act, so too are these supplementary schools being absorbed by educational reforms to 'raise standards' since 1997. What goes around comes around. For the government education is always a major election issue, but as Paulo Freire cautions, a dark cloud is enveloping education. When education is reduced to mere training, as is happening now with neoliberal education markets, it annihilates dreams (Freire 2004: 102).

This chapter has been a story of the power of love to transcend the struggle for education. We need to hold on to our love, hopes, and dreams, the fabric that makes the heart of the quilt.

Chapter 10

Writing about race and gender[1]

This conversation between myself and Jacqui MacDonald[2] weaves a personal and autobiographical narrative which contextualises many of the chapters in this book.

JMD: I'd really like to start by asking you if you can tell me something about your best piece of writing or some of your best pieces of writing. Those which you're most pleased with.

HSM: It's such a difficult question. I have been thinking long and hard about this. In my writing life which has spanned the last 25 years, different things have influenced me at different times and I can be proud of something the moment I write it then I move on to another piece and then I'm proud of that. So in different eras and different times I feel differently about my work. Sometimes I look back on a piece of work and I say, what was I thinking? So writing is about progression, it's a process. I think one of the big mistakes we make in writing is to think what we are writing at the time is final and it's got to be perfect. Perfection, I think, is the biggest enemy of a writer.

Because writing is a journey of self-growth I would have to say my favourite piece is my first book, *Young, Female and Black*[3] which I wrote in 1992. I have an emotional attachment to it. It was my Ph.D. thesis and it's become a bestselling book with Routledge. I am amazed it did so well because it was a small-scale ethnography of young Caribbean girls. I am myself from the Caribbean, but grew up and went to school in London and so I wanted to write about these experiences and the interplay between career choices and educational structures. So in a way this book was about my own life, it was a process of exploring the practices of racism and exclusion which I saw around me. I suppose it was a cathartic thing to see it in print. At the time it was very exciting for me. So that is a favourite piece of work.

JMD: So it stemmed from your Ph.D., and is perhaps autobiographical?

HSM: Yes it was autobiographical to some extent, and I think that's something that's underpinned a lot of my work. The thing with academic writing is it can be like a mask. You can use academic theory and academic conventions to articulate, in a very objective and distanced way, something that you've experienced yourself, but you're not really naming or implicating yourself in it.

When you write I do believe your personal experience is driving it but you are using academic language and nuances. I always tell my students they should write what they feel about a subject, put themselves in the text and then go back and make it 'academic'. It makes it better and more meaningful to them. I do think that sometimes we leave out the personal, or we ignore that in our writing and we should bring it to the fore.

JMD: It would appear that race and gender dominate your work; are they the main influences on your writing?

HSM: Yes, there's a connection between that very first piece of work, that cathartic outpouring if you like, and the next book which I edited, which was *Black British Feminism*.[4] I think it was a very powerful piece of work because it brought together women of colour who were writing and doing brilliant work but in isolated little 'pockets' in different universities in the UK.

Independently we were writing on similar themes. Some were just finishing their Ph.D.s, some were already established. Black British feminism opened up a moment of possibilities and brought us together to make such a powerful statement. It created a new subject area based on our collaborative writing. It was such an energetic and vibrant time. I'm very proud of this.

I remember after finishing the book I went on holiday and I saw my mum in Trinidad. She was giving me a massage because I was so stressed, and I said to her, 'Mummy, if I died now I would be so happy, I think I've done what I need to do.' I've done my opus!' I felt the book would leave a mark. And she reminded me of that the other day because I was feeling a bit low about something I was writing. With writing we do go in peaks and troughs.

We do so easily forget our achievements, because in academia you're pushed forward to do more and more and there's such little praise or chance for reflection on what you have done. You always have to do something else, be on to the next project, and you forget the value of what you've done. It's only when someone comes up to you or emails you and says, 'I read that, thank you, it made me think differently', that you realise well, actually your work is valuable. But we do work in our little pockets. It's the isolation that's so difficult.

JMD: What are the pros and cons of collaborative writing?

HSM: Working in collaboration I would say can be the best of times and the worst of times, as in *Great Expectations*! Collaborative working really makes you think differently. I've written of course with Dave Gillborn[5] here at the Institute, but I've written mainly with women, such as Diane

Reay.[6] What's challenging is to write so that it's seamless. We take responsibilities for different areas but then we interweave so that the style seems seamless, and that's very hard to do, it takes time.

Then there are always problems of ownership and that's where collaborative work can come unstuck, who owns this or that? So if you work in a very deep feminist way of saying 'let's really pool our ideas and writing styles together', then who owns it? And in academia, let's face it, it's very competitive, first authors matter and ownership matters, and it becomes difficult as people are at different phases in their careers. So I would say always, always have good ground rules that everybody understands and agrees to and talk about it openly.

I think what's really nice about working with others is that you don't get writer's block! Let's be honest, it can be really difficult, but when you've got that synergy of working together, you feel excited about what you're doing and so the passion comes through. So I would say collaborative work is creative but it can be a minefield as well.

JMD: When you talk about creative, do you find that through your co-writers you view your writing in a different way?

HSM: Well of course other people bring their own theoretical understandings so you can see something differently from their particular point of view. So yes, I think collaborative work has proven very useful for doing research work. When you're on a large team and you are working together on a huge national project like I did with SCRE,[7] and you've got researchers going up and down the country collecting data, how you pool it all together is crucial. You do learn a lot about good organisation and good leadership in those contexts. It's important that somebody has oversight over the style and presentation and knitting it together. Though, when you are finished the sense of satisfaction is very different from when you have written something yourself.

JMD: Earlier you mentioned about the difficulty of choosing your 'best' writing and you alluded to having other pieces of work where you feel it was not your best. Do you want to say anything about your least favourite and why that might be?

HSM: Ten years ago I was nominated to give the Lister Lecture at BA Festival of Science,[8] it's a huge annual jamboree. The Lister Lecture's very prestigious, it's awarded to an up-and-coming academic, and I wrote a very angry lecture. It was on racist pseudoscience and IQ. I looked at popularist right-wing academic arguments such as *The Bell Curve* which linked race to low IQ. I was so angry about the stuff I was reading at the time and the revitalisation of Social Darwinism through the new genetics discourse. I look back on that essay now and I think how angry I was. I don't feel that any more and I guess, what I'm saying is at different phases of writing you're at different places in your life, and it's always an unfinished process.

I feel similarly about *Young, Female and Black*. While it is my favourite because of its status in my life and it was my starting point, when I look back at the writing style and the simplicity of my arguments, I could crawl under a table and cringe! I can see that the style is clumsy and I would now use different theoretical approaches to the same work; in fact I am thinking of doing *Young, Female and Black* 20 years on.

I'd really love to do that because I think things have changed so enormously for young black women growing up in Britain now. I would take a different approach to the theory and methodology, which has developed. In terms of the writing and the style, I would say that it really does make me cringe! Especially when I know people are still buying and using it.

JMD: What's that 'cringe' about?

HSM: I feel I have I've moved on so much since I wrote this but I still get A level students emailing me, saying 'I'm using this book for my project; can you help me?' They see it as valuable, even though I am cringing. When you write you are putting something 'out there' and it has meaning to others but it has a different meaning to you. Writing is so personal; what matters to you is how you feel about it, not how others feel about it.

I think when you're writing you've got to learn to let go. One of my affirmations is 'trust and let go'. Whenever I'm nervous, whenever I'm not sure, I say 'just trust and let go' and let whatever I'm doing or saying float out into the ether. In your writing and your talking you have to trust people will read and hear and find their own value in it.

JMD: I like that, 'trust and let go'. Would you say that writing is a major part of your life?

HSM: Yes, it's obsessive, it dominates my thinking, I wake up in the night worried about an idea I've been working on and if it's not good enough. It's very difficult. You're always testing yourself, and it's lonely, and it's hard. Last summer there was a sculpture on Hampstead Heath, it was a massive table and the chair. It was enormous! It was the size of a house. It illustrated the loneliness of the writer and it did, because that's how big your table and chair feel to you, as big as a house! It does dominate you. Once you're in academia, and you're always being pushed for the next piece, and the next one, and the next one, and you're held up to scrutiny by your peers, you can become obsessed with the writing. So you can't easily 'trust and let go'. It's a process of just learning that you have to. Using deadlines is how I let go!

JMD: Just staying on this theme of writing being a major part of your life. If you weren't in academia would you still write?

HSM: Oh yes. I really like playing with writing styles. I did this in my inaugural lecture last year at Middlesex University.[9] The theme was love and hate in the context of educational desire. It took a year to think it through and about three months to write and in fact talking to other people who did their inaugural, that's very much the pattern. It's the most petrifying thing you can go through because it's about your life's work and not only are you up for peer review and scrutiny, it has to be meaningful to friends and family. And yet it's the most cathartic and therapeutic thing you can do, so the lecture it's my third favourite piece. I feel like I'm on *Desert Island Discs*!

The lecture was almost like a rap poem, it had a rap beat, and it was divided up into seven stories or verses. I feel very strongly in my writing that I should be able to communicate and that it's accessible. You have to break down some of the academic language and concepts, as it is a public audience, where I knew some people like my mum and my friends have not got degrees and have never been to a university. This is a totally unknown world to them and I wanted them to feel comfortable with what I was saying, and not feel excluded. We do that a lot in academia, exclude. In fact the more excluding you are the more you're valued!

The idea of the lecture was to tell a personal story about my own life and how I've come to do the work I'm doing and explore the emotions and passion that's driven me. I do feel so strongly about social justice issues. What I was able to do in that lecture with the writing style was feel confident that I'd reached a point, after all these years of writing, to write as if I'm talking to you, and not hide behind the mask of over-articulations and over-theorising. It took a long time to write, and I'm very proud of that piece, because it made people cry, and it made them laugh, it brought out emotions in people.

Part of my process of writing includes getting inspiration. So I went to the Jazz Café to see Ruby Turner singing. I love Ruby Turner because she's got that gospel power in her voice. I watched her perform, because giving a lecture is a performance, and I saw the way she worked the audience and I thought, 'Yes! I want to do that in my lecture!'

My grandfather was a minister in the Caribbean church and I wanted to be able to emulate giving a sermon, but not preaching to people of course! I wanted to bring out emotions in people. It was very difficult but I think I achieved it on the day and it was great, I really enjoyed it.

Writing this lecture allowed me to enjoy the process of writing. I'd love to write novels. Novels that have all this emotional power in them. In fact I've just come back from Trinidad where I did some research for a novel that I would like to write. You see I can't get the academia out of me, I'm still doing loads of research. Somebody said to me, 'But if you're writing a novel, just write it!' I said, 'No, no, no! I have to get the facts right!' [*laughs*]

I did go to a writing workshop, it was a week away and it's with the Arvon Foundation. They do script writing, poetry workshops, short stories, whatever. Many famous writers have contributed financially to this trust for writers. It was just amazing. We stayed In Hebden Bridge in Yorkshire in the house where Ted Hughes and Sylvia Plath lived. They get well-known novelists to come and work with you. They give you exercises like giving you postcards and say, 'there's a picture, just write what you feel', and it's so different than academic writing. 'Write what you feel'! We never do that in academic writing! I started writing in a very stiff way, and other people who'd been doing it for years, writing for women's magazines or for Radio 4, they were just flowing away. I was like 'everything had to have a political purpose', until one of the workshop leaders, who was a very famous novelist, he said to me, 'Why don't you just relax?' [*laughs*] 'Why don't you just not be so serious?' And it was an epiphany, one of those moments where you just go, 'He's so right!' But I realised I have to unlearn academic conventions if I want to . . . no, when I write my novel!

JMD: When or where did this desire to write start come from?

HSM: I think my desire to write has come from the need to have 'voice', to find a voice, to get to my own truth, whatever that is! I think that driving force has driven me even though technically I'm not a very good writer. I wasn't very good at English when I was at school in Trinidad. I was really terrible, and when I came to England I had such a strong Trinidadian accent the school wrote me off! I was 16 so I was quite old and I found spelling really difficult. I found schooling here very difficult and I still can't spell very well. Thank God for spellchecks!

I tend to write back to front, I write almost an illegible draft, only I can understand it! And then I go back and fill in the gaps and it's something I've always had to do because I'm not actually a very good writer, or at least I don't think of myself as a very good writer. No teacher ever told me I was a good writer. I read other people's work and I think, wow! That's so fabulous. I wish I could write like that. And then other people tell me they read mine and they say, wow! I wish I could write like that. So everyone's always looking to someone else.

JMD: So what should be the starting point for the less experienced writer?

HSM: I think your starting point is knowing that you've got something to say. What I've learned from my education, coming from Trinidad and going to school in Brixton is that our confidence is schooled out of us, so we come to believe we don't have anything to say.

So much of the teaching I had was about erasing who you are, instead of a teacher actually saying, 'you've written an essay, well done'! Even if it's not technically brilliant. When I worked at Middlesex and at South Bank I had many students, very often black women, who did not have a traditional education. They think they have to live up to a notion of academic writing, be something they're not, because they have learnt their experiences don't matter. They think to themselves, 'my life is of no value, I need to learn something to make me better.' It's part of our educational mindset, we've always got to be better, what we have isn't good enough. But we are good enough!

For my inaugural I was so terrified and I thought, oh, I'll be exposed, people will see me as not good enough. I went to a life-coaching session and we had to decide, if we are up against a challenge what would we do, how would we tackle it? How would we rephrase a negative thing like, 'oh I'm petrified and I'm not good enough'? And I said to myself, 'I've got something to say'. That's my positive affirmation, to the negative one, 'I'll be found out, I'm not good enough'. So I now say to myself, 'I have something to say'. And even if it's not what someone wants to hear, I still have something to say.

Even if you're working on a large team and the research isn't about your personal life, it's a so-called objective study, you still have important experiences and perspectives to include. You're the filter that is writing the work, you're the eyes that are seeing the data, so however you construct it, you are engaging in a creative process. It's not an objective process, it's a personal and subjective process.

I've learned from examining Ph.D.s that judging academic writing is so subjective. There are a few objective criteria of course, such as the structure and the form of the piece of work. That is always there and once you learn the craft then you can play with it, which I'm very privileged now to be able to do. It's like famous painters isn't it? Picasso was a very good classical painter and then he went on to abstract work because he knew the foundations. It's the same with writing, you have to get those foundations and then you can experiment. It's all about confidence really; confidence is the biggest block and the biggest help! And I guess I need to be inspired too. I think the key is confidence, inspiration, passion, good leadership – if you're working on teams, and just feeling positive about what you're doing.

Recently I was teaching on the writing of Franz Fanon.[10] He was a black philosopher and psychiatrist in the 1950s and he wrote a very famous book called *Black Skin, White Masks*. He also wrote another book called *The Wretched of the Earth*. These were seminal postcolonial texts. And in the seminar we were deconstructing the text when one of the students said, 'you know what's so amazing about this book? It's a stream of consciousness. He doesn't care who his audience is, he's just got something to say and he says it.' And it's a book of anger and of passion and it's still one of the most powerful books on race all these years on. I learnt something then that writing for an audience can be a barrier, because you're thinking of your peers or whatever, and you forget that you're also writing for yourself. In a way that is an important tip, I would say explore what *you* think.

If I'm writing a paper I'll just hammer it out. I'll do lots of reading, I get lots of inspiration, I'll get a sense of where I'm going. Then I write. It might be 2–3000 words which I just pour out on to the paper but when I go back and tidy it up I'm editing it and sorting it, fitting in the references, fitting in the data, fitting in the context. So I don't start with a blank piece of paper, it's too terrifying. So the stream of consciousness is my framework, and then I work back to front and fill in all the bits. It's just the way I have worked, it may not work for others. You may think I'm totally nuts, but it helps me to build my confidence about what I have to say.

JMD: Any other tips?

HSM: Well when I was doing my Ph.D. I was a single mum. I had a 3-year-old daughter when I started my Ph.D. and all through I did childminding among other things. I always had children around so I never had the luxury of locking myself away. When my daughter was very little I used to write through the night when she slept. I would take her to the little nursery school or as time went on to school, and I'd sleep while she was there. So my writing has always fitted around childcare [*laughs*] and so nothing would disturb me now. The TV could be on in the background, and noises here and there, and, if I'm really concentrating nothing bugs me. I'm not precious about having writing space. It just has to fit in with life. I tend to like to write at night and work through the night and hear the birds in the morning at five, when it's so quiet and still. I like a long run on something and I feel calm. I can work for five or six hours at a stretch through the night and then I feel happy with myself, it's kind of a deep satisfaction really. But I don't have any rules.

JMD: How do you juggle work responsibilities with writing, how do you find time?

HSM: It's becoming increasingly difficult, I have to say. When I first started out as a young lecturer I had loads of teaching in unfamiliar areas which required a great deal of swotting up. So that didn't give you much time for your own work but somehow I just had the energy. Now I don't have all those kind of teaching things to do, but I do have a lot of admin responsibilities. Now it's running departments or running research centres, getting budgets in and going to committee meetings. Things like that just start making me frustrated and angry because I can't get down to the real business of writing.

To write you have to switch off and move into another mode. I used to work through the night, but now I have to work through the weekends as well to get that run. So I find that I use more of my own time, which does make me feel resentful because I use my holidays. I might go away for a week or two but actually I'm using my own leave, my own time, my night time, my family time, because of what I call the increasing bureaucratisation in higher education. I think most of the meetings we have are a waste. We could make the same decisions in five minutes instead of an hour of chewing the cud, but nevertheless we have to go through the process and *when I think about* the RAE![11]

For the RAE you need to have a minimum of four pieces of work in good academic journals – I mean who decided this nonsense? I have no idea! You know some years you have good years, some years you have bad years. Sometimes you have a fabulous idea that everyone wants to publish in many journals. The other year, you're cruising along, you know? Sometimes you work on a very good research project and sometimes, politics being what they are, they don't want to publish it. This has happened to me, when the research findings are too difficult for the mainstream to accept. The RAE is like making up a rule to measure quality but it doesn't measure reality.

It's ironic that the RAE comes along at the same time as the increasing bureaucratisation of higher education has come along, so it has squeezed our time. Which makes me feel like my time in academia has a bottom and a top. I don't want to stay under this kind of pressure where I'm working harder now than when I first started. The irony is that I should be having more time to think but actually I have less time to think now.

JMD: So, where is your work–life balance?

HSM: [*laughs*] I'm not very good at it!

JMD: It doesn't sound like good news for any one entering academia. You're telling me I have to forgo family pleasures, my weekends!

HSM: I won't lie to say that it's easy to get a work-life balance. Because a project will have a deadline, and you'll just have to achieve what you have to achieve by that time, it doesn't matter if the rest of your family is going on annual leave, you have to do it. So I won't lie and say that's it's great on that score but on the other side I would say that the satisfaction of writing something is so great and being part of a research team chipping away at new horizons and saying, 'this is another way to look at something', is so deeply satisfying.

I can't think of any other professions where you could really get that from, and that's what makes us stay, despite the pay and the conditions, and the lack of office space. It makes us stay because it's an inspirational sector. But the RAE is killing our inspiration and I feel very strongly about that.

JMD: Are you arguing that the RAE hinders one's writing, creativity?

HSM: It does, it makes you panic, and I used to write because I felt passionate about things and now I find I'm writing because I'm panicking. I'm sending things into journals that I wouldn't have normally sent things into. They might be versions of the same thing, using the data differently, and I'm just thinking I wouldn't necessarily have done that a few years ago. I'm playing the game.

And the question is 'does it make one's scholarship any better?' It's made me panic and made me push more out there which takes up good creative time when I could be actually saying I want to think about this data differently. I'm not doing that, I'm just pushing it out to get the right number of hits with journals and I think it's a shame.

JMD: Do you think there's an issue here about being a woman and writing and being a success in academia?

HSM: Yes, I think it's a huge issue, and if you look at the career structure of any institution in higher ed you'll see that, yes there are lots of women, but where are they in the hierarchy? A few at the top! It is still very much a man's world. You just have to look at the career structure and criteria for promotion. And so there are definite gender issues about our productivity and how much we can do and the choices that we have to make. Because as women we do say, 'listen, forget this, I'm going to spend more time with my family' or your parents are getting older and you have to spend more time doing caring – caring issues are huge. Life is complex for women.

I would say that what I've done is not juggle so much as worked damn hard! That's what I do, to the point where it's affected my personality, it affects who you are, it affects your friendships. I'm always working and my friends say, but Heidi, we never see you, and I always feel so embarrassed and I give the same excuse, 'I'm so busy', and you know what, I really *am* busy! And so, I feel like I'm not juggling as much as intensely working. You have to be a very good organiser.

I love cooking things in the evening when I get in because it relaxes me and it stops me thinking about whatever project or paper or thing I need to work on. It's the chopping of the onions, it helps me to relax [*laughs*]. I also like salsa dancing which I did last night and I try to fit things into my life that are pleasurable because I find that academic writing is so intense that you lose your laughter. So I love to go to comedy clubs. I also do swimming, running and yoga.

JMD: Does your writing say anything about you?

HSM: You have to ask someone else that question. I feel it's hard to ask *me* that question. [*laughs*]

I think writing is very egocentric. My daughter loves literature and we were looking at something on Evelyn Waugh the other day and I was struck by the self-centredness of some writers. You have to be quite single-minded to be successful.

JMD: Well, what would you like your writing to say about you?

HSM: Yes, you're a smart cookie, Jackie! [*laughs*]

I love communicating with people, I love people, and I want my writing to be accessible and inspirational. There's a poster the ATSS[12] have made of me with a photograph and a quote of mine. It is such an honour as it is in every school in the sixth-form common-room. And it says: 'Sociology is about your life and my life, we all have something to say, our voices must be heard.'

So it goes back to that, 'if you've got something to say'. So I'm pleased I'm doing this interview. I want to encourage people to talk and write about their experiences. Maybe it's because I teach a lot of black students and I would like my writing to give them the confidence to say, 'yes if she can write that so can I'.

For example, if they are doing an essay on identity and the embodiment of difference using Bourdieu or Butler, they are actually talking about their lives, their experience, so it's about facilitating them to make that connection between theory and practice in their writing. I want my writing to make what seems inaccessible and make it accessible. Because nothing is difficult, nothing is hard, we obfuscate things, we make them unreachable but actually I think it's all within our grasp. I would like my writing to be about the search for truth in our own lives.

My most recent book, which is a jointly authored book with Reena Bhavnani and Veena Meetoo is called *Tackling Roots of Racism*.[13] It has sold 1000 copies in three months, which for an academic book on racism is pretty good. It's because it's so accessible. Schools are using it, courses are using it, and it's chatty. We start with everyday social problems and then we look back and ask what are the roots of racism that lie at the heart of the problem and how can we solve it. We look at the theories and facts behind these everyday phenomena. I think it's touched a chord with people, and it's been selling like hot cakes. It's on a second print run after six months.

JMD: That's fantastic. So is there any particular type of writing you enjoy more than others?

HSM: I really liked writing my inaugural. And I want to write more like that, which is more as if I'm talking to people. Of course, I know a lot of other black women that have written like that. There is Patricia Williams,[14] an African American law professor who did the BBC Reith Lectures. She wrote about her experiences of racism from inside out, and she received a lot of criticism, I think it was Melvyn Bragg who tore into her on Radio 4 as not 'real scholarship'. And then there's other people like bell hooks,[15] an African American cultural critic, who writes using a stream of consciousness based on her experiences. She always says, she's not considered to be a real academic, and she talks about it with pain in her voice, saying, 'why is this not acceptable? Why is my life as a black woman not theory?' I know that there's snobbery about what is real knowledge, but I think it's important that we do write like that sometimes – it is a different kind of truth.

JMD: How do you find a publisher who will publish what you want to write about?

HSM: Well, it's very interesting because I'm writing another book at the moment which is a collection of essays. I was speaking to the publishers and I said, 'Oh, I'm going to be sending you this proposal', and she didn't ask me the title, she didn't ask me about the content, she just said, 'What's the market?' [*laughs*]. That was the first question, 'What's the market?'! My daughter's working in publishing now, it's all about sales. In order for books to sell well they have to reach a wide audience, particularly an American audience, because that's a huge market. So it's about being pragmatic about that, but I think at the end of the day, a good book is a good book. They say 'cream rises', so it's got to be solid, theoretical, but entertaining; then it will sell well.

JMD: Is that all?

HSM: [*laughs*] I know the RAE is driving us in terms of these heavy academic peer-reviewed articles in refereed journals which few people read, but in the publishing world of books it's about the market and you've got to know what courses would buy your books, so the criteria for the publishing world are different than the academic world.

JMD: So you've got to really bring yourself up to speed on what they're looking for out there?

HSM: In the specialist field that I work in, which is about the intersectionality of race and gender in education, my peers are small in number. And peer review means you're competing with a select number of colleagues in similar fields. For all kinds of reasons they may not like your work. It maybe a subjective disagreement or an objective judgement based on historical differences of opinion, or on methodology or something. And the same goes for when you submit a bid for research grants. Somebody else very close to it is saying, 'oh, that's a good idea', but won't support it. So peer review is fundamentally flawed. It's against equal opportunities. It is based on academic networks and clubs and if you have a good reputation or not. It's not based on merit. But it's our main measure of quality in academia.

And when you get rejected or *if* you get rejected from a journal it isn't always just because it isn't good enough, it could be for a whole variety of factors, because it goes to two or three people who've given a subjective opinion. I've had things rejected by a journal, I've sent it to another journal and they say it's fabulous. But it's been ripped apart by another one! It's just about who reads it and where they're coming from. So, it's very difficult terrain.

JMD: Heidi, can you say something about how you discipline yourself and start writing? Where and how do you start?

HSM: I learned a technique from my supervisor when I was doing my Ph.D. The typical scenario would be me appearing in his room, with tears in my eyes, saying, 'I haven't done it' and 'it's not good enough' and 'you don't want to see it really because . . .'. And he would snatch my scraps of paper out of my hand and say, 'give it to me, let me read it anyway', which broke down my perfectionist barrier. He used to give me headings, almost like essay questions. They were in effect chapter headings and he'd say, 'go away and give me a short 5000 words, or 3000 words on this title'. It broke it down and it became doable psychologically.

I do workshops with my students who are about to embark on their Masters dissertations, or their Ph.D.s and I use a version of his method. I tell them to choose a title, a sexy, racy title, for what they are doing. I tell them to visualise it on the bookshelf, so it's tangible and fun, and give it a cover. Then think of the chapter headings and the whole big project begins to get its form.

Then we make each chapter into an essay question. So it has a bottom and a top and sides, and it really works. It's the same if you're on a research project and you've got lots of data and analysis to do. You need to ask yourself three good research questions that can frame the writing.

It's all about taking one step at a time. You break down huge chunks that seem insurmountable into small, little essays, so in the end, each chapter for your report is 5000 words. If you've got five chapters that's five 5000-word short essays. You tell yourself you can manage that! It's even better when you're doing a dissertation or a Ph.D. or a book, because each essay is on the same topic so it's easier than having five essays on five different courses in a semester.

So it's a great technique, it's what I call 'baby steps'. Don't think about an insurmountable, huge piece of work of 80,000 words!

JMD: Well that's a very good tip.

HSM: It's great to have the opportunity to reflect on my writing with you. This isn't something we often get a chance to do. Recently I got very ill, with breast cancer, and I guess for the first time I was aware of my own mortality and one of the things that gave me some solace was that whatever happens, when you write it's permanent. You leave it behind, it's something so powerful.

There are strong oral traditions in the Caribbean and among the First Nation people of America and Australia, and in African and Asian cultures too. I grew up in the Indo-Caribbean community and I've heard stories about my grandmother and stories about the history of our family which have been passed down from generation to generation, but we never write about it. I'm one of the first to write anything about that experience and I realise how powerful it is. The oral tradition is so important to our cultures but writing it down leaves a different kind of mark which is valued in Western societies.

I do often reflect on the power of writing and the power of 'voice'. It embeds you culturally and politically in other spaces. Because of *Young, Female and Black* people can say well, yes, I know what it's like to be a young black British woman growing up in a school in South London. That's an important experience that white researchers might not know about or have access to, and it's important to tell that story. I think it is really important to tell our stories. It's a way of bringing the oral tradition into the academic writing.

JMD: Heidi, it seems to me, based on what you've said, that writing is a discovery, an ongoing learning process. It's never perfect.

HSM: Exactly, and it's both petrifying and pleasing! I think the one thing that I've learned, it's all about staying power. You need to see that project through, you need to get that Ph.D. done. Somebody told me once there are people who are finishers and then there are non-finishers. A finisher has to finish it because it gets under their skin and bugs them for the rest of their life. Non-finishers can move on with no regrets. So you have to decide which one you are if you are taking on the challenge of coming into writing.

JMD: Have you ever had a coach or mentor, writing mentor or anyone like that?

HSM: Your supervisor for the Ph.D. is the nearest really.

JMD: But when you're writing as sole author, how and when do you seek the support of others?

HSM: I have a select group of feminist and critical friends and I send something to them and say, what do you think of this? But I usually do that after I've honed it quite a lot, I don't do it early on. I tend to feel very nervous about sending it out too early, I've still got that perfectionist streak in me. I really want to control it for a bit longer; I don't want too much feedback too early.

I want to actually have it all down and then incorporate the ideas of others, but I do find criticism difficult, even if it's friendly criticism, especially after working so hard on something. And when I say working hard, I mean four or five drafts later, it's a lot of drafts! So, it becomes very precious to you and you don't want to let it go and when you have someone saying 'have you thought of this, or have you thought of that?' you get protective.

I think the whole writing process is one of control, you're controlling the words, you're controlling the ideas, and it is hard to let it go, especially if you're on a team.

JMD: Do you have any final thoughts?

HSM: Everyone can learn to write. I was not good at it at school. I taught myself how to write by looking at other's examples. When I did my Ph.D. I went to the library and I read everyone's Ph.D.s around my subject. I found out which was a good one and which was a bad one. During the Civil Rights in the 1960s they had a literacy programme called 'Learning by Doing'. In order to increase voter registration the black activists would roll out literacy classes and people who learned to write, to read, would then teach others.

JMD: Like an apprenticeship, perhaps?

HSM: Yes, it's like an apprenticeship. I know it's an old-fashioned notion. My Dad did this in Trinidad in the 1940's. He learned from a more senior person in the community and then he'd become the teacher, and would teach the younger ones. So I share that same heritage. If I read someone else's work, and I'm inspired – I would try to identify what made it 'inspiring' and try to use that style in my own writing.

We need to learn from others. I've done it organically, not consciously. It's been a brilliant journey.

JMD: Heidi, Thank you for letting us hear your Desert Island Discs!

HSM: [*laughs*] Thank *you*!

Notes

Introduction: The intersectionality of race and gender in education

1 In this book 'black women' is a collective political term that embraces postcolonial 'women of colour' living in Britain who share similar racialised marginal locations. The concept of 'black' as a multiracial signifier emerged in Britain in the 1960s and was seen as a strategic political term embracing African, Caribbean and South Asian peoples living in postcolonial Britain. When specific ethnic, racial or religious groups are discussed in the book, such as African Caribbean, South Asian or Muslim women, they will be identified and highlighted in terms of their ethnicised difference. I use the term 'ethnicised women' in preference to the official and much-contested term 'black and minority ethnic women' as *being or becoming* 'ethnicised' brings into play the power relations that inform and structure the gaze of the 'other'. Women deemed as 'the other' are often 'ethnicised' or typified by the media and state agencies in terms of their perceived (backward) cultural and religious practices. While 'black and minority ethnic women' denotes the social construction of difference through visible racial (black) and cultural (ethnic) markers, it does not emphasise the *process* of racial objectification and it does not emphasise the ways in which racism is increasingly being framed in terms of visible faith-based difference since the (Muslim) terrorist attacks of 9/11. However, in chapters written for a policy audience, such as Chapters 5 and 6, this popular and widely accepted term in the UK may be used (for definitions see Bhavnani *et al.* 2005).

2 Now a special edition of the journal *Race Education and Ethnicity: Black Feminism and Post Colonial Paradigms: Researching Educational Inequalities*, March 2009 (forthcoming), edited by Heidi Safia Mirza and Cynthia Joseph.

3 According to emerging analysis of the 2006/2007 HESA staff return data it is estimated that there are 15 black female professors and 80 Asian female professors in the UK. There are 14,305 professors in Britain – 2,595 are white women and 10,705 are white men, 55 are black men and 545 are Asian men. There are 55 women and 255 men categorised as 'other' which includes mixed race. I thank HESA information service for permission to reproduce these figures (pressoffice@hesa.ac.uk) (please see HESA for definitions of staff ethnic categories). See statistics from the Higher Education Statistical agency (HESA) quoted in *The Times Higher Educational Supplement* (THES) (2004), 'Black in Ivory Towers' (22 October).

4 See Patel (2008) for a summary of Crenshaw's seminal presentation on intersectionality at the World Conference Against Racism 2001; for an additional discussion on intersectionality see Brah and Phoenix (2004); Phoenix and Pattynama (2006); Prins (2006); McCall (2005); Symington (2004).

5 The MDG 3 is concerned with gender equality and the empowerment of women. The target is to eliminate gender disparity in primary and secondary education preferably by 2005 and to all levels of education by 2015. When this target was reviewed in 2005, 49 out of 149 countries had not achieved it (Unterhalter 2007: 15).

6 The new equality legislation is discussed in Chapter 5. See also Equalities and Human Rights Commission at www.equalityhumanrights.com.

7 For a summary of black British feminism see Mirza 2007.

I Young female and black

1 Source: Mirza, H.S. (1995) 'The Schooling of Young black Women'. In S. Tomlinson and M. Craft (eds) *Ethnic Relations and Schooling: Policy and Practice*. London: Athlone Press. Reproduced by kind permission of Continuum International Publishing Group. This chapter draws on research published in Mirza, H.S. (1992) *Young, Female and Black*. London: Routledge.

2 See Cross *et al.* 1990; Drew *et al.* 1992; Mirza 1992; Skellington 1992; *Employment Gazette* 1993; Jones 1993. See also Chapter 2, this volume.

3 Research on black girls in schools during the 1980s can be loosely categorised on the one hand into feminist studies (Fuller 1982; Phizacklea 1982; Dex 1983; Griffin 1985; Riley 1985; Weis 1985; Sharpe 1987 (1976); Wright 1986; Wulff 1988; Coultas 1989; Reid 1989) and, on the other, into the 'male' tradition of liberal race relations and education research (Driver 1980; Rutter *et al.* 1982; Verma and Ashworth 1985; Eggleston *et al.* 1986; Mac an Ghaill 1988; Gillborn 1990).

4 For a more detailed description of methodology and findings see my book *Young Female and Black* (1992).

5 See Fryer 1984; Gilroy 1987; Solomos 1993.

6 In addition, 30 young women from a school in Trinidad (aged 16 to 18 years) and 16 young women from youth clubs and community centres in South London (aged 18+) participated in semi-structured interviews concerning their career choices and attitudes to marriage and relationships.

7 See e.g. Hall and Jefferson 1976; McRobbie and Garber 1975; Willis 1977; Brake 1985; Lees 1986; Brown 1987; Wallace 1987; McRobbie 1990.

8 Teachers provide easy targets, offering tangible and powerful evidence against themselves. It is not suprising, therefore, that they are assumed by many social commentators to be the central link in the transmission of social and racial inequality (Wright 1987; Gillborn 1990; Mac an Ghaill 1988). However, as Foster (1991) points out, this is a tentative link founded upon the inherent methodological shortcomings of ethnography which are highly interpretive and speculative. Foster's perspective has aroused a great deal of controversy, the response to which may be found in Wright 1990; Troyna 1991; Hammersley 1992; Gillborn and Drew 1992, 1993; Hammersley and Gomm 1993.

9 Dex 1982; Rutter *et al.* 1982; Eggleston *et al.* 1986; Cross *et al.* 1990; Drew *et al.* 1992; *Employment Gazette* 1993.

10 The media have taken a particular interest in the subject of the 'black superwoman' ('Flying Colours', *Guardian*, 12 June 1991; 'Black Men: Losers in a One-sided Sexcess Story', *Voice*, 18 June 1991; 'Sisters are Doing it for Themselves', *The Times*, 31 March 1992; 'Race Relationships', *Sunday Times*, 24 May 1992). Offering a sensational interpretation of the 1991 Labour Force statistics (*Employment Gazette* 1993), these newspapers mischievously suggest that black women are more successful than their male counterparts. But as I have argued (*Guardian*, 12 May 1992), black women are not more successful than

black men. This is a divisive representation of a simple fact: black men are locked into racially limited areas of the labour market, where there is less opportunity for educational mobility than in those open to black women.

11 Wilson's (1987) study of the black conditions in America is just such an example of this cultural redirection. He argues that public policy initiatives aimed at stemming the tide of the growing black 'underclass' should be directed towards displacing the female-headed household by restoring the economically successful, self-assured, black male breadwinner.

12 See Moynihan 1967; Murray 1984, 1990; Wilson 1987.

13 Eggleston *et al.* (1986: 95) show that African Caribbean boys are least likely of all ethnic and white groups to want their wives to stay at home upon having a child. Similarly research in the USA has shown that black husbands have a 'permissive' attitude to their wives working (Landry and Jendrek 1978).

14 The majority of Britain's ethnic minorities live in the large urban conurbations. Forty-two per cent of all ethnic minorities live in the London and Greater London area alone; 63 per cent of African Caribbeans live in the London area with 30 per cent in the West Midlands Region and Metropolitan County (Jones 1993).

2 Mapping race, class and gender

1 This chapter is based on edited extracts from Gillborn, D and Mirza H.S (2000) *Mapping Race, Class and Gender: A Synthesis of Research Evidence* (HMI 232). London: OFSTED. www.ofsted.gov.uk. Reproduced by kind permission of OFSTED and Office for Public Sector Information (PSI) HMSO. This is a jointly authored report and I acknowledge the generosity and scholarship of my colleague David Gillborn who kindly agreed for me to publish this edited extract.

2 The Stephen Lawrence Inquiry (referred to as the Macpherson Report (Macpherson 1999)), made 70 recommendations overall, four with specific reference to education: 67: Recommended amendment of the National Curriculum to value diversity, prevent racism and 'better reflect the needs of a diverse society'; 68: The duty of LEAs and school Governors to develop strategies to prevent and address racism in schools; 69: required OFSTED inspections to examine the implementation of these strategies; 70: Called for community and local initiatives to promote cultural diversity and address racism. These recommendations were broadly accepted in the Home Secretary's action plan, published in response to the Inquiry (Home Office 1999).

3 The scheme was renamed the Ethnic Minority and Travellers' Achievement Grant (EMTAG).

4 Education Provision for Gypsy and Traveller Children, ref. 4RP/200/98, DfEE.

5 For a discussion of the demographic issues concerned, see Taylor (1987). Demack *et al.* (2000) found that Chinese pupils were the most likely of all ethnic groups to attend independent schools, more than twice as likely to attend as their white peers, more than four times as likely to attend as black pupils, and eight times the rate of Bangladeshi and Pakistani children.

6 There is no universally accepted system of terminology for the social distinctions commonly associated with 'racial' and ethnic meaning. For a discussion of some of the problems see Mason (2000) and Richardson and Wood (1999).

7 The YCS uses large nationally representative samples to question a range of 16- to 19-year-olds. It has the advantage of allowing researchers to examine in detail the different attainments, experiences and viewpoints of young men and women from a variety of ethnic and social class backgrounds. Here our analysis

is concerned with the state education system and so, to avoid unrepresentative comparisons, most of our calculations exclude respondents who attended independent schools.

8 The notion of 'underachievement' has played a particularly significant role in the development of debates around ethnic diversity in British education, especially through the work of the Rampton/Swann Committees in the late 1970s and early 1980s. The label 'underachievement' has been widely used to refer to the differential educational outcomes among racial and ethnic minorities, but the term has a long and contested history. See e.g. Halsey *et al.* (1980), Gillborn (1990) and Foster *et al.* (1996).

9 It is important to remember, of course, that the relationship is far from universal. Although average differences between social classes are clear, there also remains a wide range of achievement within each group.

10 In 1988, five or more higher grade GCSEs were attained by 52 per cent of children from 'managerial/professional' backgrounds and 12 per cent of peers from 'unskilled manual' homes; in 1997, the proportions were 69 per cent and 20 per cent respectively (DfEE 1999b: 9).

11 Not all working-class households qualify for state benefits and so the proportion of FSM pupils in a school is not a good indicator of its overall class composition. In addition, some studies measure FSM take-up (rather than eligibility); such an approach can be misleading where there are cultural differences in the willingness of some communities to take advantage of state benefits. For details on differences between ethnic groups in household income, receipt of benefit and other relevant factors, see Berthoud (1998) and ONS (1996).

12 CRE (1992); Gillborn and Youdell (2000); Hallam and Toutounji (1996); Oakes (1990); Slavin (1996); and Sukhnandan and Lee (1998).

13 Unlike other subjects, maths operates a three-tier system: here pupils in the bottom tier cannot attain a higher grade GCSE (at Grade C or above) no matter how well they perform in the written exam (Gillborn and Youdell 2000).

14 We are grateful to the DfEE and to Sean Demack, David Drew and Mike Grimsley (of Sheffield Hallam University) for making available these previously unpublished analyses.

15 In 1990, 1 per cent more black pupils from a manual background attained the benchmark.

16 Indian pupils from non-manual backgrounds who were sampled in 1990 and 1993 achieved the same rate of success as the previous cohort.

17 Data refer to GCSE/GNVQ achievements of pupils aged 15 and over in England (all schools).

18 For example, girls continue to experience stereotyped advice on their subject option choices (see Gillborn and Youdell 2000) and are sometimes barred from the highest grades because of the tendency for them to be placed in the 'Intermediate Tier' in mathematics examinations (Stobart *et al.* 1992).

19 For the sake of continuity all data in Figure 2.3 are drawn from the same source, i.e. the Youth Cohort Study between 1988 and 1997 (DfEE 1999b: Table B, p. 9).

20 In 1997 the gap between boys and girls attaining five or more higher grade passes was nine percentage points; the black/white gap was 18 percentage points. The difference between managerial/professional and unskilled manual was 49 percentage points.

21 As with the previous analysis for social class and ethnic interactions within the YCS, in order to produce viable sample sizes it was necessary for the researchers to combine the Pakistani and Bangladeshi groups.

22 In 1995 the gender gaps were as follows: Pakistani/Bangladeshi pupils, 9 points; Indian and white pupils, 10 points; black pupils, 11 points.

23 Almost half of the values in Figure 2.8 represent fewer than 30 individual pupils in the original sample.

24 Figures 2.6 and 2.7 are based on data supplied by Sean Demack and his colleagues at Sheffield Hallam University.

25 This pattern held true for boys from manual backgrounds in 1988 and 1995, and for girls from manual and non-manual backgrounds in 1995. The only exception occurred for girls from manual backgrounds in 1988.

26 The research that generated these insights has been funded and conducted by a range of participants, including academic researchers, charitable foundations and statutory bodies such as OFSTED, the DfEE and the Commission for Racial Equality. Useful publications include Blair *et al.* (1998), Gillborn (1995), Osler (1997), OFSTED (1999), Siraj-Blatchford (1994) and Weekes and Wright (1999).

3 Race, gender and IQ

1 Source: Mirza H.S. (1998) 'Race, Gender and IQ: The Social Consequences of a Pseudo-scientific Discourse', *Race Ethnicity and Education* 1(1): 137–158. Reproduced by kind permission of Taylor and Francis http://www.tandf.co.uk/journals. This paper is based on the 1997 Lister Lecture, presented at the British Association for the Advancement of Science, Annual Festival of Science, University of Leeds, 10 September 1997.

2 In the late 1980s Norman Tebbit, a senior Conservative politician, publicly suggested that an appropriate test of Britishness was which national cricket team a person supported.

3 While many, both black and white, have lost their lives in needless racial violence (CRE 1997c), these three cases are well known for the mass mobilisations they evoked. In 1994 Stephen Lawrence, a 17-year-old African Caribbean young man, was stabbed while waiting at a bus-stop by a group of white youths who have never been brought to justice. In 1993 Quddus Ali, a young Bengali man, was chased, brutally beaten and permanently disfigured by a gang of white youths in the East End of London, where racial attacks increased by 300 per cent after the local election of the (fascist) British National Party. In 1993 Joy Gardner, a Jamaican woman staying with her British mother, husband and son, was suffocated to death by the immigration police who manacled her and gagged her while carrying out an order to deport her. They were found 'not guilty'.

4 On 23 February 1997 Dolly the sheep was introduced to the scientific community and press. The public debate that has ensued raises the ethical issue of human cloning (*Observer*, 2 March 1997).

5 Advanced DNA tests on Neanderthal bone by German researchers added to one of the hottest issues in the debate on human evolution (see Kohn 1996). Their findings suggest that modern humans are descendants of a common African ancestor and are not related to Neanderthals (*Guardian*, 11 July 1997).

6 The goal of the Human Genome Project is to draw up a specimen of the entire DNA code for a human being. It originated in 1991 when geneticists came together in an effort to find the clues to the evolution of the human species. Since 1993 the allied Human Genome Diversity Project has concentrated on collecting (and controversially patenting) the DNA from blood samples of indigenous peoples before many of them become 'extinct'. However, the intended subjects of the research do not see it as a benign exercise in demonstrating human unity, instead they see it as one more site of struggle (Kohn 1996).

7 In the mid-1980s the US National Library of Medicine launched a project to digitise and install on the internet two 'normal' corpses of a man and a woman. While documenting the external and internal human body in minute detail and thus fixing it in time and space forever, the disruption of boundaries of the body in cyberspace presents a new site for old anxieties about origin and reproduction (McClintock 1997).

4 A genealogy of black British feminism

1 Source: edited extracts from Mirza, H.S (1997) 'Black British Feminism: A Genealogy of the Margins'. In H. Mirza (ed.) Black British Feminism: A Reader. London: Routledge. Reproduced by kind permission of Taylor & Francis (http://www.tandf.co.uk).
2 For historical accounts of black British women see Bousquet and Douglas 1991; Bryan *et al.* 1985; Dodgson 1984; Jarrett-Macauley 1996; Prescod-Roberts and Steele 1980; Visram 1986.
3 So-called virginity testing was a recognised immigration policy; see Brah 1992a: 70; Mama 1992: 88; Parmar 1982: 245.
4 For a discussion on black British youth movements see Gilroy 1987; Keith 1993; Solomos 1988.
5 For a discussion on black feminist organising see Brah 1992b; Lewis and Parmar 1983a; Williams 1993.
6 For a discussion on feminist epistemology see Harding 1992; Weedon 1987; Yeatman 1994.
7 Black feminist writings on these subjects include Bhachu 1988; Brah 1992a; Brah and Minhas 1985; Bryan *et al.* 1985; Carby 1982b; James 1985; Lewis 1990; Lewis and Parmar 1983b; Mama 1989, 1993a, 1993b; Parmar 1982; Parmar and Mirza 1981; Phoenix 1988, 1991; Stone 1985; Wright 1987.
8 For a discussion on anti-racist feminism see Bourne 1983; Knowles and Mercer 1992; Tang Nain 1991.
9 For black women's literature see Boyce 1994; Burford *et al.* 1985; Cobham and Collins 1987; Nasta 1991; Ngcobo 1988; *Wasafiri* 1993.
10 For black women visual art and film see Boyce and Diawara 1996; Fusco 1995; Parmar 1990; Rasheed 1989; Sutler 1990; Tawadros 1996; *Ten.8* 1992; Ugwu 1995; Young 1996.
11 Barrett 1987; Brah 1992b; Maynard 1994; Scott 1990; Williams 1996.

5 Intersectionality and the marginal black woman

1 Source: edited from H. Mirza (2008) 'Ethnic Minority Women: A Prospectus for the Future' in Z. Moosa (ed.) *Seeing Double: Ethnic Minority Women's Lives.* London: Fawcett Society. Reproduced by kind permission of the Fawcett Society.
2 I use the term 'ethnicised women' in conjunction with the official policy and much-contested collective term 'Black and minority ethnic women' (Bhavnani *et al.* 2005). While the latter term denotes the social construction of difference through visible racial (black) and cultural (ethnic) markers, it does not empha-sise the *process* of racial objectification implied by the former term. Thus *being or becoming* 'ethnicised' brings into play the power relations that inform and structure the gaze of the 'other' which frames the women's experience.
3 See Brah and Phoenix 2004; Crenshaw 1991; Patel 2008; Phoenix and Pattynama 2006.
4 *Telegraph*, 17 November 2001; *Guardian*, 20 November 2001.
5 Brah 1996; Collins 1998; Mirza 1997b.

6 Blair 2006; Brown 2006.
7 See e.g. Women's National Commission Report 2006. There are also many new initiatives from the Department of Communities and Local Government with regard to black and minority ethnic women such as *Engaging with Muslim Women and Social Enterprise for Black and Minority Ethnic Women* (2006) http://www.womenandequalityunit.gov.uk/equality/min_eth.htm.

6 Multiculturalism and the gender trap

1 This chapter is based on edited extracts from Mirza, H.S. (2007) 'Multi-culturalism and the Gender Trap: Young Ethnicised Women and Domestic Violence in School', *Educational Review: Valuing Identity and Diversity* 20(2): 46–56. Reproduced by kind permission of the National Union of Teachers (NUT) and the Education Publishing Company Limited. This study has been developed from research with Veena Meetoo. I wish to acknowledge her scholarship and input into the material reported here.
2 I use the term 'ethnicised women' in preference to the official and much contested term 'Black and minority ethnic women'. While the latter term denotes the social construction of difference through visible racial (black) and cultural (ethnic) markers, it does not emphasize the *process* of racial objectification implied by the former term which frames the women's experience. Thus *being or becoming* 'ethnicised' brings into play the power relations that inform and structure the gaze of the 'other'. Despite women's agency and activism, women deemed as 'the other' are often 'ethnicised' or typified by the media and state agencies in terms of their perceived (backward) cultural and religious practices (see Bhavnani *et al.* 2005).
3 Culture is invoked only when defendants come from a racialised minority group and the crime is attributed to culture only when people from that culture seem to be lagging behind. This then leads to representations of culture that can then justify the ill-treatment of women (Phillips 2003).
4 *Boston Globe* (2006) *'For Muslim Women, A Deadly Defiance: 'Honor Killings' on Rise in Europe*. Colin Nickerson, 16 January. At http://www.boston.com/news/world/europe/articles/2006/01/16/for_muslim_women_a_deadly_defiance/?page=1 (accessed 26 July 2007).
5 Ibid.
6 FCO 2000.
7 FCO 2006.
8 *Guardian*, 'It's a Family Affair', Patrick Weir, 23 January 2002.
9 In the context of the bombings on 9/11 and 7/7 and there has been a marked media interest in anti-Muslim stories – particularly ones that focus on women. However, highlighting their plight is not an innocent act aimed at promoting their well-being and can be explained in terms of the rise of Islamophobia in the West. For an extended discussion of this phenomenon and other issues raised in this paper see Meetoo and Mirza 2007a.
10 Cultural change for migrant groups however is for the most part dynamic and reflexive and underscored by hybridity and creativity. This is particularly so with the women who renegotiate and reappropriate their traditional cultural markers, such as the wearing of the veil, making it transgressive rather than oppressive (Dwyer 1999).
11 There was a huge media debate on Muslim women that has run for several months. See Madeleine Bunting (2006) 'Straw's Storm of Prejudice'. *Guardian Unlimited Weekly*, 13 October.
12 http://www.everychildmatters.gov.uk/aims/ (accessed 23 January 2007).

13 *Guardian*, 'Special Units to Crack Down on Hounour Killings', Karen McVeigh, 16 June 2007.
14 BBC News, '*Battle to Stamp out Forced Marriage*', Barnie Choudhury, 26 January 2007. At http://news.bbc.co.uk/2/hi/uk_news/6303653.stm.
15 See FCO 2005a.
16 Amnesty International 2006.
17 BBC News, '*Battle to Stamp out Forced Marriage*', Barnie Choudhury, 26 January 2007. At http://news.bbc.co.uk/2/hi/uk_news/6303653.stm.
18 FCO 2005b; see also *Spectrum*, the DfES publication catalogue of news and issues for teachers. There are other publications dealing with child abuse and other 'culturally' sensitive issues of child abuse such as spirit possession. For these see http://publications.teachernet.gov.uk/.
19 Since the 1980s, the Organisation of Women of African and Asian Descent (OWAAD), SBS, Newham Asian Women's Project (NAWP), Refugee Women's Organisation (RWO), Women Living Under Muslim Laws (WLUML) and Women Against Fundamentalism (WAF), to name a few, have contributed to placing minority ethnic women's issues on the agenda.
20 Held by CIMEL and Interights (2001). It was recommended that it is important to raise honour crimes as a human rights violation before as many UN human rights bodies as possible such as the Human Rights Committee, Committee on the Elimination of Racial Discrimination, Committee on Economic, Social and Cultural Rights, Committee Against Torture, and Committee on the Rights of the Child.

7 Black women and real citizenship

1 Source: edited extracts from Mirza, H.S and Reay, D. (2000) 'Redefining Citizenship: Black Women Educators and the Third Space'. In M. Arnot and J-A. Dillabough (eds) *Challenging Democracy: International Perspectives on Gender Education and Citizenship*. London: Routledge/Falmer. Reproduced by kind permission of Taylor & Francis (http://www.tandf.co.uk). I would like to acknowledge the collaboration, generosity and shared scholarship with Diane Reay who co-authored this chapter.
2 This research was made possible only by the kind and open participation of the black women interviewed. Their names, and the names of the schools, have been changed.

8 (In)visible black women in higher education

1 Source: Mirza, H.S. (2006) 'The In/visible Journey: Black Women's Life-long Lessons in Higher Education'. In C. Leathwood and B. Francis (eds), *Gender and Life Long Learning: Critical Feminist Engagements*. London: Routledge/Falmer. Reproduced by kind permission of Taylor & Francis (http://www.tandf.co.uk).
2 The BBC was called 'hideously white' by Greg Dyke, the Director General of the BBC in 2001 for being 98 per cent white; with fewer than 1.3 per cent of black and minority ethnic staff in higher education in the UK (Carter *et al.* 1999; THES 2004) it too may be called hideously white.
3 This is compared to 31 per cent of young white women and 28 per cent of young white men aged 18 to 19 in full-time undergraduate degree courses (NAO 2002: 6).
4 Phoenix (1996) suggests that research on black women and mothering is characterised by the 'normative absence/pathological presence' couplet. Black

women are absent from studies on 'normative mothering' but are constructed as deviant others (i.e. single mothers, teenage pregnancy) when they do appear.

5 This paper is a reworking of a keynote address given at Trinity College, Dublin, 12 May 2004 for the symposium entitled 'Reshaping the Intellectual Landscape: Women in the Academe', to celebrate a century since women's admission to the college in 1904.

6 For another image of Cornelia Sorabji see the National Portrait Gallery website at http://www.npg.org.uk/live/search/person.asp?LinkID=mp61443.

7 I was a commissioner on the Mayor's Commission for African and Asian Heritage (MACCH) from 2003 to 2005. During this time we took evidence as to the 'forgotten' contribution of minority communities to the historical wealth of Great Britain and the institutional and organisational shortcomings in recognising and displaying this contribution (GLA 2005).

8 In the UK we have a distinction of 'old' and 'new' universities – old are the established traditional elite 'sandstone' and 'redbrick' research-based universities such as Oxford and Cambridge. The new universities are sometimes referred to as the 'post-1992' universities when polytechnics and HE colleges merged and gained university status in a new rationalising and expansion of HE.

9 However, only 7 per cent of Pakistani and Bangladeshi origin women have further and higher educational qualifications (Dale *et al.* 2002).

9 Race, gender and educational desire

1 Source: Mirza, H.S. (2006) 'Race, Gender and Educational Desire', *Race, Ethnicity and Education* 9(2): 137–158. Reproduced by kind permission of Taylor & Francis (http://www.tandf.co.uk/journals).

2 This is an edited transcript of my Inaugural Professorial Lecture 'Race, Gender and Educational Desire' delivered at Middlesex University, 17 May 2005.

3 For accounts of Ella Baker see Branch (1988) and Eyerman & Jamison (1991).

4 For information on the work of women like Lilian Cingo and Lynette Coetzee who manage the 'Phelophepa Health Care Train' also called the 'Train of Hope' or 'Miracle Train' see 'Into Africa', *Guardian*, 18 March 2003; see also the film *Act of Faith* (http://www.bullfrogfilms.com/catalog/lsact.html); or visit http://www.mhc.org.za/news/transnet_foundation.htm

5 For an analysis of the philosophy of 'back to basics' in British social policy see Jordan (1995).

6 In 1948 the ship *Empire Windrush* brought the first Caribbean migrants to work and live in Britain. Their arrival represented a significant multicultural challenge for British society, especially in terms of highlighting the inherent racism that characterised British national identity. See Phillips & Phillips (1999).

7 In the 1970s this was a pioneering interdisciplinary degree specialising in what was then called 'Third World development' focusing on agriculture, economics, cultural and social issues. It is still a thriving course today.

8 *The Sunday Times Magazine* (2004) 'Dynamite Misses', Lesley White, 10 October; the term 'Dynamite Misses' refers to young black women who are strong, independent and career minded, like the black British female rap singer Miss Dynamite.

9 Theories of black female success in education have emphasised either matriarchal social structures (see Fuller 1982), or subcultural resistance (see Mac an Ghaill 1988).

10 Although ethnic minorities show higher rates of HE participation, these statistics mask enormous variations between minority groups and the disadvantages they face getting into different types of universities and subjects. There are also

significant differences in how they progress in their degree and on from there into the labour market. For a detailed analysis see Connor *et al.* (2004); *Guardian* (2004) 'Mixed Messages', Tariq Modood and Helen Connor, 13 July.

11 As a proportion of the average 18- to 19-year-old population we find 59 per cent of young black women going to university to do a full-time undergraduate degree, as are 48 per cent of young black men. This compares to 31 per cent of young white women and 28 percent of young white men aged 18 to 19 (NAO 2002: 6).

12 For references on the policy of widening participation in higher education see Callender (2002); Connor (2001); DfES (2003a); NAO (2002); Thomas (2001).

13 Stephen Lawrence was a 17-year-old African Caribbean young man who was stabbed at a bus-stop by a gang of racist youths in 1993. Due to police racism his killers were never convicted, but the mass public mobilisation led by his parents and subsequent police inquiry and anti-racist legislation mark a watershed in race relations in Britain (see Home Office 1999).

14 *Guardian* (2005) 'The Boundaries of Race in Britain Today', Gary Younge, 25 April.

15 Roy Jenkins, Labour Home Secretary, speech to the National Committee for Commonwealth Immigrants, 23 May 1966 (quoted in Runnymede Trust 2000).

16 From November 2005 prospective British citizens have to take and pass a compulsory test in English language proficiency and British civic knowledge before being granted a passport and the right to vote. These tests are controversial as they are seen as a way of excluding certain people from British citizenship. See *Guardian* (2003) 'Immigrant Citizenship Classes Planned', Sarah Left, 3 September (and related articles); see also http://news.bbc.co.uk/1/hi/uk_politics/4391710.stm.

17 In the late 1980s Norman Tebbit, a senior conservative politician, publicly suggested that an appropriate test of Britishness was to ask young British Asians which cricket team they supported. If they supported visiting Pakistani or Indian teams their allegiance to Britain was questionable. This measure of multicultural identity has come to be known as the 'cricket test' (see Brah 1996: 195).

18 *Guardian* (2004) 'The Golden Thread that Runs Through our History', Gordon Brown, 8 July.

19 These newspaper cuttings are from the Runnymede Collection, an archive charting 40 years of the struggle for a multicultural Britain. See www.mdx.ac.uk/www/runnymedecollection) *Financial Times* (21 October 70) 'Drowned by Coloured Immigrants'; *Evening News* (21 March 78) 'Stem the Tide of Migrants'; *Guardian* (1 February 79) 'Virginity Tests on Immigrants at Heathrow'; *Mail on Sunday* (12 May 02) 'Swamped'; *Sunday Telegraph* (25 July 02) 'Wave of Migrants Descends'.

20 For accounts of racist attacks see http://www.wsws.org/articles/2001/may2001/glas-m25.shtml; http://www.ncrm.org.uk/deaths/; http://www.muslimnews.co.uk/paper/index.php?article=423.

21 This pamphlet has been reappraised 35 years on in a new collection of essays; see Richardson (2005).

22 For archives documenting the civil rights struggle for a multiracial Britain see Runnymede Collection at Middlesex University (www.mdx.ac.uk/www/runnymedecollection) and The George Padmore Institute Archives (http://www.georgepadmoreinstitute.org/archive.asp).

23 For statistics and analysis of the high rate of black and minority ethnic pupils excluded from school in the UK, see DfES (2004) and Wright *et al.* (2005).

24 Roy Jenkins' speech to the National Committee for Commonwealth Immigrants, 23 May 1966 (quoted in Runnymede Trust 2000).

25 *Guardian* (2004) 'Multiculturalism is Dead', Anthony Andrews, 8 April; more recently Trevor Phillips has also claimed, 'Britain is Sleepwalking into Segregation', (22 September 2005, Manchester Town Hall). For full text of the speech see http://www.cre.gov.uk/ A critique of this may be found at http://www.esrc.ac.uk/ESRCInfoCentre/about/CI/CP/Our_Society_Today/News _Articles_2005/segregation.aspx.

26 *Guardian* (2003) 'The Dirty D-word', Kenan Malik, 29 October.

27 In 2007 the existing anti-discrimination bodies for gender, 'race' and disability comes under one overarching single Commission for Equality and Human Rights which will also support new rights on religion and belief, age, sexual orientation and human rights; see DTi (2004); Home Office (2005).

28 See DfES (2005) for a statistical breakdown of pupil assessment across the National Curriculum. It is very detailed by subject, gender, age and social class, but the general breakdown of the main groups of ethnic minority pupils gaining five or more grade A*-C at GCSE or equivalent is: Chinese 74.2%; Indian 66.6%; White 52.3%; Bangladeshi 48.4%; Pakistani 45.2%; African 43.3%; African Caribbean 35.7% (visually represented here in Figure 9.1).

29 The General Certificate of Secondary Education (GCSE) is a national academic qualification taken at the end of compulsory schooling when pupils are aged 15 to 16. Grades are awarded from A* -G with A* being the highest. As pass grades are from A* -C gaining five or more passes at A*- C is used as a benchmark for evaluating educational attainment.

30 Trevor Phillips is Head of the Commission for Racial Equality. For his statement see 'Black Boys Separate Classes Idea', Monday, 7 March 2005 (http://news. bbc.co.uk/1/hi/education/4323979.stm).

31 See 'Minority Ethnic Pupils Make Further Progress at GCSE', 24 February 2005 (www.dfes.gov.uk/pns/display). See also 'Two Ethnic Groups Narrow Exams Gap', *Guardian*, Mathew Taylor, 2 February 2005 (www.guardian.co.uk/).

32 For texts on 'race', education and what it is to be 'human' see Fordham (1996) and Casey (1993).

33 *Guardian* (2001) 'The Quiet Riot', Helen Carter, 12 July.

10 Writing about race and gender

1 Source: This interview is an edited version of an original interview which appears as extracts in Carnell, E., Macdonald, J., Callum, B. and Scott, M. (2008) *Passion and Politics: Academics on Becoming a Published Writer*. London: Institute of Education, University of London. Reproduced by kind permission of the authors and publishers, Insitute of Education, University of London. This interview was conducted on 25 May 2006.

2 Jacqui MacDonald is Head of Staff Development at the Institute of Education, University of London. She is a trained mentor and coach and a Justice of the Peace in the Magistrate Courts in London. She is a qualified trainer for the personal and professional programme for women 'Springboard', and a Fellow of the Higher Education Academy. Publications include *Portraits of Black Achievement: Composing Successful Careers* (2000).

3 Mirza (1992).

4 Mirza (1997b).

5 Gillborn and Mirza (2000).

6 Reay and Mirza (1997).

7 Scottish Council for Research in Education (SCRE) see Powney *et al.* (2003).

8 British Association for the Advancement of Science (BA). Mirza (1998).

9 Mirza (2005); see also www.mdx.ac.uk/hssc/research/cres.htm.

10 Fanon (1986, 1990).
11 The RAE is the Research Assessment Exercise. It is an intense bureaucratic process of data gathering which involves the collating of academic outputs of individuals in higher education for funding and prestige purposes. It is undertaken every six years and research-active academics must submit, among other things, four pieces of good-quality, high-impact, peer-reviewed published work for scrutiny.
12 The Association for Teachers of Social Science.
13 Bhavnani *et al.* (2005).
14 Williams P. J. (1997).
15 hooks (1994).

Bibliography

Abdelrazack, M. and Kempadoo, M. (eds) (1999) *Directory of Supplementary and Mother-tongue Classes 1999–2000*. Resource Unit for Supplementary and Mother-Tongue Schools, Department for Education and Employment, School Inclusion Division.

Ahmad, F. (2003) 'Still in Progress? Methodological Dilemmas, Tensions and Contradicitions in Theorizing South Asian Muslim Women'. In N. Puwar and P. Raghuram (eds) *South Asian Women in the Diaspora*. Oxford: Berg.

Ahmed, S. (1997) ' "It's a Sun Tan, Isn't It?" Auto-biography as an Identificatory Practice'. In H.S. Mirza (ed.) *Black British Feminism; A Reader*. London: Routledge.

—— (2000) *Strange Encounters: Embodied others in Post-coloniality*. London: Taylor and Francis.

—— (2004) *The Cultural Politics of Emotions*. Edinburgh: Edinburgh University Press.

—— (2005) 'The Non-performativity of Anti-racism'. Paper presented at SUNY New York, 6 April.

Ainley, P. (1988) *From School to YTS: Education and Training in England and Wales 1944–1987*. Milton Keynes: Open University Press.

Alba, R.D. (ed.) (1985) *Ethnicity and Race in the U.S.A: Toward the Twenty-first Century*. London: Routledge & Kegan Paul.

Allen, S. (1987) 'Gender, Race, and Class in the 1980s'. In C. Husband (ed.) *Race in Britain, Continuity and Change: The Second Edition*. London: Hutchinson.

Amnesty International (2006) Honour Killings Conference, London. Paper presented by Jasvinder Sanghera from Karma Nirvana, 'Honour Abuse: The Victims' Story'.

Amos, V. and Parmar, P. (1981) 'Resistances and Responses: Experiences of Black Girls in Britain'. In A. McRobbie and T. McCabe (eds) *Feminism for Girls: An Adventure Story*. London: Routledge & Kegan Paul.

—— (1984) 'Challenging Imperial Feminism', *Feminist Review* Special Issue, 'Many Voices one Chant', 17 (July): 3–19.

Ang-Lygate, M. (1997) 'Charting the Spaces of (Un)Location: On Theorising Diaspora'. In H.S. Mirza (ed.) *Black British Feminism; A Reader*. London: Routledge.

Anthias, F. and Yuval-Davis, N. (1992) *Racialised Boundaries: Race, Gender, Colour and the Anti-racist Struggle*. London: Routledge.

Appiah, K. W. and Gates, H. L. (1995) 'Editors' Introduction: Multiplying Identities'. In K. W. Appiah and H. L. Gates (eds) *Identities*. Chicago, IL: The University of Chicago Press.

Arnot, M. David, M. and Weiner, G. (1996) *Educational Reforms and Gender Equality in Schools*. Manchester: Equal Opportunities Commission.

Arnot, M., Gray, J., James, M., Rudduck, J. with Duveen, G. (1998) *Recent Research on Gender and Educational Performance*. London: The Stationery Office (HMSO).

Aziz, R. (1992) 'Feminism and The Challenge of Racism: Deviance or Difference?' In H. Crowley and S. Himmelweit (eds) *Knowing Women: Feminism and Knowledge*. Cambridge: Polity Press/Blackwell/Open University.

Back, L. (2004) 'Ivory Towers? The Academy and Racism'. In I. Law, D. Phillips and L. Turney (eds) *Institutional Racism in Higher Education*. Stoke on Trent: Trentham Books.

Bakare-Yusuf, B. (1997) 'Raregrooves and Raregroovers: A Matter of Taste, Difference and Identity'. In H.S. Mirza (ed.) *Black British Feminism; A Reader*. London: Routledge.

Bar On, B. (1993) 'Marginality and Epistemic Privilege'. In L. Alcoff and E. Potter (eds) *Feminist Epistomologies*. London: Routledge.

Barrett, M. (1987) 'The Concept of 'Difference', *Feminist Review* 26 (July): 29–41.

Barrett, M. and McIntosh, M. (1982) *The Anti-social Family*. London: Verso.

—— (1985) 'Ethnocentrism and Socialist Feminist Theory', *Feminist Review* 20 (June): 23–47.

Barrett, M. and Phillips, A. (1992) 'Introduction'. In M. Barrett and A. Phillips (eds) *Destabilising Theory: Contemporary Feminist Debates*. Cambridge: Polity Press.

Barrow, C. (1986) 'Finding Support: Strategies for Survival.' *Social and Economic Studies*, Special Number: J. Massiah (ed.) 'Women in the Caribbean' (Part 1): Institute of Social and Economic Research, University of the West Indies, Vol. 35, No. 2.

Beck, U. (1992) *Risk Society*. London: Sage.

Beckett, C. and Macey, M. (2001) 'Race, Gender and Sexuality: The Oppression of Multiculturalism', *Women's Studies International Forum* 24(3/4): 309–319.

Begum, N. (1992) 'Disabled Women and the Feminist Agenda'. In H. Hinds, A. Phoenix and J. Stacey (eds) *Working Out: New Directions for Women's Studies*. London: Falmer Press.

Berthoud, R. (1998) *The Incomes of Ethnic Minorities*. ISER Report 98-1. Colchester: University of Essex, Institute for Social and Economic Research.

Besson, J. (1993) 'Reputation and Respectability Reconsidered: A New Perspective on Afro-Caribbean Peasant Women'. In J.H. Momsen (ed.) *Women and Change in the Caribbean*. London: James Currey.

Bettelheim, B. and Janowitz, M. (1977) 'The Consequences of Social Mobility'. In J. Stone (ed.) *Race, Ethnicity, and Social Change*. North Scituate, MA: Duxbury Press.

Bhabha, H. (1990) (in Interview with Rutherford) 'The Third Space'. In J. Rutherford (ed.) *Identity, Community, Culture, Difference*. London: Lawrence & Wishart.

Bhachu, P. (1988) 'Apni Marzi Kardhi. Home and Work: Sikh Women in Britain'. In S. Westwood and P. Bhachu (eds) *Enterprising Women: Ethnicity, Economy and Gender Relations*. London: Routledge.

Bhattacharyya, G. (1997) 'The Fabulous Adventures of the Mahogany Princesses'. In H.S. Mirza (ed.) *Black British Feminism: A Reader*. London: Routledge.

—— (1998) *Tales of Dark Skinned Women: Race Gender and Global Culture*. London: UCL Press.

Bhatti, G. (1999) *Asian Children at Home and at School: An Ethnographic Study*. London: Routledge.

Bhavnani, K. and Coulson, M. (1986) 'Transforming Socialist Feminism: The Challenge of Racism', *Feminist Review* 23 (June): 81–92.

Bhavnani, R. (1994) *Black Women in the Labour Market: A Research Review*, Research Series. Manchester: Equal Opportunities Commission.

Bhavnani, R., Mirza. H.S. and Meetoo, V. (2005) *Tackling the Roots of Racism: Lessons for Success*. Bristol: Policy Press.

Bhavnani, R. and PTI (2006) *Ahead of the Game: The Changing Aspirations of Young Ethnic Minority Women*. EOC.

Blair, M. and Bourne, J. with Coffin, C., Creese, A. and Kenner, C. (1998) *Making the Difference: Teaching and Learning Strategies in Successful Multi-ethnic Schools*. London: Department for Education & Employment.

Blair, M., Gillborn, D., Kemp, S. and MacDonald, J. (1999) 'Institutional Racism, Education and the Stephen Lawrence Inquiry', *Education and Social Justice* 1(3): 6–15.

Blair, T. (2006) Our Nation's Future: Multiculturalism and Integration (8 December). At http://www.number-10.gov.uk

Blanden, J., Gregg, P. and Machin, S. (2005) *Intergenerational Mobility in Europe and North America*. London: The Sutton Trust.

Bonnett, A. (1996) 'Anti-racism and the Critique of "White" Identities', *New Community* 22(1).

Bonney, N. (1998) 'The Class War Continues', *Sociology* 32(3): 601–605.

Bordo, S. (1990) 'Feminism, Postmodernism, and Gender-sceptism'. In L. Nicholson (ed.) *Feminism/Postmodernism*. London: Routledge.

Botcherby, S. (2006) *Pakistani, Bangladeshi and Black Caribbean Women and Employment Survey: Aspirations and Choices*. EOC.

Bourdieu, P. (1990) *In Other Words: Essays Towards a Reflexive Sociology*. Cambridge: Polity Press.

—— (1993) *Sociology in Question*. London: Sage.

Bourne, J. (1983) 'Towards an Anti-racist Feminism', *Race and Class* 25(1).

—— (1987) 'Homelands of the Mind: Jewish Feminism and Identity Politics', *Race and Class* 29(1): 1–24.

Bousquet, B. and Douglas, C. (1991) *West Indian Women at War*. London: Lawrence & Wishart.

Boyce Davis, C. (1994) *Black Women Writing and Identity: Migrations of the Subject*. London: Routledge.

Boyce, S. and Diawara, M. (1996) 'The Art of Identity: A Conversation'. In H. Baker, M. Diawara and R. Lindborg (eds) *Black British Cultural Studies: A Reader*. Chicago, IL: University of Chicago Press.

Brah, A. (1992a) 'Women of South Asian Origin in Britain: Issues and Concerns'. In P. Braham, A. Rattansi and R. Skellington (eds) *Race and Antiracism: Inequalities, Opportunities and Policies*. London: Sage/Open University Press. (Reproduced from *South Asia Research* 7(1) May 1987.)

—— (1992b) 'Difference, Diversity and Differentiation'. In J. Donald and A. Rattansi (eds) *'Race', Culture and Difference*. London: Sage/Open University Press.

—— (1994) 'Review Essay: Time, Place and Others: Discourses of Race, Nation and Ethnicity', *Sociology* 28(3): 805–813.

—— (1996) *Cartographies of Diaspora: Contesting Identities*. London: Routledge.

Brah, A. and Minhas, R. (1985) 'Structural Racism or Cultural Difference: Schooling for Asian Girls'. In G. Weiner (ed.) *Just a Bunch of Girls*. Milton Keynes: Open University Press.

Brah, A. and Phoenix, A. (2004) 'Ain't I a Woman? Revisiting Intersectionality', *Journal of International Women's Studies* 5(3): 75–86.

Brake, M. (1985) *Comparative Youth Culture: The Sociology of Youth Subcultures in America, Britain and Canada*. London: Routledge.

Branch, T. (1988) *Parting the Waters: Martin Luther King and the Civil Rights Movement 1954–63*. New York: Simon & Schuster.

Brewer, M. R. (1993) 'Theorising Race, Class and Gender: The New Scholarship of Black Feminist Intellectuals and Black Women's Labour'. In S.M. James and A.P. Busia (eds) *Theorizing Black Feminisms: The Visionary Pragmatism of Black Women*. London: Routledge.

Brown, G. (2006) 'The Future of Britishness', Fabian Society (14 January). At http://www.fabiansociety.org.uk/press_office/news_latest_all.asp?pressid=520.

Brown, P. (1987) *Schooling Ordinary Kids: Inequality, Unemployment, and the New Vocationalism*. London: Tavistock.

Bryan, B., Dadzie, S. and Scafe, S. (1985) *The Heart of the Race: Black Women's lives in Britain*. London: Virago Press.

Bunting, M. (2006) 'Straw's Storm of Prejudice', *Guardian Unlimited Weekly*, 13 October.

Burford, B., Pearce G., Nichols G. and Kay, J. (eds) (1985) *A Dangerous Knowing: Four Black Women Poets*. London: Sheba Press.

Burlet, S. and Reid, H. (1998) 'A Gendered Uprising: Political Representation and Minority Ethnic Communities', *Ethnic and Racial Studies* 21(2): 270–287.

Burton, A. (1998) *At the Heart of the Empire: Indians and the Colonial Encounter in Late-Victorian Britain*. Berkeley: University of California Press.

Butler, J. (1990) *Gender Trouble: Feminism and the Subversion of Identity*. New York: Routledge.

Cabinet Office (2001) *Towards Equality and Diversity: Implementing the Employment and Race Directive*. London: Cabinet Office.

Callender, C. (2002) 'The Costs of Widening Participation: Contradictions in New Labour's Student Funding Policies', *Social Policy and Society* 1(2): 83–94.

Carby, H. (1997) 'White women listen! Black feminism and the boundaries of sisterhood'. In H.S Mirza (ed.) *Black British Feminism*. London: Routledge

Carby, H.V. (1982a) 'Schooling in Babylon'. In CCCS *The Empire Strikes Back: Race and Racism in 70s Britain*. London: Hutchinson.

—— (1982b) 'White Woman Listen! Black Feminism and the Boundries of Sisterhood'. In CCCS *The Empire Strikes Back: Race and Racism in 70s Britain*. London: Hutchinson.

Caribbean Quarterly (1986) Special issue: 'East Indians, West Indians', 32 (3 and 4): 1–92.

Carter, J., Fenton, S. and Modood, T. (1999) *Ethnicity and Employment in HE*. London: Policy Studies Institute.

Casey, K. (1993) *I Answer with My Life: Life Histories of Women Teachers Working for Social Change*. New York: Routledge.

Castells, M. (2004) 'Universities and Cities in a World of Global Networks'. Sir Robert Birley Lecture, City University, 17 March. At http://www.city.ac.uk/social/birley2004.html.

(charles), H. (1992) 'Whiteness – The Relevance of Politically Colouring the "Non". In H. Hinds, A Phoenix and J. Stacey (eds) *Working Out: New Directions for Women's Studies*. London: Falmer Press.

—— (1997) 'The Language of Womanism: Rethinking Difference'. In H.S. Mirza (ed.) *Black British Feminism: A Reader*. London: Routledge.

Chevannes, M. (1979) 'The Black Arrow Supplementary School Project', *The Social Science Teacher* 8(4).

Christian, B. (1990) 'But What do We Think We are Doing Anyway: The State of Black Feminist Criticism(s) Or My Version of a Little Bit Of History'. In C.A. Wall (ed.) *Changing Our Own Words: Essays On Criticism, Theory and Writing by Black Women*. London: Routledge.

—— (1994) 'Diminishing Returns: Can Black Feminism(s) Survive the Academy?' In D. T. Goldberg (ed.) *Multiculturalism: A Critical Reader*. Oxford: Blackwell.

—— (1995) 'The Race for Theory'. In B. Ashcroft, G. Griffiths and H. Tiffin (eds) *The Post Colonial Studies Reader*. London: Routledge.

CIMEL/Interights (2001) 'Roundtable on Strategies to Address "Crimes of Honour": Summary Report'. Women Living Under Muslim Laws Occasional Paper 12 November. At http://www.wluml.org/english/pubs/pdf/occpaper/OCP-12.pdf.

Clark, R.M. (1983) *Family Life and School Achievement: Why Poor Black Children Succeed or Fail*. Chicago, IL: University of Chicago Press.

Coard, B. (1971) *How the West Indian Child is Made: ESN in the British School System*. London: New Beacon Books.

Cobham, R. and Collins, M. (eds) (1987) *Watchers and Seekers: Creative Women's Writing by Black Women in Britain*. London: The Women's Press.

Collins, Hill P. (1991) *Black Feminist Thought: Knowledge Consciousness and the Politics of Empowerment*. London: Routledge.

—— (1993) 'Whose Story is it Anyway? Feminist Antiracist Appropriations of Anita Hill'. In T. Morrisson (ed.) *Rac-ing Justice, En-gendering Power: Essays on Anita Hill, Clarence Thomas and the Construction of Social Reality*. London: Chatto & Windus.

—— (1994) 'Shifting the Centre: Race Class and Feminist Theorising about Motherhood'. In D. Bassin, M. Honey and M. Kaplan (eds) *Representations of Motherhood*. New Haven, CT: Yale University Press.

—— (1998) *Fighting Words: Black Women and the Search for Justice*. Minneapolis: University of Minnesota Press.

Compton, R. (1998) *Class and Stratification: An Introduction to Current Debates*. Oxford: Polity Press.

Connolly, P. (1998) *Racism, Gender Identities and Young Children: Social Relations in a Multi-ethnic, Inner-city Primary School*. London: Routledge.

Connor, H. (2001) 'Deciding For or Against Participation in Higher Education: The Views of Young People from Lower Social Class Backgrounds', *Higher Education Quarterly* 55(2): 204–224.

Connor, H., Tyers, C., Modood, T. and Hillage, J. (2004) *Why the Difference? A*

Closer Look at Higher Education Minority Ethnic Students and Graduates. DfES Research Report. At 552www.dfes.gov/research.

Cosslett, T., Lury, C. and Summerfield, P. (eds) (2000) *Feminism and Autobiography: Texts, Theories, Methods*. London and New York: Routledge.

Coultas, V. (1989) 'Black Girls and Self-esteem', *Gender and Education*, Special Issue: Race, Gender and Education 1 (3).

CRE (Commission for Racial Equality) (1992) *Set to Fail? Setting and Banding in Secondary Schools*. London: Commission for Racial Equality.

—— (1997a) *Factsheet: Employment and Unemployment*. London: Commission for Racial Equality.

—— (1997b) *We Regret to Inform You . . .'. Testing for Racial Discrimination in Youth Employment*. London: Commission for Racial Equality.

—— (1997c) *Factsheet: Racial Attacks and Harassment*. London: Commission for Racial Equality.

—— (1997d) *Factsheet: Ethnic Minority Women*. London: Commission for Racial Equality.

Crenshaw, K. (1989) 'Demarginalising the Intersection of Race and Sex: A Black Feminist Critique of Antidiscrimination Doctrine, Feminist Theory and Antiracist Politics', *University of Chicago Legal Forum* 138–167.

—— (1991) 'Mapping the Margins: Intersectionality, Identity Politics, and Violence against Women of Color', *Stanford Law Review* 43(6): 1241–1299.

Cross, M., Wrench, J. and Barnett, S. (1990) *Ethnic Minorities and the Career Service: An Investigation into Processes of Assessment and Placement*. Research Paper Series No. 78. Employment Department, Sheffield, HMSO.

Dale, A., Fieldhouse, F., Shaheen, N. and Kalra, V. (2002) 'Routes into Education and Employment for Young Pakistani and Bangladeshi Women in the UK', *Work, Employment and Society* 16(1): 5–27.

David, M. and Weiner, G. (1997) 'Keeping Balance on the Gender Agenda', *Times Educational Supplement*, 23 May, p. 23.

Davis, A. (1982) *Women, Race and Class*. London: The Women's Press.

Dean, M. (1994) *Critical and Effective Histories: Foucault's Methods and Historical Sociology*. London: Routledge.

Demack, S., Drew, D. and Grimsley, M. (1998) 'Myths about Underachievement: Gender, Ethnic and Social Class Differences in GCSE Results 1988–93'. Paper presented at the *British Educational Research Association Annual Conference*, Belfast, August.

Demack, S., Drew, D. and Grimsley, M. (1999) 'Subjective Educational Stratification in Britain at the End of the 20th Century: Socio-economic, Ethnic and Gender Differences in Mathematics and English Attainment 1988–95. Paper presented at the International Sociological Association (RC28 – Social Stratification) conference, Madison, Wisconsin, USA.

Demack, S., Drew, D. and Grimsley, M. (2000) 'Minding the Gap: Ethnic, Gender and Social Class Differences in Attainment at 16, 1988–95', *Race Ethnicity and Education* 3 (2): 117–143.

Department for Education and Employment (DfEE) (1997) *Excellence in Schools*. Cm 3681. London: HMSO.

—— (1998) *Minority Ethnic Pupils in Maintained Schools by Local Education Authority Area in England*. 452/98. London: DfEE.

——— (1999a) *Ethnic Minority Pupils and Pupils for whom English is an Additional Language: England 1996/97*. Statistical Bulletin Issue No. 3/99. London: The Stationery Office.

——— (1999b) *Youth Cohort Study: The Activities and Experiences of 16 Year Olds: England and Wales 1998*. Issue 4/99. London: The Stationery Office.

Department of Communities and Local Government (DCLG) (2006a) *Engaging with Muslim Women*. London: HMSO.

——— (2006b) *Social Enterprise for Black and Minority Ethnic Women*. At http://www.womenandequalityunit.gov.uk/equality/min_eth.htm.

——— (2007a) *The Equalities Review: Fairness and Freedom: The Final Report of the Equalities Review: A Summary*. London, HMSO. At http://www.theequalities review.org.uk/upload/assets/www.theequalitiesreview.org.uk/equalities_review_f airness_freedom_summary.pdf.

——— (2007b) *A Framework for Fairness: Proposals for a Single Equality Bill for Great Britain – A Consultation Paper*. At http://www.communities.gov.uk/ index.asp?id=1511211.

Dex, S. (1982) 'West Indians, Further Education and Labour Markets', *New Community* 10, (2): 191–205.

——— (1983) 'The Second Generation: West Indian Female School Leavers'. In A. Phizacklea (ed.) *One Way Ticket*. London: Routledge & Kegan Paul.

DfES (2003a) *Widening Participation in Higher Education*, April DfES/0301/2003. Department for Education and Skills. London: HMSO.

——— *Aiming High: Raising Achievement of Ethnic Minority Pupils*. Consultation, March DfES/0183/2003. Department for Education and Skills. London: HMSO.

——— *Minority Ethnic Exclusions and the Race-Relations (Amendment Act) 2000*. Research Report RR616. Department for Education and Skills. London: HMSO. At http://www.dfes.gov.uk/exclusions/uploads/RR616.pdf.

——— *National Curriculum Assessment GCSE and Equivalent Attainment and Post-16 Attainment by Pupil Characteristics, in England 2004*. National Statistical First Release, SFR 08/2005, 24 February. At www.dfes.gov.uk/rsgateway/DB/ SFR.

——— (2007) *Gender and Education: The Evidence on Pupils in England*, RT POL-07. London: DfES HMSO. See www.dfes.gov.uk/research.

Dodgson, E. (1984) *Motherlands: West Indian Women in Britain in 1950s*. Oxford: Heinemann.

Dore, R. (1976) *The Diploma Disease: Education Qualification and Development*. London: George Allen & Unwin.

Douglas, M. (1992) *Risk and Blame: Essays in Cultural Theory*. London: Routledge.

Drew, D. (1995) *'Race', in Education and Work: The Statistics of Inequality*. Aldershot: Avebury.

Drew, D., Fosam, B. and Gillborn, D. (1995) 'Race, IQ and the Underclass; Don't Believe the Hype', *Radical Statistics* 60 (Spring/Summer): 2–21.

Drew, D. and Gray, J. (1991) 'The Black and White Gap in Examination Results: A Statistical Critique of a Decade of Research', *New Community* 17 (2).

Drew, D., Gray, J. and Sime, N. (1992) *Against the Odds: The Education and Labour Experiences of Black Young People*. Research Paper Series No. 68. Employment Department, Sheffield, HMSO.

Driver, G. (1980) *Beyond Underachievement: Case Studies of English, West Indian and Asian School Leavers at Sixteen Plus*. London: CRE.

DTi (2004) *Fairness for All: A New Commission for Equality and Human Rights*. White Paper, May, Department for Trade and Industry. London: HMSO.

Dunant, S. (ed.) (1994) *The War of the Words: The Political Correctness Debate*. London: Virago.

Durant-Gonzalez, V. (1982) 'The Realm of Female Familial Responsibility'. In J. Massiah (ed.) *Women in the Caribbean Research Papers Vol 2: Women and the Family*. Cave Hill, Barbados: ISER, UWI.

Dwyer, C. (1999) 'Veiled Meanings: Young British Muslim Women and the Negotiation of Difference', *Gender, Place and Culture* 6 (1): 5–26.

ECU and JNCHES (2003) *Partnership for Equality: Action for Higher Education*. London: Equality Challenge Unit (ECU) and Joint Negotiating Committee for Higher Education Staff (JNCHES).

Eggleston, J., Dunn, D., Anjali, M. and Wright, C. (1986) *Education for Some. The Educational and Vocational Experiences of 15–18 year old Members of Minority Ethnic Groups*. Stoke-on-Trent: Trentham.

Eggleston, S.J., Dunn, D.K. and Anjali, M. (1986) *Education for Some: The Educational and Vocational Experiences of 15-18-year-old Members of Minority Ethnic Groups*. Stoke-on-Trent: Trentham.

Ellison, N. (1997) 'Towards a New Politics; Citizenship and Reflexivity in Late Modernity', *Sociology* 31 (4): 697–717.

Ellison, R. (1965) *The Invisible Man* (4th edn). London: Penguin Books.

Elwood, J. (1995) 'Undermining Gender Streotypes: Examination Performance in the UK at 16', *Assessment in Education* 2(3): 283–303.

Elwood J. and Comber, C. (1996) *Gender Differences in Examinations at 18+*. London: Institute of Education, University of London.

Employment Gazette (1993) 'Ethnic Origin and the Labour Market', London: Employment Department (January). HMSO.

EOC (2006) *Moving On Up? Bangladeshi, Pakistani and Black Caribbean Women and Work*. At http://www.eoc.org.uk/PDF/BME_GFI_early_findings_England.pdf.

Epstein, D., Elwood, J., Hey, V. and Maw, J. (eds) (1998a) *Failing Boys? Issues in Gender and Achievement*. Buckingham: Open University Press.

Epstein, D., Maw, J., Elwood, J. and Hey, V. (1998b) Guest Editorial: 'Boys' Underachievement', *International Journal of Inclusive Education* 2(2): 91–94.

Essed, P. (2000) 'Dilemmas in Leadership: Women of Colour in the Academy', *Ethnic and Racial Studies*, Special Issue: 'Gender and Ethnicity' 23(5): 888–904.

Etzioni, A. (1993) *The Spirit of Community*. New York: Crown.

Eyerman, R. & Jamison, A. (1991) *Social Movements: A Cognitive Approach*. Cambridge: Polity Press.

Eysenck, H. J. (1973) *The Inequality of Man*. London: Temple Smith.

Fanon, F. (1986; 1st edn 1952) *Black Skin White Masks*. London: Pluto Books.

—— (1990; 1st edn 1961) *The Wretched of the Earth*. London: Penguin Books.

Fawcett Society (2005) *Black and Minority Ethnic Women in the UK*. London: Fawcett Society. At http://www.fawcettsociety.org.uk/index.asp?PageID=46.

—— (2006) *The Veil, Feminism and Muslim Women: A Debate*. 14 December. At http://www.fawcettsociety.org.uk/index.asp?PageID=378.

Feldman, R., Stall, S. and Wright, P. (1998) 'The Community Needs to be Built by Us'. In N. Naples (ed.) *Community Activism and Feminist Politics*. New York: Routledge.

Feminist Review (1993) Special Issue, 'Thinking Through Ethnicities' 45 (Autumn).

Ferree, M.M. (1992) 'The Political Context of Rationality: Rational Choice Theory and Resource Mobilisation'. In D. Aldon, M. and C. McClurg Mueller (eds) *Frontiers in Social Movement Theory*. New Haven, CT: Yale University Press.

Figueroa, P. (1991) *Education and the Social Construction of Race*. London: Routledge.

Fischer, C., Hout, M., Jankowski, M., Lucas, S., Swidler, A. and Voss, K. (1996) *Inequality by Design: Cracking The Bell Curve Myth*. Princeton, NJ: Princeton University Press.

Flannery, M. (2001) 'Quilting: A Feminist Metaphor for Scientific Inquiry', *Qualitative Enquiry* 17 (5): 628–645.

Foner, N. (1979) *Jamaica Farewell. Jamaican Migrants in London*. London: Routledge & Kegan Paul.

Fordham, S. (1996) *Blacked-out: Dilemmas of Race, Identity and Success at Capital High*. Chicago, IL: University of Chicago Press.

Foreign and Commonwealth Office (FCO) (2000) 'A Choice by Right: Working Group on Forced Marriage'. At www.fco.gov.uk.

—— (2004) *Young People and Vulnerable Adults Facing Forced Marriage: Practice Guidance for Social Workers*. London: FCO. At www.fco.gov.uk.

—— (2005a) *Forced Marriage: A Wrong Not a Right. London: FCO.*

—— (2005b) *Dealing with Cases of Forced Marriage: Guidance for Education Professionals* (1st edn). London: FCO. At www.fco.gov.uk.

—— (2006) *Forced Marriage: A Wrong Not a Right – Consultation Report*. London: FCO.

Foster, P. (1991) 'Case Still Not Proven: A Reply to Cecile Wright', *British Educational Research Journal* 17 (2).

—— (1992) 'Equal Treatment and Cultural Difference in Multi-ethnic Schools: A Critique of the Teacher Ethnocentrism Theory', *International Studies in Sociology of Education* 2(1): 89–103.

Foster, P., Gomm, R. and Hammersley, M. (1996) *Constructing Educational Inequality: An Assessment of Research on School Processes*. London: Falmer.

Frankenberg, R. (1993) *White Women, Race Matters: The Social Construction of Whiteness*. London: Routledge.

Fraser, N. (1994) 'Rethinking the Public Sphere: A Continuation to the Critique of Actually Existing Democracy'. In H.A. Giroux and P. McLaren (eds) *Between Borders: Pedagogy and the Politics of Cultural Studies*. New York: Routledge.

Fraser, S. (ed.) (1995) *The Bell Curve Wars*. New York: Basic Books.

Fredman, S. (2002) *The Future of Equality in Britain*. Working Paper Series No. 5. Manchester: Equal Opportunities Commission.

Freire, P. (2004) *Pedagogy of Indignation*. Boulder, CO: Paradigm.

Fryer, P. (1984) *Staying Power: The History of Black People in Britain*. London: Pluto.

Fuller, M. (1978) Dimensions of Gender in a School. Unpublished Ph.D., University of Bristol.

—— (1980) 'Black Girls in a London Comprehensive School'. In R. Deem (ed.) *Schooling for Womens' Work*. London: Routledge & Kegan Paul.

—— (1982) 'Young, Female and Black'. In E. Cashmore and B. Troyna (eds) *Black Youth in Crisis*. London: George Allen & Unwin.

Fusco, C. (1995) *English is Broken Here: Notes on Cultural Fusion in the Americas*. New York: The New Press.

Fuss, D. (1989) *Essentially Speaking: Feminism, Nature and Difference*. New York: Routledge.

Gaita, R. (2000) *A Common Humanity: Thinking about Love and Truth and Justice*. London: Routledge.

Gardner, H. (1995) 'Cracking Open the IQ Box'. In S. Fraser (ed.) *The Bell Curve Wars*. New York: Basic Books.

Gates, H. L. (1995) 'Why Now?' In S. Fraser (ed.) *The Bell Curve Wars*. New York: Basic Books.

Gibson, A. with Barrow, J. (1986) *The Unequal Struggle: The Findings of a West Indian Research Investigation into the Underachievement of West Indian Children in British Schools*. London: Centre for Caribbean Studies.

Giddens, A. (1994) *Beyond Left and Right: The Future of Radical Politics*. Oxford: Polity Press.

Gill, A. (2003) 'A Question of Honour'. *Community Care*, 27 March. At www.communitycare.co.uk/articles/.

Gillborn, D. (1990) *'Race', Ethnicity and Education: Teaching and Learning in Multi-ethnic Schools*. London: Unwin Hyman.

—— (1995) *Racism and Antiracism in Real Schools: Theory. Policy. Practice*. Buckingham: Open University Press.

—— (2008) *Racism and Education: Coincidence or Conspiracy?* London: Routledge.

Gillborn, D. and Mirza, H. (2000) *Educational Inequality: Mapping Race, Class and Gender: A Synthesis of Research Evidence*. London: OFSTED. At www. ofsted.gov.uk.

Gillborn, D. and Drew, D. (1992) ' "Race", Class and School Effects', *New Community* 18(4).

—— (1993) 'The Politics of Research: Some Observations on Methodological Purity', *New Community* 19(2).

Gillborn, D. and Gipps, C. (1996) *Recent Research on the Achievements of Ethnic Minority Pupils*. London: OFSTED.

Gillborn, D. and Youdell, D. (2000) *Rationing Education: Policy, Practice, Reform and Equity*. Buckingham: Open University Press.

Gilroy, P. (1987) *There Ain't No Black In the Union Jack*. London: Hutchinson.

—— (1990) 'The End Of Anti-Racism', *New Community* 17 (1).

—— (2004) *After Empire: Melancholia or Convivial Culture?* Oxon: Routledge.

Giroux, H.A. and Giroux, S.S. (2004) *Take Back Higher Education: Race, Youth and the Crisis of Democracy in the Post-civil Rights Era*. New York: Palgrave Macmillan.

GLA (2005) *Delivering a Shared Heritage: The Mayor's Commission on African and Asian Heritage*. London: Greater London Authority.

—— (2007) Equality in Our Life Time? The Discrimination Law Review Green Paper – what is needed from Single Equality Act'. Seminar, 27 June. At http://www.london.gov.uk/mayor/equalities/docs/dlr-briefing2-jun07.pdf.

Glazer, N. and Moynihan, D.P. (1963) *Beyond the Melting Pot: The Negroes, Puerto Ricans, Jews, Italians and Irish of New York City.* Cambridge, MA: MIT Press.

Gonzalez, N.S. (1985) 'Household and the Family in the Caribbean: Some Definitions and Concepts'. In F.C. Steady (ed.) *The Black Woman Cross-culturally.* Cambridge, MA: Schenkman Books.

Gould, S. J. (1981) *The Mismeasure of Man.* New York: W.W. Norton.

—— (1988) 'Jensen's Last Stand'. In *An Urchin in The Storm.* London: Collins Harvill.

—— (1995) 'Curveball'. In S. Fraser (ed.) *The Bell Curve Wars.* New York: Basic Books.

Gourevitch, P. (2000) *'We Wish to Inform You that Tomorrow we Will be Killed with Our Families': Stories from Rwanda.* London: Picador.

Grewal, S., Kay, J., Landor, L., Lewis, G. and Parmar, P. (1988) *Charting the Journey: Writings by Black and Third World Women.* London: Sheba.

Griffin, C. (1985) *Typical Girls? Young Women from School to the Job Market.* London: Routledge & Kegan Paul.

—— (1996) 'Experiencing Power: Dimensions of Gender, "Race", and Class'. In N. Charles and F. Hughes-Freeland (eds) *Practicing Feminism: Identity, Difference and Power.* London: Routledge.

Grossberg, L. (1996) 'Identity and Cultural Studies – Is That All There Is?' In S. Hall and P. duGray (eds) *Questions of Cultural Identity.* London: Sage.

Gunaratnam, Y. (2003) *Researching 'Race' and Ethnicity: Methods Knowledge Power.* London: Sage.

Gupta, R. (2003) 'Some Recurring Themes: Southall Black Sisters 1979–2003 – and Still Going Strong'. In R. Gupta (ed.) *From Homemakers to Jailbreakers; Southall Black Sisters.* London: Zed Books.

Guy, W. and Menter, I. (1992) 'Local Management of Resources: Who Benefits?' In D. Gill, B. Mayor and M. Blair (eds) *Racism and Education.* London: Sage/Open University.

Hacker, A. (1995) 'Cast, Crime and Precocity'. In S. Fraser (ed.) *The Bell Curve Wars.* New York: Basic Books.

Haider, A. J. (2003) 'Domestic Violence: An Islamic Perspective'. Paper delivered at the Conference on Tackling Domestic Violence in the Asian Community. Cardiff, September. At Alijanhaider@hotmail.com.

Hall, S. (1992) 'New Ethnicities'. In J. Donald and A. Rattansi (eds) *'Race', Culture and Difference.* London: Sage/Open University press.

—— (1996) 'The After-life of Franz Fanon: Why Fanon? Why Now?' In A. Read (ed.) *The Fact Of Blackness.* London: ICA.

—— (2000) 'The Multicultural Question'. In B. Hesse (ed.) *Un/Settled Multiculturalisms: Diasporas, Entanglements, 'Transruptions'.* London: Zed Books.

Hall, S. and Jacques, M. (eds) (1989) *New Times: The Changing Face of Politics in the 1990s.* London: Lawrence & Wishart.

Hall, S. and Jefferson, T. (eds) (1976) *Resistance Through Rituals: Youth Sub-cultures in Post War Britain.* London: Hutchinson.

Hallam, S. (1999) 'Set to See Rise in Standards', *Times Educational Supplement*, 23 July, p. 19.

Hallam, S. and Toutounji, I. (1996) *What Do We Know About the Grouping of Pupils by Ability? A Research Review.* London: University of London Institute of Education.

Halsey, A.H., Heath, A.F. and Ridge, J.M. (1980) *Origins and Destinations: Family, Class, and Education in Modern Britain.* Oxford: Clarendon Press.

Hammersley, M. (1992) 'A Response to Barry Troyna's "Children Race and Racism: The Limits of Research and Policy", *British Journal of Educational Studies* 40 (2).

Hammersley, M. and Gomm, R. (1993) 'A Response to Gillborn and Drew on "Race Class and School Effects" ', *New Community* 19(2).

Haque, Z. (2000) 'The Ethnic Minority "Underachieving" Group? Investigating the Claims of "Underachievement" amongst Bangladeshi Pupils in British Secondary Schools', *Race Ethnicity and Education* 3 (2): 145–168.

Haraway, D. (1992) *Primate Visions: Gender, Race and Nature in the World of Modern Science.* London: Verso.

Harding, S. (1992) 'The Instability of the Analytical Categories of Feminist Theory'. In H. Crowley and S. Himmelweit (eds) *Knowing Women: Feminism and Knowledge.* Cambridge: Polity Press/Open University Press.

Hargreaves, I. and Christie, I. (eds) (1998) *Tomorrow's Politics: The Third way and Beyond.* London: Demos.

Hatcher, R. and Thomas, S. (2000) 'Equity and School Effectiveness Research', *Race Ethnicity and Education* 3 (1): 103–109.

Hennessy, R. (1993) *Materialist Feminism and the Politics of Discourse.* London: Routledge.

Herrnstein, R.J. and Murray, C. (1994) *The Bell Curve: Intelligence and Class Structure in American Life.* New York: Free Press.

Hesse, B. (ed.) (2000) *Un/Settled Multiculturalisms: Diasporas, Entanglements, Transruptions.* London: Zed Books.

Hey, V. (1998) 'Reading the Community: A Critique of Some Post/modern Narratives about Citizenship and Civil Society'. In P. Bagguley and G. Hearn (eds) *Transforming the Political.* London: Macmillan.

Higginbotham, E. (1992) 'African-American Women's History and the Metalanguage of Race', *Signs* 17(2): 251–274.

Higher Education Funding Council England (HEFCE) (2000) *Diversity in Higher Education: HEFCE Policy Statement.* Bristol: HEFCE Ref 00/33.

Hillage, J., Pearson, R., Anderson, A. and Tamkin, P. (1998) *Excellence in Research on Schools.* London: Department for Education and Employment.

Home Office (1999) *Stephen Lawrence Inquiry: Home Secretary's Action Plan.* London: The Home Office. Available at www.homeoffice.gov.ak/ppd/oppu/slpages.pdf.

—— (2005) *Improving Opportunity, Strengthening Society: The Government's Strategy to Increase Race Equality and Community Cohesion.* London: Home Office.

hooks, b. (1981) *Ain't I a Woman: Black and Women Feminism.* Boston, MA: Southend Press.

—— (1991) *Yearnings: Race, Gender and Cultural Politics.* Boston, MA: South End Press.

—— (1992) *Black Looks: Race and Representation.* London: Turnaround Press.

—— (1994) *Teaching to Transgress: Education as the Practice of Freedom*. New York: Routledge.

—— (1995) *Killing Rage: Ending Racism*. London: Penguin Books.

Housee, S. (2004) 'Unveiling South Asian Female Identities Post September 11: Asian Female Students' Sense of Identity and Experiences of Higher Education'. In I. Law, D. Phillips and L. Turney (eds) *Institutional Racism in Higher Education*. Stoke on Trent: Trentham Books.

Hull, G., Bell Scott. P. and Smith, B. (1982) *All the Women are White, All the Blacks are Men, But Some of Us are Brave*. Black Women's Studies. New York: The Feminist Press.

Ifekwunigwe, J.O. (1997) 'Diaspora Daughters, Africa's Orphans? On Lineage, Authenticity and "Mixed Race" Identity'. In H. S. Mirza (ed.) *Black British Feminism; A Reader*. London: Routledge.

James, S. (ed.) (1985) *Strangers and Sisters: Women, Race and Immigration*. London: Falling Wall Press.

James, W. and Harris, C. (1993) *Inside Babylon: The Caribbean Diaspora in Britain*. London: Verso.

Jarrett-Macauley, D. (1996) 'Exemplary Women'. In D. Jarrett Macauley (ed.) *Reconstructing Womanhood, Reconstructing Feminism: Writings on Black Women*. London: Routledge.

Jensen, A.R. (1973) *Educability and Group Differences*. London: Methuen.

Johnson, R. (1988) 'Really Useful Knowledge 1790–1850: Memories for Education in the 1980s'. In T. Lovett (ed.) *Radical Approaches to Education: A Reader*. New York: Routledge.

Jones, J. (1985) *Labour of Love Labour of Sorrow: Black Women, Work and the Family, from Slavery to the Present Day*. New York: Vintage Books.

—— 'Back to the Future with the Bell Curve: Jim Crow, Slavery, and G'. In S. Fraser (ed.) *The Bell Curve Wars*. New York: Basic Books.

Jones, T. (1993) *Britain's Ethnic Minorities*. London: PSI.

Jordan, B. (1995) 'Are New Right Policies Sustainable? Back to Basics and Public Choice', *Journal of Social Policy* 24(3): 363–384.

Jordan, B., Redley, M. and James, S. (1994) *Putting the Family First: Identities, Decisions, Citizenship*. London: UCL Press.

Justus, J.B. (1985) 'Women's Role in West Indian Society'. In F.C. Steady (ed.) *The Black Woman Cross-culturally*. Cambridge, MA: Schenkman Books.

Kanneh, K. (1995) 'Feminism and the Colonial Body'. In B. Ashcroft, G. Griffiths and H. Tiffin *The Post Colonial Studies Reader*. London: Routledge.

Kay, J. (1995) 'So you Think I'm a Mule?' In B. Burford, G. Pearce, G. Nichols and J. Kay (eds) *A Dangerous Knowing: Four Black Women Poets*. London: Sheba Press.

Kazi, H. (1986) 'The Beginning of a Debate Long Over Due: Some Observations on Ethnocentrism and Socialist Feminist Theory', *Feminist Review*, 'Feedback: Feminism and Racism' 22 (Spring).

Keith, M. (1993) *Race, Riots and Policing: Lore and Disorder in a Multiracist Society*. London: UCL Press.

Kelly, L. (2005) 'Inside Outsiders: Mainstreaming Violence against Women into Human Rights Discourse and Practice', *International Feminist Journal of Politics* 7(4): 471–495.

Kelly, P. (2007) 'Governing Individualised Risk Biographies: New Class Intellectuals and the Problem of Youth at Risk', *British Journal of Sociology of Education* 28(1): 39–53.

Kirby, M., Kidd, W., Koubel, F., Barter, J., Hope, T., Kirton, A., Madry, N., Manning, P. and Triggs, K. (1997) *Sociology in Perspective*. Oxford: Heinemann.

Knowles, C. and Mercer, S. (1992) 'Feminism and Antiracism: An Exploration of the Political Possibilities'. In J. Donald and A. Rattansi (eds) *'Race', Culture and Difference*. London: Sage.

Kohn, M. (1996) *The Race Gallery: The Return of Racial Science*. London: Vintage.

La Rose, J. (1999) *Remembering the Past Forging Forward to the Future*. Martin Luther King Memorial Lectures, Martin Luther Twelve. Crofton Park: Root and Branch Consultancy.

Landry, B. and Jendrek, M. (1978) 'The Employment of Wives from Black Middle Class Families', *Journal of Marriage and the Family*, November.

Lash, S. (1996) 'Tradition and the Limits of Difference'. In P. Heelas, S. Lash and P. Morris (eds) *Detradtionalisation*. Oxford: Blackwell.

Law, I., Phillips, D. and Turney, L. (eds) (2004) *Institutional Racism in Higher Education*. Stoke on Trent: Trentham Books.

Lawton, D. (1992) *Education and Politics in the 1990s*. London: Falmer.

LDA (2004) *The Educational Experiences and Achievements of Black Boys in London Schools 2000–2003*. The Education Commission. London: London Development Agency.

Lee, J. (1982) 'Society and Culture'. In F. Litton (ed.) *Unequal Achievement: The Irish Experience 1957–1982*. Dublin: Institute of Public Administration.

Lees, S. (1986a) *Losing Out: Sexuality and Adolescent Girls*. London: Hutchinson.

—— (1986b) 'Sex, Race and Culture: Feminism and the Limits of Cultural Pluralism', *Feminist Review*, 'Feedback: Feminism and Racism' 22 (Spring).

Leicester, M. and Taylor, M. (eds) (1992) *Ethics, Ethnicity and Education*. London: Kogan Page.

Lester, A. and Clapinska, L. (2005) 'An Equality and Human Rights Commission Worthy of the Name', *Journal of Law and Society* 32 (1): 169–186.

Lewis, G. (1990) 'Audre Lorde: Vignettes and Mental Conversations', *Feminist Review* 34 (Spring): 100–114.

—— (1993) 'Black Women's Employment and the British Economy'. In W. James and C. Harris (eds) *Inside Babylon: The Caribbean Diaspora in Britain*. London: Verso.

Lewis, G. and Parmar, P. (1983a) 'Black Feminism: Shared Oppression, New Expression', *City Limits*, 4–10 March.

—— (1983b) 'Review Article: Black Women's Writing', *Race and Class* 25(2).

Lister, R. (1990) 'Women, Economic Dependency and Citizenship', *Journal of Social Policy* 21 (1): 445–468.

—— (ed.) (1996) *Charles Murray and the Underclass: The Developing Debate*. London: IEA.

Lopez, I.H. (1993) 'Community Ties and Law School Faculty Hiring: The Case of Professors Who Don't Think White'. In B. Thompson and S. Tyagi (eds) *Beyond a Dream Deferred: Multicultural Education and the Politics of Excellence*. Minneapolis: University of Minnesota Press.

Luttrell, W. (1992) 'Working Class Women's Ways of Knowing: Effects of Gender,

Race and Class'. In J. Wrigley (ed.) *Education and Gender Equality*. London: Falmer Press.

—— (1997) *School-smart and Mother-wise: Working-class Women's Identity and Schooling*. London: Routledge.

Mac an Ghaill, M. (1988) *Young, Gifted and Black: Student-Teacher Relations in the Schooling of Black Youth*. Milton Keynes: Open University Press.

—— (1989) 'Coming of Age in 1980s England: Reconceptualising Black Students' Schooling Experiences', *British Journal of Sociology of Education* 10(3).

—— (1991) 'Black Voluntary Schools: The "Invisible" Private Sector'. In G. Walford (ed.) *Private Schooling: Tradition, Change and Diversity*. London: Paul Chapman.

—— (1993) 'Beyond the White Norm: The Use of Qualitative Methods in the Study of Black Youths' Schooling in England'. In P. Woods and M. Hammersley (eds) *Gender and Ethnicity in Schools: Ethnographic Accounts*. London: Routledge/ Open University.

—— (1994) *The Making of Men: Masculinities, Sexualities and Schooling*. Buckingham: Open University Press.

—— (ed.) (1996) *Understanding Masculinities: Social Relations and Cultural Arenas*. Buckingham: Open University Press.

Macpherson, W. (1999) *The Stephen Lawrence Inquiry*. CM 4262-I. London: The Stationery Office.

Malik, K. (1996) *The Meaning of Race: Race, History and Culture in Western Society*. London: Macmillan.

—— (2003) 'The Dirty D-word', *Guardian*, 29 October.

Mama, A. (1984) 'Black Women, The Economic Crisis and the British State', *Feminist Review*, Special Issue, 'Many Voices one Chant' 17 (July) 3–19.

—— (1989) 'Violence Against Black Women: Gender, Race and State Responses', *Feminist Review* 32 (Summer): 30–48.

—— (1992) 'Black Women and the British State: Race Class and Gender Analysis for the 1990s'. In P. Braham, A. Rattansi and R. Skellington (eds) *Racism and Antiracism: Inequalities, Opportunities and Policies*. London: Sage/Open University Press.

—— (1993a) 'Woman Abuse in London's Black Communities'. In W. James and C. Harris (eds) *Inside Babylon: The Caribbean Diaspora in Britain*. London: Verso.

—— (1993b) 'Black Women and the Police: A Place Where the Law is Not Upheld'. In W. James and C. Harris (eds) *Inside Babylon: The Caribbean Diaspora in Britain*. London: Verso.

—— (1995) *Beyond the Masks: Race, Gender and Subjectivity*. London: Routledge.

Mani, L. (1992) 'Multiple Mediations: Feminist Scholarship in the Age of Multinational Reception'. In H. Crowley and S. Himmelweit (eds) *Knowing Women: Feminism and Knowledge*. Cambridge: Polity Press/Open University Press.

Marshall, G. (1997) *Repositioning Class: Social Inequality in Industrial Societies*. London: Sage.

Mason, D. (2000) *Race and Ethnicity in Modern Britain* (2nd edn). Oxford: Oxford University Press. First published 1995.

Mason-John, V. (1995) *Talking Black*. London: Cassell.

Massiah, J. (1986) 'Work in the Lives of Caribbean Women', *Social and Economic Studies*, Special Issue: J. Massiah (ed.) 'Women in the Caribbean' (Part 1): Institute of Social and Economic Research, University of the West Indies, Vol. 35, No. 2.

Maynard, M. (1994) ' "Race", Gender and the Concept of Difference in Feminist Thought'. In H. Afshar and M. Maynard (eds) *The Dynamics of 'Race' and Gender: Some Feminist Interventions*. London: Taylor & Francis.

McAdoo, Pipes, H. (ed.) (1988) *Black Families: Second Edition*. London: Sage.

McCall, L. (2005) 'The Complexity of Intersectionality', *SIGNS Journal of Women Culture and Society* 30(31): 1771–1802.

McClintock, A. (1992) *Race Gender and Sexuality in the Colonial Contest*. New York: Routledge.

—— (1995) *Imperial Leather: Race, Gender and Sexuality in the Colonial Contest*. New York: Routledge.

—— (1997) 'Transexions: Race, Queer and Cyber Crossings'. Paper presented at Transformations: Thinking Through Feminism. Lancaster University, Institute of Women's Studies, 17–19 July.

McDowell, D.E. (1990) 'Reading Family Matters'. In C.A. Wall (ed.) *Changing Our Own Words*. London: Routledge.

McKittrick, K. (2006) *Demonic Grounds: Black Women and the Cartography of Struggle*. Minneapolis: University of Minnesota Press.

McLaughlin, E. and Neal, S. (2004) 'Misrepresenting the multicultural nation; the policy making process, news media management and the Parekh report', *Policy Studies* 25(3): 155–174.

McRobbie, A. (1990) *Feminism and Youth Culture*. London: Macmillan Education.

McRobbie, A. and Garber, J. (1975) 'Girls and Subcultures: An Exploration'. In S. Hall and T. Jefferson (eds) *Resistance Through Rituals: Youth Subcultures in Post-war Britain*. London: Hutchinson.

Meetoo, V. and Mirza, H.S. (2007a) 'There is Nothing Honourable About Honour Killings: Gender, Violence and the Limits of Multiculturalism', *Women's Studies International Forum* 30 (3): 187–200.

—— (2007b) 'Lives at Risk: Multiculturalism, Young Women and "Honour" killings. In B. Thom, R. Sales and J. Pearce (eds) *Growing up with Risk*. Bristol: Policy Press.

Melucci, A. (1989) *Nomads of the Present: Social Movements and Individual Needs in Contemporary Society*. London: Radius.

Metcalf, H. and Forth, J. (2000) *Business Benefits of Race Equality: Race Research for the Future*. Research Report No. 177. London: Department for Education and Employment (DFEE), 6 March.

Milner, D. (1975) *Children and Race*. Harmondsworth: Penguin.

Mirza, H.S. (1986) 'The Dilemma of Socialist Feminism: A Case for Black Feminism', *Feminist Review*, 'Feedback: Feminism and Racism' 22 (Spring).

—— (1992) *Young, Female and Black*. London: Routledge.

—— (1993) 'The Social Construction of Black Womanhood in British Educational Research: Towards a New Understanding'. In M. Arnot and K. Weiler (eds) *Feminism and Social Justice in Education*. London: Falmer Press.

—— (1995) 'Black Women in Higher Education: Defining a Space/Finding a Place'. In L. Morley and V. Walsh (eds) *Feminist Academics: Creative Agents For Change*. London: Taylor & Francis.

—— (1997a) 'Mapping a Genealogy of Black British Feminism'. In H. Mirza (ed.) *Black British Feminism*. London: Routledge.

—— (1997b) *Black British Feminism: A Reader*. London: Routledge.

—— (1997c) 'Black Women in Education: A Collective Movement for Social Change'. In H.S. Mirza (ed.) *Black British Feminism: A Reader*. London: Routledge.

—— (1998) 'Race, Gender and IQ: The Social Consequences of a Pseudo-scientific Discourse', *Race Ethnicity and Education* 1(1): 137–158.

—— (2003) ' "All Women are White, All the Blacks are Men – But Some of Us are Brave": Mapping the Consequences of Invisibility for Black and Minority Ethnic Women in Britain'. In D. Mason (ed.) *Explaining Ethnic Differences*. Bristol: Policy Press.

—— (2005) 'Race, Gender and Educational Desire'. Inaugural Professorial Lecture, 17 May, Middlesex University. At www.mdx.ac.uk/hssc/research/cres.htm.

—— (2006a) 'The In/visible Journey: Black Women's Life-long Lessons in Higher Education'. In C. Leathwood and B. Francis (eds), *Gender and Life Long Learning: Critical Feminist Engagements*. London: Routledge/Falmer.

—— (2006b) 'Race, Gender and Educational Desire', *Race, Ethnicity and Education* 9(2): 137–158.

Mirza, H. S. and Reay, D. (2000a) 'Redefining Citizenship: Black Women Educators and the Third Space'. In M. Arnot and J. Dillabough (eds) *Challenging Democracy: International Perspectives on Gender, Education and Citizenship*. London: Routledge Falmer.

—— (2000b) 'Spaces and Places of Educational Desire: Rethinking Black Supplementary Schools as a New Social Movement', *Sociology* 34 (3): 521–544.

—— (2007) 'Feminism, Black British', in D. Dabydeen, J. Gilmore and C. Jones (eds) *Oxford Companion to Black British History*. Oxford: Oxford University Press.

Modood, T. (1994) 'Political Blackness and British Asians', *Sociology* 28(4): 859–876.

Modood, T. and Acland, T. (eds) (1998) *Race and Higher Education*. London: Policy Studies Institute.

Modood, T. and Shiner, M. (1994) *Ethnic Minorities and Higher Education: Why Are There Differential Rates of Entry?* London: PSI Publishing.

Modood, T., Berthoud, R., Lakey, J., Nazroo, J., Smith, P., Virdee, S. and Beishon, S. (1997) *Ethnic Minorities in Britain: Diversity and Disadvantage*. London: Policy Studies Institute.

Mohammed, P. (1988) 'The Caribbean Family Revisited'. In P. Mohammed and C. Shepherd (eds) *Gender in Caribbean Development*. Women and Development Studies Project. St Augustine, Trinidad: University of the West Indies.

Mohanty, C.T. (1988) 'Under Western Eyes: Feminist Scholarship and Colonial Discourses', *Feminist Review* 30 (Autumn): 65–88.

—— (1993) 'On Race and Voice: Challenges for Liberal Education in the 1990s'. In B. Thompson and S. Tyagi (eds) *Beyond a Dream Deferred: Multicultural Education and the Politics of Excellence*. Minnesota: University of Minnesota Press.

Momsen, J. (1993) 'Development and Gender Divisions of Labour in the Rural Caribbean'. In J. Momsen (ed.) *Women and Change in the Caribbean*. Bloomington: Indiana University Press.

Morley, L. and Rassool, N. (1999) *School Effectiveness: Fracturing the Discourse*. London: Falmer.

Morrison, T. (1993a) 'Friday on the Potomac'. In T. Morrison (ed.) *Race-ing, Justice – Engendering Power*. London: Chatto and Windus.

—— (ed.) (1993b) *Race-ing Justice, En-gendering Power: Essays on Anita Hill, Clarence Thomas and the Social Construction of Reality*. London: Chatto & Windus.

Morrow, V. (1999) 'Conceptualising Social Capital in Relation to Health and Well Being for Children and Young People; A Critical Review', *Sociological Review* 47 (4): 744–765.

Mortimore, P. (1998) *The Road to Improvement: Reflections on School Effectiveness*. Abingdon: Swets & Zeitlinger.

—— (1999) *Does Educational Research Matter? Presidential Address to the British Educational Research Association*. University of Sussex, September.

Mortimore, P. and Whitty, G. (1997) *Can School Improvement Overcome the Effects of Disadvantage?* London: University of London Institute of Education.

Moses, Y.T. (1985) 'Female Status, the Family, and Male Dominance in a West Indian Community'. In F. Steady (ed.) *The Black Woman Cross Culturally*. Cambridge, MA: Schenkman Books.

Mouffe, C. (1993) *The Return of the Political*. London: Verso.

Moynihan, D. (1967) 'The Negro Family: A Case for National Action'. In L. Rainwater and W.L. Yancey (eds) *The Moynihan Report and the Politics of Controversy*. Cambridge, MA: The MIT Press.

Multiverse (2004) *Exploring Diversity and Achievement*. Newsletter 1, February. London: London Metropolitan University IPSE. At http://www.multiverse.ac.uk/.

Murphy, P. and Elwood, J. (1998) 'Gendered Experiences, Choices and Achievement – Exploring the Links', *International Journal of Inclusive Education* 2(2): 95–118.

Murray, C. (1984) *Losing Ground: American Social Policy 1950–80*. New York: Basic Books.

—— (1990) 'Underclass', *The Sunday Times Magazine*, 26 November.

—— (1994) *Underclass: The Crisis Deepens*. London: IEA Health and Welfare Unit.

Nasta, S. (1991) *Motherlands: Black Women's Writing from Africa, The Caribbean and South Asia*. London: The Woman's Press.

National Audit Office (NAO) (2002) *Widening Participation in Higher Education in England*. HC 485 session 2001–2002. London: National Audit Office.

Ngcobo, L. (ed.) (1988) *Let it be Told: Black Women Writers in Britain*. London: Virago.

Nowotny, H. (1981) 'Women in Public Life in Austria'. In C. F. Epstein and R. L. Coser (eds) *Access to Power; Cross National Studies of Women and Elites*. London: George Allen & Unwin.

O'Cinneide, C. (2007) 'Purpose Clauses – Giving Coherence and Direction to Anti-discrimination Law'. At http://www.drc-gb.org/the_law/equality_and_human_rights/single_equality_act_green_pape.aspx.

Oakes, J. (1990) *Multiplying Inequalities: The Effects of Race, Social Class, and Tracking on Opportunities to Learn Mathematics and Science*. Santa Monica, CA: The Rand Corporation.

Office for National Statistics (ONS) (1996) *Social Focus on Ethnic Minorities*. London: HMSO.

Office For Standards in Education (OFSTED) (1993) *Access and Achievement in Urban Education*. London: HMSO

—— (1999) *Raising the Attainment of Minority Ethnic Pupils*. London: OFSTED.

Okin, S. M. (with respondents) Cohen, J. Howard, M. and Nussbaum (eds) (1999) *Is Multiculturalism Bad for Women?* Princeton, NJ: Princeton University Press.

Ong, A. (1987) *Spirits of Resistance and Capitalist Discipline: Factory Women in Malaysia*. Albany, NY: State University of New York Press.

Osler, A. (1997) *Exclusion from School and Racial Equality*. London: Commission for Racial Equality.

Palmer, F. (ed.) (1987) *Antiracism: An Assault on Education and Value*. London: Sherwood Press.

Parkes, S.M. (2004) *A Danger to the Men? A History of Women in Trinity College Dublin 1904–2004*. Dublin: Lilliput Press.

Parmar, P. (1982) 'Gender, Race and Class: Asian Women's Resistance'. In Centre for Cultural Studies *The Empire Strikes Back: Race and Racism in 70s Britain*. London: Hutchinson.

—— (1989) 'Other Kinds of Dreams', *Feminist Review* Special Issue, 'The Past is Before Us: Twenty Years of Feminism', 31 (Spring): 55–65.

—— (1990) 'Black Feminism and the Politics of Articulation'. In J. Rutherford (ed.) *Identity, Community, Culture, Difference*. London: Lawrence & Wishart.

Parmar, P. and Mirza, N. (1981) 'Growing Angry: Growing Strong', *Spare Rib* 111.

Patel, P. (1997) 'Third Wave Feminism and Black Women's Activism'. In H.S. Mirza (ed.) *Black British Feminism; A Reader*. London: Routledge.

—— (accessed 24 February 2008) Notes on Gender and Racial Discrimination. See http://www.eurowrc.org/13.institutions/5.un/un-en/12.un_en.htm.

Patterson, S. (1965) *'Dark Strangers': A Study of West Indians in London*. Harmondsworth: Penguin Books.

Pearson, D. (1981) *Race, Class and Political Activism: A Study of West Indians in Britain*. Farnborough: Gower Press.

Persram, N. (1997) 'In My Fathers House There are Many Mansions: The Nation and Postcolonial Desire'. In H.S. Mirza (ed.) *Black British Feminism; A Reader*. London: Routledge.

Phillips, A. (2003) 'When Culture Means Gender: Issues of Cultural Defence in English Courts', *The Modern Law Review* 66(4): 510–531.

—— (2007) *Multiculturalism Without Culture*. Princeton, NJ: Princeton University Press.

Phillips, M. & Phillips, T. (1999) *Windrush: The Irresistible Rise of Multi-racial Britain*. London: Harper Collins.

Phizacklea, A. (1982) 'Migrant Women and Wage Labour: The Case of West Indian Women in Britain'. In J. West (ed.) *Work, Women and the Labour Market*. London: Routledge & Kegan Paul.

—— (1983) 'In The Front Line'. In Phizacklea (ed.) *One Way Ticket*. London: Routledge & Kegan Paul.

Phoenix, A. (1987) 'Theories of Gender and Black Families'. In G. Weiner and M. Arnot (eds) *Gender Under Scrutiny*. London: Hutchinson and the Open University Press.

—— (1988) 'Narrow Definitions of Culture: The Case of Early Motherhood'. In S. Westwood and P. Bhachu *Enterprising Women: Ethnicity, Economy and Gender Relations*. London: Routledge.

—— (1991) *Young Mothers?* London: Polity Press.

—— (1996) 'Social Constructions of Lone Motherhood; A Case of Competing Discourses'. In E. Bortolia Silva (ed.) *Good Enough Mothering?* London: Routledge.

Phoenix, A. and Pattynama, P. (2006) 'Editorial: Special Issue on Intersectionality', *European Journal of Women's studies* 2006 13(3): 188–192.

Platt L. (2006) *Pay Gaps: The Position of Ethnic Minority Women and Men.* Manchester: EOC.

—— (2007) *Poverty and Ethnicity: A Review.* Bristol: Policy Press.

Powell, D. (1986) 'Caribbean Women and their Response to Familial Experiences', *Social and Economic Studies*, Special Issue: J. Massiah (ed.) 'Women in the Caribbean' (Part 1): Institute of Social and Economic Research, University of the West Indies, Vol. 35, No. 2.

Powney, J., Hall, S., Wilson, V., Davidson, J., Kirk, S., Edward S. and Mirza, H.S. (2003) *Teachers' Careers: The Impact of Age, Disability, Gender, Ethnicity and Sexual Orientation.* DFES Research Report 488: 1–81.

Prescod-Roberts, M. and Steele, N. (eds) (1980) *Bringing it All Back Home.* Bristol: Falling Wall Press.

Prins, B. (2006) 'Narrative Accounts of Origins: A Blind spot in the Intersectional Approach?', *European Journal of Women's Studies* 13(3): 277–290.

Puwar, N. (2001) 'The Racialised Somatic Norm and the Senior Civil Service', *Sociology* 35(3): 351–370.

—— (2003) 'Melodramatic Postures and Constructions'. In N. Puwar and P. Raghuram (eds) *South Asian Women in the Diaspora.* Oxford: Berg.

—— (2004) 'Fish In or Out of Water: A Theoretical Framework for Race and the Space of Academia'. In I. Law, D. Phillips and L. Turney (eds) *Institutional Racism in Higher Education.* Stoke on Trent: Trentham Books.

Ramazanoglu, C. (1986) 'Ethnocentrism and Socialist-feminist Theory: A Response to Barrett and McIntosh', *Feminist Review*, 'Feedback: Feminism and Racism' 22 (Spring).

Ramdin, R. (1999) *Arising from Bondage: The History of the Indo-Caribbean Peoples.* London: IB Taurus.

Rampton, A. (1981) *West Indian Children in Our Schools.* Cmnd 8273. London: HMSO.

Rasheed, A. (1989) *The Other Story.* Exhibition Catalogue, London: Hayward Gallery.

Rassool, N. (1997) 'Fractured or Flexible Identities? Life Histories of "Black" Diasporic Women in Britain'. In H.S. Mirza (ed.) *Black British Feminism; A Reader.* London: Routledge.

Ratcliffe, P. (1988) 'Race, Class and Residence: Afro-Caribbean Households in Britain'. In C. Brock (ed.) *The Caribbean In Europe: Aspects of the West Indian Experience in Britain, France and the Netherlands.* London: Frank Cass.

Rattansi, A. (1992) 'Changing the Subject? Racism, Culture and Education'. In J. Donald and A. Rattansi (eds) *'Race', Culture and Difference.* London: Sage/Open University.

Razack, S. (1998) *Looking White People in the Eye: Gender Race and Culture in Courtrooms and Classrooms.* Toronto: University of Toronto Press.

Reay, D. (1998) *Class Work: Mothers' Involvement in Their Children's Primary Schooling.* London: University College Press.

Reay, D. and Mirza, H.S. (1997) 'Uncovering Genealogies of the Margins: Black Supplementary Schooling', *British Journal of Sociology of Education* 18(4): 477–499.

Reay, D., David, M. and Ball, S. (2005) *Degrees of Choice: Social Class, Race and Gender in Higher Education*. Stoke on Trent: Trentham Books.

Reid, E. (1989) 'Black Girls Talking', *Gender and Education*, Special Issue: 'Race, Gender and Education' 1(3).

Reynolds, T. (1997) '(Mis)representing the Black (Super)woman'. In H.S. Mirza (ed.) *Back British Feminism*. London: Routledge.

Richardson, B. (ed.) (2005) *Tell It Like It Is: How our Schools Fail Black Children*. London: Bookmark Publications in association with Trentham Books.

Richardson, R. and Wood, A. (1999) *Inclusive Schools, Inclusive Society: Race and Identity on the Agenda*. Report produced for Race on the Agenda in partnership with Association of London Government and Save the Children. Stoke-on-Trent: Trentham.

Riley, K. (1985) 'Black Girls Speak for Themselves'. In G. Weiner (ed.) *Just a Bunch of Girls*. Milton Keynes: Open University Press.

Rivera Fuentes, C. (1997) 'Two Stories, Three Lovers and the Creation of Meaning in a Black Lesbian Autobiography: A Diary'. In H.S. Mirza (ed.) *Black British Feminism; A Reader*. London: Routledge.

Rose, S., Lewontin, R.C. and Kamin, L.J. (1984) *Not in our Genes: Biology, Ideology and Human Nature*. London: Penguin Books.

Runnymede Trust (2000) *The Parekh Report: Commission on the Future of Multi-ethnic Britain*. London: Profile.

Rutherford, J. (1990) 'A Place Called Home: Identity and the Cultural Politics of Difference'. In J. Rutherford (ed.) *Identity, Community, Culture, Difference*. London: Lawrence & Wishart.

Rutter, M., Gray, G., Maughan, B. and Smith, A. (1982) 'School Experiences and the First Year of Employment'. Unpublished Report to the DES.

Sahgal, G. and Yuval-Davis, N. (eds) (1992) *Refusing Holy Orders*. London: Virago.

Salim, S. (2003) 'It's About Women's Rights and Women's Rights are Human Rights'. An interview with Sawsan Salim, Coordinator of Kurdistan Refugee Women's Organisation (KRWO). London: KRWO received at Stop Violence Against Women Honour Killing Conference, London, 28 October.

Samantrai, R. (2002) *AlterNatives: Black Feminism in the Post Imperial Nation*. Stanford, CA: Stanford University Press.

Sammons, P. (1999) *School Effectiveness: Coming of Age in the Twenty-first Century*. Lisse: Swets & Zeitlinger.

Sandoval, C. (1991) 'U.S. Third World Feminism: The Theory and Method of Oppositional Consciousness in the Post Modern World', *Genders* 10: 1–24.

Savery, L. (2002) 'Women's Human Rights and Changing State Practices: A Critical Realist Approach', *Journal of Critical Realism* 4 (1): 89–111.

Sawicki, J. (1991) *Disciplining Foucault: Feminism Power and Body*. London: Routledge.

Scarman Report (1981) *The Brixton Disorders 10–12 April 1981: Report of an Inquiry*. London: HMSO.

Schneider-Ross Consultants (2001) *Equality in the University: Setting the New*

Agenda: A Report on Equality Audit for Cambridge University. Andover: Schneider-Ross Ltd.

Scott, J.W. (1990) 'Deconstructing Equality-versus-difference: Or the Uses of Poststructuralist Theory for Feminism'. In M. Hirsch and E. Fox-Keller (eds) *Conflicts in Feminism.* New York: Routledge.

—— (1992) 'Experience'. In J. Bulter and J. Scott (eds) *Feminists Theorise the Political.* New York: Routledge.

SEU (1998) *Bringing Britain Together: A National Strategy for Neighbourhood Renewal.* Report by the Social Exclusion Unit CD 4045. London: HMSO.

Sewell, T. (1997) *Black Masculinities and Schooling: How Black Boys Survive Modern Schooling.* Stoke-on-Trent: Trentham.

Sharpe, S. (1987; 1st edn 1976) *Just like a Girl: How Girls Learn to be Women.* Harmondsworth: Penguin.

Shotter, M. (1993) *The Cultural Politics of Everyday Life.* Buckingham: Open University Press.

Siddiqui, H. (2003) 'It was Written in her Kismet: Forced Marriage'. In R. Gupta (ed.) *From Homebreakers to Jailbreakers.* London: Zed Books.

—— (2008) 'Making the Grade? Meeting the challenge of tackling violence against ethnic minority women'. In Z. Moosa (ed.) *Seeing Double: Ethnic minority women's lives.* London: Fawcett Society.

Simmonds, N. F. (1997) 'My Body Myself: How Does a Black Woman do Sociology?' In H.S. Mirza (ed.) *Black British Feminism; A Reader.* London: Routledge.

Siraj-Blatchford, I. (1994) *The Early Years: Laying the Foundations for Racial Equality.* Stoke-on-Trent: Trentham.

Skeggs, B. (1997) *Formations of Class and Gender: Becoming Respectable.* London: Sage.

Skellington, R. (1992) *'Race' in Britain Today.* London: Sage/Open University.

Skelton, C., Francis, B. and Valkanova, Y. (2007) Breaking Down the Stereotypes: Gender and Achievement in Schools, Working Paper No. 59 EOC (Equal Opportunities Commission), Manchester. See www.eoc.org.uk/research.

Slavin, R.E. (1996) *Education for All.* Lisse: Swets and Zeitlinger.

Smith, D.J. and Tomlinson, S. (1989) *The School Effect: A Study of Multi-Racial Comprehensives.* London: Policy Studies Institute.

Social Exclusion Unit (1999) *Bridging the Gap: New Opportunities for 16–18 Year Olds Not in Education, Employment or Training.* London: The Stationery Office.

Solomos, J. (1988) *Black Youth, Racism and the State.* Cambridge: Cambridge University Press.

—— (1993: 2nd edn) *Race and Racism in Britain.* London: Routledge.

Spelman, E. (1990) *Inessential Woman: Problems of Exclusion in Feminist Thought.* London: The Women's Press.

Spivak, G. (1988) 'Can the Subaltern Speak?' In C. Nelson and L. Grossberg (eds) *Marxism and the Interpretation of Culture.* London: Macmillan.

—— (1993) Outside in the Teaching Machine. New York: Routledge.

Stack, C. (1982; 1st edn 1974) *All Our Kin: Strategies for Survival in a Black Community.* New York: Harper & Row.

Steinberg, D.L., Epstein, D. and Johnson, R. (1997) *Border Patrols.* London: Cassell.

Stephan, Leys N. (1990) 'Race and Gender: The Role of Analogy in Science'. In D. Goldberg (ed.) *The Anatomy of Racism.* Minneapolis: University of Minnesota Press.

Stobart, G., Elwood, J., Hayden, M., White, J. and Mason, K. (1992) *Differential Performance in Examinations at 16+: English and Mathematics*. London: University of London Examinations and Assessment Council.

Stone, K. (1983) 'Motherhood and Waged Work: West Indian, Asian and White Mothers Compared'. In A. Phizacklea (ed.) *One Way Ticket*. London: Routledge & Kegan Paul.

Stone, M. (1985; 1st edn 1981) *The Education of the Black Child: The Myth of Multi-cultural Education*. London: Fontana Press.

Sudbury, J. (1998) *'Other Kinds of Dreams': Black Women's Organisations and the Politics of Transformation*. London: Routledge.

—— (2001) '(Re)constructing Multicultural Blackness: Women's Activism, Difference and Collective Identity in Britain', *Ethnic and Racial Studies* 24, 1: 29–49.

Sukhnandan, L. and Lee, B. (1998) *Streaming, Setting and Grouping by Ability*. Slough: National Foundation for Educational Research.

Suleri, S. (1993) 'Woman Skin Deep: Feminism and the Postcolonial Condition'. In P. Williams and L. Chrisman (eds) *Colonial Discourse and Post-colonial Theory: A Reader*. Hemel Hempstead: Harvester Wheatsheaf.

Sutler, M. (ed.) (1990) *Passion: Discourses on Black Women's Creativity*. Hebden Bridge, West Yorkshire: Urban Fox Press.

Sutton, C. and Makiesky-Barrow, S. (1977) 'Social Inequality and Sexual Status in Barbados'. In A. Schlegel (ed.) *Sexual Stratification: A Cross-cultural View*. New York: Columbia University Press.

Swann Report (1985) *Education for All: Final Report of the Committee of Inquiry into the Education of Children from Ethnic Minority Groups*. Cmnd 9453. London: HMSO.

Symington, A. (2004) 'Intersectionality; A Tool for Gender and Economic Justice', *Women's Rights and Economic Change* 9(August).

Tang Nain, G. (1991) 'Black Women, Sexism and Racism: Black or Antiracist Feminism?', *Feminist Review* 37 (Spring) 1–22.

Tawadros, G. (1996) 'Beyond the Boundary: The Work of Three Black Women Artists in Britain'. In H. Baker, M. Diawara and R. Lindeborg (eds) *Black British Cultural Studies: A Reader*. Chicago, IL: University of Chicago Press.

Taylor, M.J. (1987) *Chinese Pupils in Britain: A Review of Research into the Education of Pupils of Chinese Origin*. Windsor: NFER-Nelson.

Taylor, M.J. with Hegarty, S. (1985) *The Best of Both Worlds . . .? A Review of Research into the Education of Pupils of South Asian Origin*. Windsor: NFER-Nelson.

Ten.8 (1992) 'Critical Decade: Black British Photography in the 80s', 2(3).

Thomas, L. (2001) Power, Assumptions and Prescriptions: A Critique of Widening Participation in Policy making', *Higher Education Policy* 14: 361–376.

Thorogood, N. (1987) 'Race, Class, and Gender: The Politics of Housework'. In J. Brannen and G. Wilson (eds) *Give and Take in Families*. London: Allen & Unwin.

Times Higher Education Supplement (THES) (2004) 'Distinct Lack of Ebony in Ivory Towers', 22 October.

Tomlinson, S. (1982) 'Response of the English Education System to the Children of Immigrant Parentage'. In M. Leggon (ed.) *Research in Ethnic Relations* 3.

—— (1983) *Ethnic Minorities in British Schools*. London: Heinemann Educational Books.

—— (1985) 'The "Black Education" Movement'. In M. Arnot (ed.) *Race and Gender*. Oxford: Pengamon Press/Open University.

—— (1993) 'The Multicultural Task Group: The Group That Never Was'. In A. King and M. Reiss (eds) *The Multicultural Dimension of the National Curriculum*. London: Falmer Press.

—— (2008) *Race and Education: Policy and Politics in Britain*. Maidenhead: Open University Press.

Troyna, B. (1984) Fact or Artefact? The ' "Educational Underachievement" of Black Pupils', *British Journal of Sociology of Education*, 5(2): 153–166.

—— (1991) 'Children, "Race" and Racism: The Limitations of Research and Policy', *British Journal of Educational Studies* 39(4).

—— (1992) 'Can You See the Join? An Historical Analysis of Multicultural and Antiracist Education Policies'. In D. Gill, B. Mayor & M. Blair (eds) *Racism and Education: Structures and Strategies*. London: Sage.

Ugwu, C. (ed.) (1995) *Let's Get It On: The Politics of Black Performance*. London: ICA.

Unterhalter, E. (2007) *Gender, Schooling and Global Justice*. London: Routledge.

Vadgama, K. (2004), *Cornelia Sorabji*. Lecture at the seminar, 'Politics and Pioneers of South Asian History'. Museum of London, 27 March.

Verma, G. K. and Ashworth, B. (1985) *Ethnicity and Educational Attainment*. London: Macmillan.

Visram, R. (1986) *Ayahs, Lascars and Princes: Indians in Britain 1700–1947*. London: Pluto.

—— (2002) *Asians in Britain: 400 Years of History*. London: Pluto Press.

Walby, S. (1994) 'Is Citizenship Gendered?', *Sociology* 28 (2): 379–395.

Wallace, C. (1987) *For Richer for Poorer: Growing up in and Out of Work*. London: Tavistock.

Wasafiri (1993) 'Black Women Writers in Britain', Special Issue 17 (Spring).

Ware, V. (1992) *Beyond the Pale: White Women, Racism and History*. London: Verso.

Weedon, C. (1987) *Feminist Practice and Poststructuralist Theory*. Oxford: Blackwell.

Weekes, D. (1997) 'Shades of Blackness: Young Female Constructions of Beauty'. In H.S. Mirza (ed.) *Black British Feminism; A Reader*. London: Routledge.

Weekes, D. and Wright, C. (1999) *Improving Practice: A Whole School Approach to Raising the Achievement of African Caribbean Youth*. London: Runnymede Trust in association with Nottingham Trent University.

Weiner, G., Arnot, M. and David, M. (1997) 'Is the Future Female? Female Success, Male Disadvantage, and Changing Gender Patterns in Education'. In A.H. Halsey, H. Lauder, P. Brown and A.S. Wells (eds) *Education: Culture, Economy and Society*. Oxford: Oxford University Press.

Weis, L. (1985) *Between Two Worlds: Black Students in an Urban Community College*. London: Routledge & Kegan Paul.

West, C. (1990) 'The New Cultural Politics of Difference'. In R. Ferguson, M. Gever, T. Minh-ha and C. West (eds) *Out There: Marginalisation and Contemporary Cultures*. New York: New Museum of Contemporary Art.

—— (1993) *Keeping the Faith: Philosophy and Race in America*. London: Routledge.

Wetherell, M., Lafleche, M. and Berkeley, R. (2007) *Identity, Ethnic Diversity and Community Cohesion*. London: Sage.

WEU (2002) *Key Indicators of Women's Position in Britain*. At www.women andequalityunit.gov.uk or DTI publications HMSO 6309/1.8/11/02/NP.

Whitty, G. (1998) 'New Labour, Education and Disadvantage', *Education and Social Justice* 1(1): 2–8.

Williams, C. (1993) 'We are a Natural Part of Many Different Struggles: Black Women Organising'. In W. James and C. Harris (eds) *Inside Babylon: The Caribbean Diaspora in Britain*. London: Verso.

Williams, F. (1996) 'Postmodernism, Feminism and the Question of Difference'. In N. Parton (ed.) *Social Work, Social Theory and Social Change*. London: Routledge.

Williams, P.J. (1991) *The Alchemy of Race and Rights: The Diary of a Law Professor*. Cambridge, MA: Harvard University Press.

—— (1997) *Seeing a Colour-blind Future: The Paradox Of Race – The 1997 Reith Lectures*. London: Virago.

Willis, P. (1977) *Learning to Labour: How Working Class Kids Get Working Class Jobs*. Farnborough: Saxon House.

Wilson, A. (1978) *Finding a Voice: Asian Women in Britain*. London: Virago.

Wilson, W.J. (1987) *The Truly Disadvantaged: The Inner City, The Under Class, and Public Policy*. Chicago, IL: University of Chicago Press.

Wiltshire-Brodber, R. (1988) 'Gender, Race and Class in the Caribbean'. In P. Mohammed and C. Shepherd (eds) *Gender in Caribbean Development*. Women and Development Studies Project. St Augustine, Trinidad: University of the West Indies.

Women's National Commission (WNC) (2006) *She Who Disputes: Muslim Women Shape the Debate*. At http://www.thewnc.org.uk/wnc_work/muslim_women.html.

Wong, L. H. (1994) 'Di(s)-secting and Dis(s)-closing "Whiteness": Two Tales about Psychology'. In K. Bhavnani and A. Phoenix (eds) *Shifting Identities, Shifting Racisms: A Feminism and Psychology Reader*. London: Sage.

Wragg, T. (1997) 'Oh Boy! Sixth Annual TES/Greenwich Lecture', *Times Educational Supplement*, 16 May, p. 4 (TES2).

Wright, C. (1986) 'School Processes: An Ethnographic Study'. In J. Eggleston, D. Dunn and M. Anjali (eds) *Education for Some: The Educational and Vocational Experiences of 15–18 Year old Members of Ethnic Minority Groups*. Stoke on Trent: Tretham.

—— (1987a) 'The Relations Between Teachers and Afro-Caribbean Pupils: Observing Multi-Cultural Classrooms'. In G. Weiner and M. Arnot (eds) *Gender Under Scrutiny*. London: Hutchinson/Open University.

—— (1987b) 'Black Students – White Teachers'. In B. Troyna (ed.) *Racial Inequality in Education*. London: Tavistock.

—— (1990) 'Comments in Reply to an Article by P. Foster: A Case not Proven', *British Education Journal* 16(4).

Wright, C., Standen, P., John, G., German, G. and Patel, T. (2005) *School Exclusion and the Transition into Adulthood in African-Caribbean Communities*. York: Joseph Rowntree Foundation. At www.jrf.org.uk.

Wulff, H. (1988) *Twenty Girls: Growing Up, Ethnicity and Excitement in a South London Microculture*. Stockholm Studies in Anthropology 21. Stockholm: University of Stockholm.

Yeatman, A. (1994) 'Postmodern Epistemological Politics and Social Science'. In K. Lennon and M. Whitford (eds) *Knowing the Difference: Feminist Perspectives in Epistemology*. London: Routledge.

Young, I. M. (1990) 'The Ideal of Community and the Politics of Difference'. In L. Nicolson (ed.) *Feminism/Postmodernism*. London: Routledge.

Young, L. (1996) *Fear of the Dark: Race, Gender and Sexuality in the Cinema*. London: Routledge.

Young, M. and Willmott, P. (1957) *Family and Kinship in East London*. Harmondsworth: Penguin Books.

Young, R. (1995) *Colonial Desire: Hybridity in Theory, Culture and Race*. London: Routledge.

Young, S. (1997) *Changing the Wor(l)d: Discourse, Politics and the Feminist Movement*. London: Routledge.

Yuval-Davis, N. (1997) *Gender and Nation*. London: Sage.

—— (2006) 'Intersectionality and Feminist Politics', *European Journal of Women's Studies* 13(3): 193–209.

Index